HENRY ADAMS

The Myth of
FAILURE

HENRY ADAMS

The Myth of
FAILURE

WILLIAM DUSINBERRE

University Press of Virginia

Charlottesville

THE UNIVERSITY PRESS OF VIRGINIA
Copyright © 1980 by the Rector and Visitors
of the University of Virginia

First published 1980

Library of Congress Cataloging in Publication Data

Dusinberre, William, 1930–
  Henry Adams, the myth of failure.

  Bibliography: p.
  Includes index.
  1. Adams, Henry, 1838–1918. 2. Adams, Henry, 1838–1918. History of the United States of America. 3. United States—History—1801–1809. 4. United States—History—1809–1817. 5. History—Philosophy. 6. Historians—United States—Biography. I. Title. E175.5.A2D84 973'.07'2024 [B] 79–16096 ISBN 0–8139–0833–7

Printed in the United States of America

For Charlotte, my mother,
and to the memory of Merrick, my father

Contents

Acknowledgments		ix
Chronology		xii
Introduction		1

I   LIFE
    1 *Family*   7
    2 *England*   34
    3 *Clover*   54
    4 *Historian*   86

II   HISTORY
    5 *History as Art*   111
    6 *History as Science*   147

III   STATURE
    7 *Macaulay and Gibbon*   165

IV   FAME
    8 Mont-Saint-Michel and Chartres *and* The Education
      of Henry Adams   187
    9 *The Sense of Failure*   219

Genealogical Chart   224
Notes   225
Bibliographical Note   245
Index   247

Acknowledgments

I am deeply indebted to Prof. David Levin, Prof. J. C. Levenson, Prof. John Clive, Prof. Marcus Cunliffe, Dr. Philip Taylor, Dr. Stephen Spackman, and Prof. Robert Bannister. Each of these scholars read and criticized the manuscript, and I shall always be grateful to them for the time and intelligence they gave so generously to a thankless task. Their suggestions, strictures, and encouragement were indispensable. While they saved me from numerous mistakes, they bear of course no responsibility for those that remain.

Prof. Levenson, Prof. Charles Vandersee, and Dr. Viola Winner were extraordinarily openhanded in sharing with me their learning and the fruits of their work on the Adams letters. Prof. W. R. Brock's encouragement has meant a great deal to me. Dr. Howard Temperley and Prof. Arnold Goldman made many valuable suggestions about chapter 2. Prof. Ernest Samuels's authoritative biography of Adams was helpful on innumerable points. I am most grateful to each of these men and women.

Prof. Earl Harbert shared with me his knowledge of Adams family history. Professors Vincent Capowski, Norman Risjord, and Grant Gilmore kindly assisted my research. I wish also to express my debt to Dr. Harold Cater and to other Adams scholars.

Miss Winifred Collins created a constantly friendly atmosphere in the reading room of the Massachusetts Historical Society. The staffs of the Massachusetts Historical Society and of the libraries at Harvard, Warwick, Oxford, and Brown universities, of the University of Virginia, and of St. Anselm's College were most helpful. Mrs. Mary Caswell was very generous as well as utterly professional in her typing of the manuscript.

The University of Warwick most kindly granted liberal sabbatical leave and a substantial supplement from its American Travel and Research Fund.

Juliet Dusinberre worked tirelessly on the book's content and form. She also goaded by example and infused into a few pages a particle of her own spirit.

For permission to quote manuscript and printed materials I would like to thank the following.

Acknowledgments

Quotations from the Adams Papers at the Massachusetts Historical Society, through 1889, are from the microfilm edition, by permission of the Massachusetts Historical Society. The Massachusetts Historical Society also granted permission to quote from the Adams Papers since 1889, the Theodore Dwight Papers, the Shattuck Papers, and the Harold Dean Cater Papers. Quotations from the Adams Papers at Houghton Library, the J. G. Palfrey Papers, and the E. L. Godkin Papers are by permission of the Houghton Library. Quotations from the Henry James Papers are by permission of the Houghton Library and of Alexander R. James. Quotations from the Oliver Wendell Holmes, Jr., Papers are by permission of the Harvard Law School Library and of Professor Grant Gilmore. A quotation from the John Hay Papers is by permission of Brown University Library.

Quotations from the following books are reprinted by permission of Houghton Mifflin Company: *Letters of Henry Adams* edited by Worthington C. Ford (copyright renewed 1958 and 1966 by Emily F. Lowes); *A Cycle of Adams Letters* edited by Worthington C. Ford (copyright renewed 1958 by Emily F. Lowes); *Henry Adams and His Friends* edited by Harold Dean Cater (copyright renewed 1975 by Harold Dean Cater); *The Education of Henry Adams* by Henry Adams (copyright 1946 by Charles F. Adams); *Mont-Saint-Michel and Chartres* by Henry Adams (copyright 1933 by Charles F. Adams); *An Autobiography* by Charles Francis Adams (copyright 1916 by Massachusetts Historical Society).

Quotations from Henry Adams, *History of the United States*, and from Henry James, *The Portrait of a Lady* and *Roderick Hudson*, are by permission of Charles Scribner's Sons; from Edward Gibbon, *The History of the Decline and Fall of the Roman Empire* (ed. J. B. Bury) are by permission of Methuen & Co. Ltd.; from Thomas Babington Macaulay, *History of England from the Accession of James the Second* (ed. C. H. Firth) are by permission of Macmillan, London and Basingstoke; from John Lothrop Motley, *The Rise of the Dutch Republic* (George Bell and Sons) are by permission of Bell & Hyman; from Francis Parkman, *Montcalm and Wolfe* and *The Old Regime in Canada*, are by permission of Little, Brown and Company; from W. H. Prescott, *The Conquest of Mexico*, and from F. O. Matthiessen and K. Murdock, eds., *The Notebooks of Henry James*, are by permission of Oxford University Press; and from Ernest Samuels, *The Young Henry Adams*, *Henry Adams: The Middle Years*, and *Henry Adams: The Major Phase*, are by permission of Harvard University Press. Quotations from *Letters of Mrs. Henry Adams* edited by Ward Thoron (copyright 1936 by Ellen Sturgis Hooper Potter; © renewed 1964) are by permission of Little, Brown and Company in association with the Atlantic Monthly Press. An earlier version of chapter 2 appeared in the *Journal of American Studies*, August 1977, and is reprinted by permission of Cambridge University Press.

HENRY ADAMS

The Myth of
FAILURE

Henry Adams: Chronology

1838	Born in Boston
1854–58	Student at Harvard College
1858–60	Student in Germany and European travel
1860–61	Private secretary to his father, Congressman Charles Francis Adams, in Washington, D.C.
1861–68	Private secretary to his father, the American minister in London
1868–70	Free-lance journalist in Washington, D.C., especially for the *North American Review*
1870–77	Teacher of history at Harvard and editor of the *North American Review*
1872	Married Marian Hooper
1872–73	Wedding trip to Europe and Egypt
1877–90	Writer of history, two biographies, and two novels, in Washington, D.C.
1879–80	Research trip to Europe
1885	Death of his wife
1889–91	*History of the United States* published, 9 vols.
1904	*Mont-Saint-Michel and Chartres*, privately printed
1907	*The Education of Henry Adams*, privately printed
1918	Died in Washington, D.C.
	The Education of Henry Adams published

Introduction

ACROSS THE canyon of twenty years—from the time of his courting Clover Hooper until the moment of his reluctant return to Washington after his *History* was published—the accomplished author of *The Education of Henry Adams* leaped with such dexterity that one might have supposed it a mere garden ditch. Here lay buried the two great passions of his life—and what he felt were his greatest failures; and he aimed with skill to divert public attention from these important circumstances. So successful was this diversion that the most remarkable historical writer of the United States is remembered primarily as the author of a brilliant autobiography and of a study of twelfth- and thirteenth-century France. Such a success would have delighted the imp of the perverse ever lurking in Adams's breast. He was amused to substitute a diminutive "manikin" for the man himself. Yet only half wishing his *Education* to mislead, Adams admitted that he had tailored the dummy as well as its educational clothes and he raised the question whether it may not indeed have had a life of its own. "Who knows? Possibly it had!"

Although *The Education of Henry Adams* contains accurate and suggestive autobiographical information, it is a purposeful travesty of the meaning of Adams's life. I have attempted to recreate that life, especially during the years before Adams's wife died, as part of a revaluation of his literary career. My interpretation of Adams is consonant with that of Carl Becker, the well-known historian; of Adams's friend Justice Oliver Wendell Holmes; and of the literary critic Yvor Winters. These three very different observers all admired Adams' *History of the United States*, 1801–17, regarding it as the best such work written in America—"a history," Becker exclaimed in 1935, "which for clarity, tight construction, and sheer intelligence applied to the exposition of a great theme, had not then, and has not since, been equaled by any American historian." But these men, while fascinated by *The Education of Henry Adams*, doubted the cogency of Adams's philosophical thought. "In the later chapters [of the *Education*], in which he deals with the dynamic

1

theory of history," Becker mildly protested, "the problem was so vague, even to [Adams] himself, that we too often do not know what he wishes to convey." Yvor Winters adopted a more extreme position: "The later work of Adams ... represents the radical disintegration of a mind. The mind, however, had been a great one."[1]

The views of Holmes, Winters, and Becker have not been fully accepted by the scholars who in recent years have done so much to elucidate Adams's life and writings. William Jordy, author of the first important study of Adams's historical writing, focused on Adams's scientific side—his debt to Comte, his identification with German scientific history, his speculations about historical laws. J. C. Levenson, who initiated the serious literary study of Adams's *History*—Levenson called it Adams's "masterwork"—seemed to imply that *The Education of Henry Adams*, for all of its "imaginative vitality," was a slightly limited achievement. Yet Levenson's book does not explicitly present a base from which to challenge the interpretation later formulated by Ernest Samuels. In Samuels's opinion, Adams's "Major Phase" comprised the period when he wrote *Mont-Saint-Michel and Chartres* and *The Education of Henry Adams*.[2]

My own view is somewhat different. I regard Adams's *History* as his most impressive work, because he had mastered there both his subject and his artistic form. *Mont-Saint-Michel and Chartres* appears, by contrast, dilettante; and the *Education*—despite its wonderful portrayal of Adams's mid-nineteenth-century world—seems to me to be weakened by the author's querulous, self-important tone and by the inconsequential theorizing of its concluding chapters. But in the *History* Adams controlled his penchant for overgeneralization. Based on years of research, his story of diplomacy, politics, and war was told with both critical detachment and passionate involvement. Adams was at this time a perfectionist concerning sentence structure, diction, and the elements of literary workmanship, and his imagination bubbled with satire and invention. He fused German scientific history with English literary history, and this fusion remains, I believe, his greatest achievement.

In the 1880s, when writing his *History*, Adams acknowledged to himself his ambition: He thought automatically, and frequently, of Gibbon. But his wife's mental breakdown, together with his own growing self-doubt, precipitated in Adams a revulsion against his earlier self. So strong was his reaction—so anxious was Adams to hide the literary purpose that had given his life meaning—that he contrived *The Education of Henry Adams* carefully to deceive. Only a few disguised allusions in the *Education* pointed toward Adams's literary ambition; everything was designed to show him instead as a frustrated politician and a social butterfly.

No picture of his early life could have been more misleading. Adams's passionate interest in literary craftsmanship already glowed when he was in his twenties, writing combatively from England to his critical elder brother Charles. During seven years in Great Britain, Henry had found a tradition to nourish his own literary inclination, and his marriage to Clover Hooper further encouraged this bent. Clover's family had been closely associated with the literary world of Boston—with Transcendentalists, with the elder Oliver Wendell Holmes, Harvard College, Henry James—when the Adamses were still, above all, politicians. Clover's raillery sharpened Henry Adams's satirical power, and the happy years of their marriage were the foundation upon which Adams built his literary career.

Other books on Adams examine his intellectual heritage;[3] I have concentrated instead upon the vigorous individuals surrounding him, through whom this heritage made itself felt. My reconstruction of their personalities is based on the Adams Papers in Boston, which were not open to the public when Ernest Samuels published *The Young Henry Adams* thirty years ago. I have attempted a full portrait of Henry Adams's wife, whose influence upon him was deep; and there are also pictures of the two friends who most affected him before his marriage, his brother Charles and his English companion Charles Milnes Gaskell. I have sketched the personality of Henry's mother, suggesting how her chronic melancholy affected the tone of *The Education of Henry Adams*. Henry's scholarly debt to his father and his ambivalent feelings about his grandfather, John Quincy Adams, are explored, as is the triangular relation between Henry James, Henry Adams, and Adams's wife. I have analyzed the intellectual and artistic power that distinguished Adams's writing, but also the self-esteem and hunger for the world's applause that afflicted him.

The existence in mid-nineteenth-century Boston of a significant school of historians was a prerequisite to the development of Adams's own talent, but the British tradition of literary history was the deepest intellectual influence upon his life. Gibbon and, to a lesser degree, Macaulay were to Adams the most important exemplars of that tradition. From his father and his elder brother, from lessons in rhetoric at Harvard College, from his long sojourn in England, and from Boston friends like Motley and Parkman, Adams learned to regard history as a branch of literature. Bishop Whately's *Rhetoric* guided Adams in literary usage when he was an undergraduate, while Frank Palgrave acted in England as a kind of graduate supervisor. Intimacy with Milnes Gaskell encouraged Henry to diverge from the path of his elder brother Charles Adams and to pursue literary history upon principles rather different from those of his Boston friends and predecessors.

Adams's *History* requires to be placed in its literary context—to be seen as an outgrowth of the work of Prescott, Motley, and Parkman—and to be set against the accomplishments of British historians. Yvor Winters once expressed the suspicion that Adams's *History* "is the greatest historical work in English, with the probable exception of *The Decline and Fall of the Roman*

Empire."[4] The only way to evaluate this apparently extravagant claim is to examine the achievements of historians in Britain. I believe Adams's *History* deserves a place in American letters comparable to that of Macaulay's or Gibbon's in England, and I hope my comparison of these writers with Adams may suggest something of the truths and errors implicit in Winters's assertion.

Nearly every other study of Henry Adams has been written by a literary critic or an art historian, and my being a political historian doubtless colors the judgments expressed here. In assessing Adams's *History*, I have attempted to answer a question that neither Ernest Samuels, Adams's accurate and illuminating biographer, nor J. C. Levenson, his most penetrating critic, set for themselves: How reliable was Adams as a historian? And in discussing the qualities that make his *History* a masterpiece, I have stressed the craftsmanship of individual passages and the author's effervescent spirit rather than his philosophy or the *History*'s structure.

But I share with all other students of Adams an interest in history as a form of literature. The literary critic David Levin, through his *History as Romantic Art* and *In Defense of Historical Literature*, has done most in the American field to promote this interest. Two well-known historians have recently fostered a growing tendency to take literary history seriously, by their studies of Adams's European masters: John Clive's *Macaulay* and Peter Gay's *Style in History*. My discussion of Adams's *History* is intended as a contribution to this movement.

Adams's fame derives largely from the two books of his old age. Beyond its interesting sketch of French medieval culture, *Mont-Saint-Michel and Chartres* contains moving confessional passages; and *The Education of Henry Adams* is not only an absorbing autobiography but a significant work of iconoclasm. Yet Adams's grasp of subject matter and literary form may be regarded as less sure in *Mont-Saint-Michel*—and even in the *Education*—than in his earlier work. The time may be ripe for further examination of certain defects, as well as the virtues, of these two extraordinary volumes.

Failure—so Adams alleged in the *Education*—was the keynote of his life: failure to gain a useful education, failure to acquire political power, failure to understand the world in which he lived. Yet Adams was, in a true sense, the most successful historian his country had ever produced. His paradox lies in the dramatic contrast between his achievement and his imputed failure. In his embittered old age, Adams could not publicly acknowledge the heights to which he had once aspired. His whole experience before 1885 contributed to the remarkable work toward which ambition had directed him; but the disintegration of his life after his wife's death in 1885 and the unappeased hungers of his peculiar psyche led him to denominate that life a failure. To reconsider the elements of success and failure in Adams's career—to help to rescue him from the myth he created about his own life—is the object of the following pages.

4

PART I · *Life*

CHAPTER 1 · *Family*

ARTISTS ARE not only born, they are made. Mozart's genius was nurtured by his father's care and shaped by his bountiful experience in the musical capitals of Europe. The forces that most affected Henry Adams's development sprang from his grandfather, father, and elder brother; from his living abroad for nearly the whole decade of his twenties; and from his marrying a quick-minded Boston woman. *The Education of Henry Adams* furnishes a vivid picture of Adams's childhood and his undergraduate years, but the character of his relation to his family, to England, and to his wife demands examination if his life is to be fathomed.

Many of Adams's traits emerged during three epochs of his life between his graduation from Harvard in 1858 at the age of twenty and the completion of his *History* in 1890. The decade 1858–68 was decisive for his development, and during this time he resided almost entirely in England and Germany or traveled on the Continent: It included seven years when he was private secretary to his father, who held a diplomatic post as American minister in London. From 1868 to 1877 he pursued a more conventional career, first briefly as free-lance political journalist in Washington, then as teacher of history at Harvard. The span from 1877 to 1890, when Adams spent the winters in Washington and the summers in the seaside community of Beverly Farms, Mass., was devoted to historical writing. Each of these periods was varied by a year across the Atlantic: In 1860–61 the young man returned from Europe and witnessed the secession crisis; in 1872–73 he left Harvard for a year's wedding journey in Europe and Egypt; and in 1879–80 he abandoned Washington for a year's research in London, Paris, and Madrid. Thus between 1858 and 1890 he lived eleven years abroad, resided many winters in Washington, and passed six winters and most summers in Massachusetts. The main themes of his historical writing during this period—for which his life in Washington, London, and Boston had prepared him well—were the diplomatic relations of the United States and Great Britain, and the conflict between democrats in Washington and the extreme Federalists of Massachusetts.

One of the deepest influences on his early life was that of his father, and Adams's unusual circumstances as a young man were certain to magnify this force. Although he had inherited from relatives capital producing an annual income of rather less than $1,000, Henry relied for his principal support during the 1860s on a $2,000 yearly allowance from his father. This payment compensated the son's otherwise unremunerated labor as private secretary in London. Financial dependence harmonized with official duty and personal inclination: The young secretary felt obliged, as a sort of civil servant, to support every political act of his superior, and in any case he was far from wishing to criticize his father's handling of Palmerston and Lord John Russell. Henry's school of politics, as he informed his brother, was situated athwart his own desk: "The Chief and I are as merry as grigs, writing in this delightful old study all day long, opposite to each other"; and of one of his father's diplomatic maneuvers he later effused, "The Minister was grand. I studied his attitude with deep admiration." This regard was reciprocated. "The two sit up stairs there exchanging views on all subjects," the assistant secretary of the legation confided enviously to his diary, "and . . . each considers the other very wise."[1]

Henry's enduring interest in politics was nourished by his father's political career. Charles Francis Adams, the most fortunate child of John Quincy Adams, whose New England severity contributed to the suicide of another son, had succeeded to a sort of archbishopric in the antislavery movement after his father's death. The Free-Soilers had nominated him for the vice presidency in 1848; and later, when he was in Congress during the secession winter of 1860–61, his unimpeachable antislavery credentials had permitted him to pursue a course not entirely popular with his Massachusetts constituents. This characteristic independence from local interests soon contributed to his immense success as a diplomat. During the Civil War his personal character and self-respecting attitude did much to neutralize England's anti-American sentiment; while in 1872 his conciliation earned him credit for the amicable settlement of America's postwar claims against Britain. Chilly reserve, so effective for a nineteenth-century American diplomat dealing with Englishmen, finally cost him the Liberal Republican nomination for the presidency in 1872, though he led on three of the seven ballots. From the beginning of this distinguished career Charles Francis Adams painstakingly opened doors to his favored son:

As the boy grew up to be ten or twelve years old, his father gave him a writing-table in one of the alcoves of his Boston library, and there, winter after winter, Henry worked over his Latin Grammar and listened to these four gentlemen [Charles Sumner, Richard Henry Dana, Adams, and Dr. John Palfrey] discussing the course of anti-slavery politics. The discussions . . . were habitual because Mr. Adams had undertaken to edit a newspaper as the organ of these gentlemen, who came to discuss its policy and expression.[2]

The boy's early affinity for politics, thus intelligently fostered by a parent's indulgence, matured through the quarter century of Henry's attachment to his father's career.

Yet Charles Francis Adams always thought himself most happy as a scholar, and this bent of mind, rather than his political interest, was his greatest legacy to Henry. "My father," Charles Francis proudly reminisced, "predicted that I should be a hermit [and a bookworm, like my uncle Johnson] and live in a cave far away from the busy haunts of men." "I stopped that off by an early marriage—But the tendency has always been more or less strong."[3] In lieu of a cave he erected a fireproof stone library that can still be visited behind the family home at Quincy; here he immured himself daily during the 1870s, completing that task of scholarship and family piety that had already consumed his most regular energies for years before the war. He had published during the 1840s letters of John Adams and his wife, and from 1850 to 1856 an edition of John Adams's *Works*, in ten volumes. His biography of John Adams was finished in the latter year. The twelve volumes of the most remarkable American diary—that of John Quincy Adams—appeared in his edition by 1877. These publications he considered the great work of his career, and in 1878 he recalled with satisfaction that editing his father's papers had cost him "a large share of twenty years. I look back upon that period as on the whole the most agreeable of my life."[4]

For recreation Charles Francis turned with Puritanic persistence to Greek literature. During one four-month period, he lamented to Henry, "my usual hour's relaxation in the ancient languages has only produced one reading of Plato's Gorgias so unsatisfactory that I am going over it again more effectively."[5] He did not find it unnatural to preface another letter to Henry with five words in Greek taken from Demosthenes, whom he was rereading. He dreamed of teaching history at Harvard (John Quincy Adams had been professor of rhetoric there) and regretted that the college authorities would have thought him competent only to hear recitations in Greek. Thus, when in 1870, as one of the most influential Overseers, he made the decisive suggestion to President Eliot that Harvard appoint Henry to be a professor of history, he was living vicariously through his son.

Charles Francis Adams fostered his children's taste for literature by reading aloud and giving them the run of his library, but mainly by presenting the example of his own interest.* He brought home the first volume of Macaulay's *History of England* soon after its publication in 1848: "I took the book up," Henry's elder brother Charles remembered, "and almost instantly got absorbed in it."[6] It was a milestone in Charles's life, for it precipitated an

*"Charles Francis Adams" designates Henry's father.

"Charles Adams" always refers here to Henry's older brother, whose full name was Charles Francis Adams, Jr. A genealogical chart showing Adams family relationships appears ahead of the notes on page 224.

interest in writing that led him to publish nearly a dozen books, mainly on history, during an active career as railroad reformer and tycoon. Charles Francis Adams was still reading Macaulay's *History* (the later volumes) as he sailed for England in 1861, accompanied by Henry, but he concluded that this popular rhetorician could not match the standard of eighteenth-century historians. "For him," the son Charles complained in 1897 with quadruple emphasis,

there was absolutely no merit at all in any thinker, writer or observer of this century,—Darwin was an infidel, Macaulay a "bag of wind," Carlisle a literary humbug, Tennyson a passing fashion, Browning a pure unintelligible mystery, while in Dickens and Thackeray there was only a poor echo of Smollett and LeSage; Pope was still the climax of English poetry; Hume and Robertson the models of historical style; and, to the very end I think, he believed in the Mosaic cosmogeny, including the Deluge. [7]

Beyond exposing Henry to this salutary dissent from the fashions of Victorian taste, Charles Francis exercised a more direct influence on his son's early literary work. It was in 1877 that he completed the publication of John Quincy Adams's diary, and Henry issued in the same year John Quincy Adams's previously unpublished 220-page disquisition "To the Citizens of the United States" as the heart of his *Documents Illustrating the History of New England Federalism*. The father gave public lectures on the history of America's claims to neutral rights, and the son devoted years to studying the same topic. The literary style of Charles Francis's diplomatic notes excited Henry's admiration, and when Henry himself set pen to paper, his father occasionally evinced interest: He felt it his duty, austere New England gentleman as he was, to admonish the young man about personal failings that marred his style. The Springfield *Republican* had objected early in 1869 to the contemptuous tone of a political essay just published by Henry, and circumlocution warred with psychological insight in Charles Francis's own criticism of the piece. We "generally like it," he wrote coolly; but "upon one of . . . [the *Republican*'s] criticisms I shall take the liberty to dwell for a single moment, and trust that you will see in my remark only a suggestion prompted as much by my pride in as by my parental affection for you. I think there is a little modicum of justice in the objection to the tone of parts of the article as savoring of conceit more or less. . . . Shy natures are given to it from a necessity to support themselves from within against the first struggles with the opinion of the world without."[8]

A principal source of Henry's conceit, whose origin Charles Francis specified so understandingly, was the father's own example. He inculcated into his offspring that scorn of the world for which he at the same time castigated them. "If you do not like Massachusetts and its population," he wrote testily after Henry had resigned from Harvard, "you are under no obligation whatever to stay there. But if you do, it is not worth your while to be sarcastic about them." "Do not let the habit grow upon you." "As to the political state I see nothing to redeem it from utter contempt." The personality of this caustic judge of mankind did not commend itself to every observer. "The general impression [was] that he was an 'icicle,'" admitted one favorably disposed young visitor to the Adams household. But Henry's brother Charles was their father's most relentless critic. In classic rebellion against his own New England heritage, Charles alleged that his father resembled John Quincy Adams: "Neither of them had any real taste . . . for innocent outdoor amusement. . . . [Both were] afflicted with an everlasting sense of work to be accomplished. . . . [They were] ingrained Puritans, and no Puritan by nature probably ever was really companionable. Of the two, however, my grandfather was incomparably the more active-minded and interesting."9

In 1842 Charles Francis had purchased for his family's winter residence in Boston what Charles came to consider an excessively dreary house on Beacon Hill, and in his view his father's subsequent behavior surpassed mere bookishness: He appropriated for his own library the "one large and handsome room on the second floor into which the sun poured, and which occupied the entire front. The only really desirable room in the house, my father fixed on it for his library regardless of other considerations." The concern for his own well-being was joined to an irritable nature: He was "selfcentred, unsympathetic and uncongenial, set in his ways and unable to express his own feelings, except in bursts of uncontrolable temper, or to elicit the expression of feeling from others."10

Charles submitted to his father's prejudices, one of which constrained young men to pass directly from college into the business of life: "For young men just out of college he held Europe in horror, because a classmate of his— Alleyne Otis—after graduation chanced to go to Europe, and came home an ass, and remained an ass all the long continuing days of life. My father didn't realize that Alleyne Otis was born an ass."11 Yet Henry circumvented his father's prejudice against the Grand Tour and added two peripatetic years in Europe to his college education. Charles followed his father's precepts and forty-five years later was still fighting those battles against the deceased parent that he had not waged as a young man; Henry evaded his father's dominion and lived to pay homage to the older man.

Evasion began early and continued long: "When his father offered [the boy Henry] his own set of Wordsworth as a gift on condition of reading it through, he declined." And as a young man of twenty-five, bypassing his father's provincialism, Henry let the experience of London society develop his taste for aesthetic refinement and luxury. Mrs. Russell Sturgis, wife of an American banker long resident in Britain, offered at her country house— depicted in *The Portrait of a Lady* as the residence of the expatriate American banker Daniel Touchett—hospitality to soothe the nerves of a shy young

11

man pursued by the hot, dry, anti-American blasts of London. From this oasis Henry explained to Charles, youthfully patronizing their father, how he avoided family conflict. Mrs. Sturgis

is a charming woman as women go; fond of luxury, eating, drinking, and display. . . . She is hospitable as her house is large. . . . I have repeatedly taken refuge there when disagreeable things were making London a smokey hell, and I never failed to get back my courage and spirits there. . . . Your mother and father are not exactly the people to admire the pattern [of Mrs. Sturgis], even though their minds have developed considerably within three years. Accordingly we differ in our tastes quietly. . . . If I were to maintain in argument the points of difference between myself and the elders, my residence with them would be brief.[12]

Henry managed to accept the beneficial tutelage without sacrificing his spiritual independence. Perhaps his greatest luck was in being only the fourth of Charles Francis's children, for this relieved him from the full burden of the Adams heritage. The first three children were named for Adamses: Louisa for John Quincy Adams's wife, John for the president himself, and Charles for his father. But "the fourth, being of less account, was in a way given to his mother, who named him Henry Brooks, after a favorite brother just lost." This gift to his mother grew to understand her better than did any of the other children, and during the 1860s he helped his father considerably in caring for her. The minister, relieved by Henry for weeks at a time from the responsibilities of traveling with his wife, transferred to his son a share of that affection that might otherwise have gone to Mrs. Adams. When Henry finally left his parents in 1868 to follow a journalist's career in Washington, his father—this reserved, forbidding, apparently chill figure—gave way, with only a hint of egotism, to a rare expression of emotion: He would miss his son "every day and every hour of the rest of my life, as a companion and friend. Nobody has known so much of me, as he."[13]

The father bequeathed to Henry his own objectivity. Charles Francis's mother, half-American but half-English and born and bred in England, never felt at home in the United States, and this no doubt had contributed to her son's independent judgment of British-American disputes. In December 1861 an American war vessel stopped a British mail steamer on the high seas and removed the Confederate envoys to England and France. The "Mason-Slidell affair," much resented in England, was greeted by an outburst of jubilant jingoism in the northern United States, but Charles Francis Adams could see the matter from a British standpoint. He knew that a proud naval people would not tolerate the treatment it had once meted out to others. "It has given us here an indescribably sad feeling to witness the exultation in America," he wrote from London. "Putting ourselves in the place of Great Britain, where would be the end of the indignation that would be vented against the power committing it? Yet it seems everywhere to have been very coolly taken for granted that because she did outrageous things on the ocean to other powers, she would remain quiet when such things were done to her." Adams was equally free from the passions of his native New England: Attorney General Rockwood Hoar, he once confided to Henry, "has in his composition a little of that old federal New England leaven which has so often run into excess ultimately fatal to its own object."[14]

How well Henry assimilated his father's training appeared during a family crisis of 1872. Charles Francis Adams had returned to Europe on a diplomatic mission in November 1871, leaving his wife in Boston. During a long adjournment of the Geneva arbitration he set off on a trip to Italy and Egypt; his wife, distraught at his absence, desperately implored her children to urge him to return temporarily to America. Charles, supposing in a panic that his mother was losing her sanity, urged immediate return. John, fearful that leaving Europe would impair his father's prospects for the presidency, advised against homecoming. Henry understood that what was required was not exhortation but a detailed, dispassionate statement of Mrs. Adams's condition so that his father could decide for himself what to do; his dispatches were a model of lucidity and clearheaded observation amidst a tempest of family passion. The same quality of objective appraisal, acquired during long apprenticeship to his father, marks Adams's *History*:

In the end, far more than half the territory of the United States was the spoil of Spanish empire, rarely acquired with perfect propriety. . . .

. . . . .

[Americans] were persistent aggressors, while Spain, even when striking back, as she sometimes timidly did, invariably acted in self-defence. That the Spaniards should dread and hate the Americans was natural; for the American character was one which no Spaniard could like, as the Spanish character had qualities which few Americans could understand. Each party accused the other of insincerity and falsehood; but the Spaniards also charged the Americans with rapacity and shamelessness. In their eyes, United States citizens proclaimed ideas of free-trade and self-government with no other object than to create confusion, in order that they might profit by it.[15]

The origin of Henry Adams's mordant humor is less easily specified, yet here again he owed something to his father. The best spur to wit is a responsive audience, and even Charles could recall with satisfaction his father's "laughing until he had to wipe the tears from his eyes over an account I gave of the usual procedure of the . . . [House of Representatives] of which he was a member. . . . 'It is n't very respectful,' said my father, 'but it's dreadfully true.'" Henry too remembered Adams's risibility:

From childhood the boys were accustomed to hear, almost every day, table-talk as good as they were ever likely to hear again. The eldest child, Louisa, was one of the most sparkling creatures her brother met in a long and varied experience of bright women. . . . Palfrey and Dana could be entertaining when they pleased, and though Charles Sumner could hardly be called light in hand, he was willing to be amused, and smiled grandly from time to time; while Mr. Adams, who talked relatively little, was always a good listener, and laughed over a witticism till he choked.

By way of educating and amusing the children, Mr. Adams read much aloud, and was sure to read political literature, especially when it was satirical.

Henry became a different man from his father, yet not so different as to fail to benefit most from him. Charles Francis Adams had earned his affection and respect without thwarting his independence.[16]

While his father's influence upon Henry is reasonably plain, his mother's has remained obscure. Abigail Brooks Adams, daughter of a Boston merchant reckoned in 1849 the wealthiest man in New England, was not, like her daughter Louisa, one of those sparkling women to whom Henry paid tribute in the *Education*. That book was written partly as an act of piety toward Henry's father, but in it he seldom mentioned Abigail and then usually with deprecation: "Certainly no one was strong enough to control [the Adams children], least of all their mother." Henry acknowledged her social success but affected contempt for the wealth she brought from the Brooks family: When he was a baby his grandfather, former President John Quincy Adams, characteristically had presented him with "a little volume of critically edited Nursery Rhymes. . . . Of course there was also the Bible, given to each child at birth, with the proper inscription in the President's hand on the fly-leaf; while their grandfather Brooks supplied the silver mugs." In private correspondence, as in the *Education*, Adams was unobtrusively more affectionate toward his father: When both parents suffered the afflictions of old age, he wrote to a close friend, "My poor father is a complete wreck, and my mother almost a cripple."[17]

The reasons for this coolness toward one parent are quickly told. Weak and easily overborne by her imposing spouse and fast-developing children, Mrs. Adams grew into a habit of complete dependence on her husband and could not make a decision alone. Her husband always thought she had been faultily educated, and she neither nourished her mind by serious reading nor profited greatly from travel. Her tendency to fretful querulousness drove her family frantic. When Charles Francis employed Henry as private secretary, a fair share of the duty was mother-minding.

This aspect of Henry's career was illustrated early in 1865 when Adams packed his wife off from their establishment at Portland Place, London, for a long trip to southern Italy. Ostensibly the journey was for the sake of Henry's twenty-year-old sister, Mary, who suffered from frequent sore throats. Henry was in charge of the expedition, and by the time they reached Sorrento he and Mary were wild at their mother's spoiled fussing amidst the luxurious trappings and furnishings of upper-class travel. She is "one of the most devoted of mothers!" he assured Charles; yet

Mary rises into humor in describing her, after a lovely day's journey, and an excellent dinner, eaten with excellent appetite, in a most comfortable hotel, sitting before a crackling wood fire, with her feet on the fender, entertaining us thus before going to her warmed and neat bed. "Well, for my part I confess I do not understand at my time of life the pleasures of traveling. I have seen nothing yet on this journey that any one could call pleasure, and if it weren't for Mary's sake, I never would have left home. Mary's health was our single reason for taking this journey and I do think that Mary is the most perverse and obstinate girl I ever saw in all my life. She will not take care of herself.... It does make me utterly miserable, this never staying two nights in one place; there! it does! and I can't help it. I do want rest so! I get so fatigued with this continual motion.... Dear me, what a draught there is! Mary, you are crazy not to wear your jacket! Oh Henry, how you do look with that beard! I really think it is wicked in you to go so, when you know how it pains and disgusts me to have you seen so!.... Oh dear! there, I am *too* homesick!"

... [The example I have given] is far from exaggerated.... This perpetual feeble worrying; this unvarying practice of dwelling on the dark points of a picture, and bearing hardest on me at the most difficult moments, make me contemplate a journey with alarm and complete it with relief.[18]

Like a mother caring for a demanding child, Henry complained of his charge with mixed affection and exasperation. So curiously were these elements entwined that twenty years later an observant Englishman imagined him to be passionately fond of his mother.[19] Constantly acting the devoted son while dissimulating his feelings except in an occasional outburst to his brother or sister, Henry suffered the dilemma that Jane Austen set for Elizabeth Bennet: He must bear with a mother "of mean understanding, little information, and uncertain temper [who], when she was discontented ... fancied herself nervous."

Her influence on him was not an intellectual one; Mrs. Adams's mind, indeed, was prosaic to a degree. After two years as wife to the American minister in London, this heiress to Boston mercantile wealth was still as naive and artlessly impressed by royalty and dukedom as a barefoot country girl. There was no end to her astonishment at the variations between British and American usage of everyday language; she was painfully conscious that her provincial background might cause her to blunder before her awesome British cousins; and her earnest soul meandered across the hills and dales of national difference:

I did not call a Loch a pond once, or an English Lake either. The Duke took great delight, in telling me, of *one* American gentleman calling the Loch by the Castle—a "pretty pond." I have found *them* out in two years, and am careful, although as I remarked to him, and others, why they should resent our saying pond, when we used the word, for bigger sheets of water at home, I did not understand. I was sure we should never resent their calling our *ponds, lakes*. They none of them are satisfied. I always make one mistake and call, their rivers, "brooks, and little streams," but sel-

15

dom, do that beyond my own family, who do the same. They are after all mostly nothing but brooks, but I am dreadfully afraid of mistakes here.[20]

Yet Henry was conscious of resembling his mother: "I have inherited her disposition." His notorious melancholy, far from being a fin de siècle secretion, entered his organism with his mother's milk. Her chronic prevision of disaster—a "constitutional self-torture," as her son John termed it—was well understood within the family; and when Charles portrayed in his *Autobiography* his mother's despond, he might equally have been evoking the cheerless outlook Henry later incorporated into the *Education*. As Charles explained, his father's greatest stroke of political fortune was his selection as American minister to England, yet when the unexpected news of this nomination reached Boston in March 1861, " 'my mother at once fell into tears and deep agitation; foreseeing all sorts of evil consequences, and absolutely refusing to be comforted'. . . . My mother, in some respects remarkably calculated for social life, took a constitutional and sincere pleasure in the forecast of evil. She delighted in the dark side of anticipation; she did not really think so; but liked to think, and say, she thought so. She indulged in the luxury of woe."[21] Once Mrs. Adams arrived in England, the war news from America afforded limitless scope to sibylline gloom. "Mamma made day ghastly by her wails," Henry reported after the Seven Days Battle, "and it was all Mary and I could do to keep any sort of cheerfulness up in the house." Her son may have assumed a forced gaiety in the service of family diplomacy, but his private letters to Charles, an officer in the Union army, were so despondent as to excite the soldier's indignation. Unlike Mrs. Adams, Henry possessed the power of aggrandizing his predisposition into a general philosophy. He espoused a point of view which, "whether it calls itself submission to the will of God, or to the laws of nature, rests in bottom simply and solely upon an acknowledgment of our own impotence and ignorance." The arrival in London of a pessimistic American friend irked him, for the visitor was "disposed to look on his own affairs and those of the world in general, through rather brown media; and that is an amusement that I generally prefer to reserve to myself, because I can do it on a more universal and radical scale than anyone else."[22]

Henry's thorough dissatisfaction with the world as it was, which underlay occasional lapses into irritability in the *History*, stemmed partly from his mother's example. If in 1861 Charles did not join the army, Abigail complained that it behooved the Adamses to contribute a son to the Northern ranks; but if he should join, her dissatisfaction would not be dissipated: "As for mamma she drives us all crazy by worrying to let you go. When you are gone she will give us no rest worrying till you're killed." In 1872 it was arranged that she sit to have her portrait painted, but Henry was "so much afraid of giving her any new occasion for worry, that I daren't get her to

16

begin. I have had so much annoyance from similar small obligations working on her mind, that I do not willingly disturb her quiet. She cannot even dine out quietly without a day's unhappiness, and I do not believe she would sit often without finding the burden intolerable, especially as she is sure to dislike the portrait."[23] Full of weakness, indecision, and self-reproach, Mrs. Adams could not persuade herself to place any confidence in the capacities of her children, and her son grew up a shy, self-distrusting young man. Despite his two years on the Continent and his rich social opportunities at the American legation, he moped through four years of social isolation in London before making his first real friendship with a young Englishman. Henry did gain self-assurance in the 1870s and 1880s, when he was married and was active as a historian; and the tone of authority which rings from the pages of the *History* seldom falters. But after Henry's wife died, his earlier tendency toward melancholy was reactivated and it strongly affected him for the rest of his life.

Mrs. Adams was an indulgent mother, and Henry profited from her great affection; she afforded him an escape from his father's austerity, and—especially when he was first striking out for himself on the Continent in 1858–60—she made it easy for him in his letters to adopt toward her a jocular, self-mocking tone; yet he could not respect Abigail. "Our good mother, as usual, has been frightened and talks nonsense," he wrote of his worst London scrape. He was certain to react against the protracted exasperation of managing his mother's weakness: "I am at it again," he wrote to Charles in 1867 from the holiday resort of Baden, "trying hard to drive my team of women. . . . I have three shrinking women to protect."[24] When he married at the age of thirty-four, it was natural that he should turn from the feeble type of his mother toward a strong-minded woman who seemed in every way a contrast to Mrs. Adams. The strange thing was that, during some of the thirteen happy but care-stricken years of this marriage, he was to need to the full those powers of succour developed over long years with his mother. His experience with Abigail perhaps developed in him a fascination for a woman whose almost masculine strengths were inseparable from a special helplessness.

However that may be, before Adams's marriage in 1872 his most intimate relations were with two young men, of whom the first was his brother Charles, nearly three years his elder. Charles had character, energy, and varied talents; nevertheless, throughout his life he pursued certain false gods, and, dividing his energies among a half dozen separate careers, he never completely succeeded at any one of them. In his first—military—undertaking he became a twenty-nine-year-old colonel commanding the 1,200 black cavalrymen who rode into Richmond on Lee's heels in 1865. An idealist who disclaimed idealistic motives, he had persuaded his superiors to issue horses to his Negro soldiers so that they could fight instead of remaining on guard duty; he had declined the offer of a choice staff job in order to stay with his black regiment; and, not recovered from illness, he had returned from sick leave to lead this regiment into active service. But the experience was not a happy one. He concluded that, while Negroes made reasonably good infantrymen, they were "wholly unfit for cavalry service."[25] Certainly Charles was not wholly fit for this particular post; never a popular man, he seems to have commanded with unsuitable New England rigor, and his army service ended in bad blood between himself and his soldiers.

He showed equal sense of duty and eagerness to undertake a difficult task in his second venture, railroading, but here ambition betrayed him into a fatal blunder. He was successively a courageous journalist exposing the swindles of the Erie Railroad, a pioneering commissioner of railroads in Massachusetts, and a government director of the Union Pacific Railroad. But he was tempted into accepting the presidency of the Union Pacific, its assets having been gutted in the Crédit Mobilier scandal and in the operations of Jay Gould, and he was finally driven from that post by Gould before completing reforms he had imagined he could impose.[26]

While busy with the railroads, he was also engaged in moneymaking. His investments in the real estate and stockyards of Kansas City were immensely lucrative, yet at the end of his life he regretted, in a pathetic commentary upon the objects of the Gilded Age, that he had not succeeded better: "I would like to have accumulated . . . one of those vast fortunes of the present day rising up into the tens and scores of millions. . . . What I would now like the surplus tens of millions for would be to give them to Harvard. . . . I would like to be the nineteenth-century John Harvard—the John Harvard-of-the-Money-Bags, if you will."[27]

Besides all this he adopted the role of local worthy. He helped to renovate the town government of Quincy, launched a widely publicized reform of the local schools, worked hard as a Harvard Overseer to improve the college, and was long president of the Massachusetts Historical Society. His connection with this society was congruent with his view of himself as a man of letters, which by 1890 he felt to have been his true vocation. His ten bound and two unbound volumes of publications made a useful attack upon New England's complacent filiopietism and helped to inaugurate that onslaught upon New England Puritanism that continued its ravages until after 1930. But Charles did not understand his subject thoroughly enough, nor was his mental acuity sufficient, for his writings to survive. His achievements were far overshadowed by those of three earlier generations of Adamses and by those of his brilliant younger brother, and despite his amazing energy and versatility in public works, his private role as Henry's mentor, friend, and critic was not least valuable to the world.

On Valentine's Day, 1862, nearing his twenty-fourth birthday, Henry commenced from London his weekly letter to his soldier-brother in Virginia:

> Good morrow, 'tis St Valentine's day
>> All in the morning betime.
> And I am a maid at your window
>> To be your Valentine.[28]

This mocking salutation, adapted from Ophelia's distracted song, told something of Henry's fraternal affection, as did the great array of greetings on the scores of letters Henry faithfully inscribed throughout the war. "My dear boy" was a frequent opening, varied by

> My dear Warrior,
> My dear old boy,
> Leefteenant,
> My dear Fellow,
> My bould Sojer-boy,
> My dear Rank-hero,
> Most admirable Captain,
> Sir Charles de Quincey,
> Noble Captain,
> My dear Lieut-Col-Major-Captain,
> Oh my friend and mentor.

Fearing for Charles's safety during the holocaust, Henry adverted nostalgically to the good times of "that dimly distant period when we were boys and you used to box my ears because your kite wouldn't fly, and were the means of getting them boxed by disseminating at the tea-table truthless stories that I was painting myself a moustache with pear-juice." He recalled happy memories of riding horseback with Charles in springtime through the woods of Arlington, Mass., when they were undergraduates together at Harvard. When Charles was on leave in 1864, they took a week's spree together in Paris, and a year later Henry longed for Charles to enliven him: "I grow horribly solemn. I haven't had a good time for an age, nor laughed for a year. . . . However, I hope to see you before long, and till then—basta! We will have a quiet talk somewhere some day." The *Education* disguises how fond Henry once was of Charles. Henry there acknowledged his boyhood habit of following Charles about, and his respect as a young man for Charles's opinion; but he approached nearer to the truth in writing privately after his brother's death, "I loved Charles, and in early life our paths lay together."[29]

As good sons of Charles Francis Adams, Henry and Charles ranged in their correspondence over political and military history, diplomacy, literature, and art. Charles believed in the autumn of 1861 that an indignant public should force Lincoln to transform his policy and dismiss Simon Cameron from the War Department; but from London, Henry failed to see the need for change, and he turned naturally to British history for an argument: "When the English nation in the year 1795 were struggling with revolutionary France, their armies were beaten, their allies conquered and forced to sue for peace. . . . But did the English people hesitate to give a firm and noble support to Pitt, their Prime Minister, in spite of his gross failures? Not a bit of it." The older brother thought Henry misunderstood the position: "Your historical examples are not good. When was England greatest? Was it not when an angry people drove the drivellers from office and forced on an unwilling King the elder Pitt, who reversed at once the whole current of a war? I want to see Mr. Holt in the War Department."[30] Charles's touch was less sure when in 1864 he turned to military history; it was as if he had been doing hasty camp-bed reading to supplement his earlier studies and was eager to overbear his bookish father and brother. Nevertheless, he had grasped the principal military lesson of the Civil War:

Where skill is nearly equal and luck alone decides, the chances are ten to one against the assailant. Probably the most famous assault in history was that of McDonald's column at Wagram (I think). I doubt if it was more determined or better deserved success than Longstreet's at Gettysburg. Read the campaigns of Frederick of Prussia. See how rarely he by direct assault carried positions—never when opposed by Daun, except once and then by pure luck when the day was lost. Look at Napoleon at Borodino. Marlborough was more successful. Malplaquet, in respect to defensive preparations and advantages of position, was more like our battles here than any old world action that I can call to mind; yet Marlborough carried it much as Grant carried Spottsylvania. It was a nominal victory. The same of the Crimea, etc.[31]

Henry's letters discussed diplomatic affairs as frequently as Charles's did military: The young men educated each other in the two fields in which, in his mature work, Henry was to write with the greatest authority. The younger brother sent not only epistles but the quarry of London bookshops—volumes of military biography, sketches of English life, tomes on finance, and Buckle's *History of Civilization in England*. Responding to Henry's gift of the life of Sir William Napier, Charles made an uncompromising pronouncement on this literary form: "The English are getting to understand the art of biography for they let a man tell his own story and reflect his own character in his own words."[32] Henry embraced this principle too wholeheartedly in his subsequent, overpraised biography of *Gallatin*, but by then Charles perceived the error of his advice and, by using almost brutal methods, saw to it that the author's mistake of submerging himself too much in his material was not repeated in the *History*.

Henry and Charles also practiced imagery on each other. Henry understood that metaphors ought not to be altered in midstream, yet his youthful efforts could be painfully self-conscious, even ridiculous. Thus in 1862 he was explaining how the London *Times*'s satire of a newspaper article of his had obliged him temporarily to desist from journalism. The *Times*'s savage tone originated in the eagerness of the anti-American faction to strike an indirect blow against the American minister: "I form a convenient head to punch when people feel vicious and pugnacious. I have, therefore, to change the metaphor, found it necessary to take in every spare inch of canvas and to run (on a lee-shore) under double-close-reefed mizzen to' gallant skysails, before a tremendous gale." Henry's execution was not always so mannered. Of their father's friend, author of *Two Years before the Mast*, he observed, Dana's "fear of Democracy [i.e., the Democratic party] is very like an English Bishop's hatred of dissent"; and this turn of mind led easily in his published work to the remark that Senator Pickering's "hatred for Jefferson resembled the hatred of Cotton Mather for a witch." When late in 1861 Charles discounted Senator Sumner's further utility in politics, his image was too pat: Sumner has "been a useful man in his day, but he's as much out of place now as knights in armor would be at the head of our regiments."[33] Henry, twenty years later, revitalized the image in his *History*: In the Europe of 1800, so the democratic Adams believed, class distinctions, the fixity of residence, and entrenched local customs

raised from birth barriers which paralyzed half the population. . . . All this might have been borne; but behind this stood aristocracies, sucking their nourishment from industry, producing nothing themselves, employing little or no active capital or intelligent labor, but pressing on the energies and ambition of society with the weight of an incubus. Picturesque and entertaining as these social anomalies were, they were better fitted for the theatre or for a museum of historical costumes than for an active workshop preparing to compete with such machinery as America would soon command. From an economical point of view, they were as incongruous as would have been the appearance of a mediaeval knight in helmet and armor, with battle-axe and shield, to run the machinery of Arkwright's cotton-mill.[34]

All was not harmony between the two young men. Charles admired Henry's literary talent, persistently urged him to write for publication, and got his articles printed in the Boston *Courier*. But he himself also wrote for the *Courier*, and Henry felt the pinch of competition: Some articles by Charles in 1861 were "devilish good and made me blue for a day, thinking of my own weak endeavors in the same way." Henry labored at reading and writing during long years in London, and by 1867 his tone was different. Both by then were writing for the *North American Review*, and Henry was blunt: "I've read your article. In style I don't think it better than mine, and mine I frankly assure you is damned bad. Yours too is flabby in places and wants squeezing to take the fat out. . . . I am now going through a course of training, with the idea of sweating off my superfluous words." Henry tried in later years to create the picture of himself as trifler and social butterfly, so reluctant was he to confess that writing history had been one of the two

21

pivots of his life, but when he lectured his older brother on what Charles must do to improve his style, something of his own feeling showed through: "Nothing but work will do. It breaks one's spirit and crushes one's hopes to keep one's eyes fixed on an unattainable standard; but it's the only way for a man who is not a dunce or an ass."[35]

Charles was never a tactful man—perhaps this family weakness was the source of the Adamses' vigorous, independent clearsightedness—and in his desire to improve Henry he regularly applied three parts of aggressive criticism to one portion of praise. The brothers used each other as a whetstone, and years later, when Henry sharpened his wit at the expense of one of Charles's pamphlets, his brother was delighted: "Your comments on the manner of my argument pleased me amazingly. They were of the old time. The truth is, however, as I go on I grow reckless. The average American legislator is a man to be scorned. . . . Nothing tells like being contemptuous. . . . Let me hear from you from time to time, and do slash round in your letters. The middle years of life I find frightfully common place." Even when Charles praised his brother's efforts, Henry saw their relation as a combat: "Your two letters in reply to my two pugnacious epistles, were very satisfactory indeed. . . . The skilful manner in which you turn my flank and rout me with an attack of flattery on my weakest points, satisfies me."[36]

Henry's satisfaction was smaller when in 1879 he read the *Nation's* two-part review of his first serious historical work, *The Life of Gallatin*. He was by this time embarked on his thirteen-year study of the Jefferson and Madison administrations, and his biography of Jefferson's secretary of the treasury was an outrider for the main work published a decade later. Henry and Charles had for various reasons begun to grow apart—Henry's years in England had helped him to find his own feet, he had found an English comrade at about the time Charles married in 1865, and his own selection of a wife in 1872 was by no means to Charles's taste. Thus when Charles decided to publish an anonymous onslaught upon certain features of the book, he took great pains to protect the secret of his authorship from Henry. It was all meant for Henry's own good, and the vehicle he chose was America's most reputable weekly magazine, edited by Henry's confidential friend E. L. Godkin. The review annoyed Henry and his wife, who betrayed pique to Godkin. The editor passed this information on to Charles, who replied with ecstasy:

I laughed consumedly as I read it [Oct. 24], for it showed me that my *medicine* was working. You know *perfectly* well that my review was very complimentary in its *substance*, merely criticising sharply certain defects in detail. If Henry and his wife can't stand that, but insist on pure and solid taffy, he'd better stop writing.

My good sister-in-law don't favor me much now, and if she finds it is I who dared to criticise her adored Henry, my goose will be finally cooked.

The *Nation*'s review opened urbanely with an anecdote:

About the year 1802 Albert Gallatin's tailor spoiled a coat for him in the making, whereat the then Secretary of the Treasury expressed the energetic opinion to his wife that "every man, from John Adams to John Hewitt, who undertakes to do what he does not understand, deserves a whipping." Upon first handling the ponderous volume in which Mr. Henry Adams undertakes to tell the story of a very remarkable life, one is irresistibly tempted to substitute for the name of John Adams in the foregoing sentiment that of his great-grandson. In its superficial make-up this volume falls little short of being an outrage both on Albert Gallatin and on every one who wishes to know anything about him. It at once recalls Macaulay's remark on Nares's "Burleigh"—that it "might, before the Deluge, have been considered light reading by Hilpa and Shallum."

. . . [Mr. Adams] set to work in a spirit of defiance, and made every detail of publication as repelling to the general reader as he knew how. . . .

[Mr. Adams has] kept himself altogether too far in the background—sunk the author in the editor.

Each volume, Charles complained, was oppressively large and heavy; the typography was monotonous; and the printing of letters in French seemed "to say, as clearly as if in words, that the book is not for general readers."[37] Not one of these arrows failed to pierce its target. When Henry later published his *History*, he saw to it that the volumes could each be held easily in the hand, and the weight of each was well under half that of *Gallatin*. Long quotations were clearly distinguished from the text, everything was in English, huge pains were taken with the maps, and, much more important, the author commented continually upon his sources instead of presenting undigested material.

Charles praised the research in *Gallatin*, the clarity of much of the narrative, and its occasional eloquence, but even so Henry wrote that he was "used to cuffs, not compliments, and my poor style has been hardened into unnatural rigidity by the blows of criticism."[38] Although Henry seems to have learned Charles's secret, he was still to turn to his brother for criticism of the *History*. He was rewarded by a careful reading, and the evidence of this fraternal collaboration—Charles's detailed comments on the style, content, and overall construction of the work—can still be seen in the margins of a prepublication version preserved in the Massachusetts Historical Society.

Time had not abated the vigor of Charles's blows, which usually were meant to induce conciseness or discourage hyperbole. When Henry wrote, "The next morning, January 19, Parliament came together, and American affairs were instantly made the subject of attack on ministers," Charles waxed statistical: " 'Met' is one word of three letters; 'came together' are two words and contain twelve letters." In the final version brevity won the day. When Henry's florid imagination suggested to him that in 1805 "Gallatin already meditated schemes of internal improvements, which included four great thoroughfares across the Alleghanies, while Fulton was nearly ready with the steamboat which was to tame the winds and turn the waters of the Mississippi back to their source," Charles's query caused the deletion of all of the words after "steamboat." Of the British captain of the *Little Belt*, a small war vessel much damaged in 1811 by the attack of an American frigate, Henry planned to declaim that "two years afterward he would have thought himself the happiest of men to escape from the 'President' on any terms." "In writing history," Charles intoned, with an elder brother's undiminished confidence in his own superiority, "suppress the patriotic glow." The words "thought himself the happiest of men" became "been well content."[39]

In many similar skirmishes Charles helped to curb the excesses of Henry's hyperbole, but he lost the major battle. Charles believed, justly, that some of Henry's elaborate accounts of diplomacy were "excellent material for history in a condensed form; but they are not a condensed historical narrative. You are writing for historians, but only indirectly writing history."[40] The definition of "history," unconsciously presumed by Charles, indicated that Henry stood at a crossroads: The tradition of literary history was still vital, yet the era of the modern monograph had begun. Henry sought to traverse both highways at once, but in writing a detailed monograph he ran the danger, no matter how fine the art, of repelling all except expert readers. His painstaking dissection of James Monroe's diplomacy in 1805 provoked Charles's fulmination, "This chapter is, to my mind, long, obscure and dull. It could be compressed into half the space to advantage. Verbose and inconclusive diplomacy can be spared in history. It will bear boiling down." But Henry expected too much from his audience. "Nonsense!" he inscribed below Charles's marginal comment. "This is the most important chapter in [volume 3] . . . , and readers must not only read, but study it."[41] Charles had touched the artist's most sensitive nerve.

Adams cannot have found it entirely easy to possess an older brother so vigorous and critical. Henry—only five feet three inches tall, slight of build, perhaps permanently affected by his childhood bout of scarlet fever—had long stood exposed to Charles's assault. When, nearing his twenty-fourth birthday, Henry had ventured to express from London some of his most fatuous young-man's thoughts, Charles was crushing:

You set up for a philosopher. You write letters a la Horace Walpole; you talk of loafing around Europe; you pretend to have seen life. Such twaddle makes me feel like a giant Warrington talking to an infant Pendennis. *You* "tired of this life"! *You* more and more "callous and indifferent about your own fortunes!" Pray how old are you and what has been your career? . . . Fortune has done nothing but favor you and yet you are "tired of this life". . . . What do you mean by thinking, much less writing such stuff?

A year later Charles returned to the attack: "Your mind has become morbid and is in a bad way. . . . Make a bolt into the wilderness, go to sea before the mast, volunteer for a campaign in Italy, or do anything singularly foolish and exposing you to uncalled for hardship. . . . I here suggest what you most need, and what you will never be a man without. . . . All a man's life is not meant for books, or for travel in Europe." To defend himself against this strenuous philosophy, Henry needed to find in England a tradition to which he could attach himself and which would let him flourish upon his own terms. His brother, visiting England briefly in 1864, suspected Henry's inclination: Henry "seeks the society of the profound," Charles reported, "and had better return to America." The younger man soon found in the Englishman Milnes Gaskell a style of life that suited him, and by 1867 he was taking a lofty tone toward Charles's Americanism: "Keep your temper, my boy. Above all, forget that you are a national eagle."[42] Ostensibly their disagreement was about Radical Reconstruction, but Charles was goaded to ridicule Henry's diminutive stature, and his epithets suggested that their proper roles had become inverted: "Damned little cuss . . . damnedest collection of panic-stricken howls . . . *you* lecture *me*. . . . Here's richness."[43]

By 1869 Henry was well-launched in Washington upon his career as a writer, and he was ready to rebuff Charles's allegation that he thought too much about himself and did not write popularly enough. Henry asserted that he was following his own path: "Of course a man can't do this without appearing to think a great deal about himself, and perhaps doing so in fact." He felt the strain of his return to America after nearly a decade's absence. He had to risk unpopularity if he were to find his own way. He believed there was in England a class of people who could cultivate their own taste and mode of writing without regard for its popularity, but "in America there is no such class, and the tendency is incessant to draw everyone into the main current. I have told you before that I mean to be unpopular," he cried, in his sharpest explosion against Charles's influence: "I must do it, or do as other people do and give up the path I chose for myself years ago. Your ideas and mine don't agree, but they never have agreed. You like the strife of the world. I detest it and despise it. You work for power. I work for my own satisfaction. You like roughness and strength; I like taste and dexterity. For God's sake, let us go our ways and not try to be like each other."[44]

Despite this outburst, in 1869 Henry and Charles entered into a fruitful collaboration as reformist journalists, tracking down the Erie Railroad mismanagement and the "Great Gold Conspiracy." The next year Charles helped persuade Henry to take the editorship of the *North American Review* and to accept the Harvard assistant professorship that subsidized this post. Henry edited the magazine in the reform interest with Charles contributing some of the most substantial articles. Henry's marriage more or less terminated this collaboration; but in 1885, after the death of Henry's wife, Charles was probably the only person to whom he told the full story. By then the brothers had grown much farther apart. Recognizing the brilliance of the *History*, Charles secured the offer of a Harvard LL.D. to Henry, but his brother refused it rudely. Henry felt that Charles had been captured by "State Street"—as indeed he had—and he was contemptuous of Charles's literary style. Charles nevertheless changed his residence from Massachusetts to Washington, partly in order to be near Henry, and when Charles died Henry paid tribute to the ruin of what had once been his closest friendship, a partnership of vital consequence to his development: "Now that he is gone, nothing remains but for me to go too."[45]

Although another of the brothers, Brooks Adams, affected Henry after 1890, Brooks was ten years the junior, and the early lines of influence ran almost exclusively from Henry toward Brooks. Upon Henry's own development a far more important influence arose from his convoluted relation to his grandfather, John Quincy Adams, who died when Henry was ten but who exercised the historian's imagination for the rest of his life. That Henry admired some of his grandfather's qualities is certain, for he made him the central figure of the glowing first chapter in the *Education*. The golden haze that enveloped Henry's recollection of his grandfather at Quincy was associated with the enchantment of a boy's summer freedom in the country after winter confinement in Boston; but it was formed when the warm draft of Henry's family pride touched the cool features of a New England antislavery hero already apotheosized into marble, like one of Houdon's busts, during his lifetime. As recently as the 1960s John Quincy Adams was sometimes regarded merely as a competent diplomatist, unequal to the presidency, who afterwards in the House of Representatives gave free rein to a passion for self-righteous denunciation of the South. But as misunderstanding of the antislavery movement has lifted, it has become clear that he of all early national leaders was most honorable and resolute in attacking his countrymen's acquiescence in slavery. His grandson had reason to be proud of him.

Henry inherited his grandfather's repugnance for the abettors of slavery. He published in the *Revue Historique*, at a moment when most French historians were glorifying Napoleon, an exposé of Bonaparte's treachery in restoring human bondage to Santo Domingo,[46] and his subsequent tribute to the Negroes of that island has not lost resonance with the passage of years:

Had Toussaint [L'Ouverture] not been betrayed by his own generals, and had he been less attached than he was to civilization and despotic theories of military rule, he would have achieved a personal triumph greater than was won by any other man of his time. . . .

. . . . .

In these days of passion, men had little time for thought; and the last subject on which Bonaparte thereafter cared to fix his mind was the fate of Toussaint and Leclerc. That the "miserable negro," as Bonaparte called him, should have been forgotten so soon was not surprising; but the prejudice of race alone blinded the American people to the debt they owed to the desperate courage of five hundred thousand Haytian negroes who would not be enslaved.[47]

Although Henry Adams was willing as early as 1867 to abandon the freedmen to the mercies of their former owners, he inherited the independence that characterized John Quincy Adams's position on slavery. As boys, Charles and Henry learned to stand alone. Charles recalled having been "from childhood a part of the anti-slavery agitation. . . . Always at school I was in the small minority. . . . The very name of my grandfather was to the Webster Whig gall and wormwood."[48] John Quincy Adams was one of the earliest New England Federalists to go over to Jefferson's Democratic Republican party, and in his later career he displayed further indifference to party ties. Henry's eldest brother, John, was a leader of the Massachusetts Democrats after the Civil War. Henry, an early Republican, was an Independent in 1876 and a supporter of the Democrats in 1884. It was not surprising that the *History* grew out of Henry's criticism of Federalists and Jeffersonians alike and from his willingness to challenge both British and American national susceptibilities.

He esteemed John Quincy Adams's writings as the most important single source for early nineteenth-century American history, and some historians suspect that Henry, loyal to his grandfather, uncritically adopted his prejudices in the *History*. But Henry's discussion of Adams's service as an American peace commissioner after the War of 1812 does not suggest a writer maimed by ancestor worship. President Madison had at first nominated Albert Gallatin to head the five-man commission, but the Senate, refusing to accept Gallatin at once as a commissioner, caused Adams to be made chairman. Henry declared that

Gallatin was peculiarly fitted to moderate a discordant body like the negotiators, while Adams was by temperament little suited to the post of moderator, and by circumstances ill-qualified to appear as a proper representative of the commission in the eyes of its other members. . . .

. . . . .

In this delicate situation only the authority and skill of Gallatin saved the treaty. At the outset of the discussion, October 30 [1814], Gallatin quietly took the lead from Adams's hands. . . .

. . . . .

The extraordinary patience and judgment of Gallatin, aided by the steady support of Bayard, carried all the American points without sacrificing either Adams or Clay.[49]

This negotiation has recently been restudied by a diplomatic historian who shows that Henry Adams exaggerated the quarrelsomeness of the British envoys and the significance of the dispute between Adams and Clay but otherwise substantially erred only in undervaluing his own grandfather's achievement.[50]

As American minister to Russia, John Quincy Adams secured in December 1810 the czar's defiance of Napoleon on the issue of neutral trade. Napoleon wished Russia to enforce his own ban on American commerce with the Continent, and when the czar refused, it was a sign that Russia and France would soon be at war. While Henry's praise of Adams is hyperbolic at this point in his narrative, esteem does not preclude insight into character: "Anxious by temperament, with little confidence in his own good fortune,—fighting his battles with energy, but rather with that of despair than of hope,—the younger Adams never allowed himself to enjoy the full relish of a triumph before it staled, while he never failed to taste with its fullest flavor, as though it were a precious wine, every drop in the bitter cup of his defeats."[51]

Henry published in the *History* his belief that John Quincy Adams, as senator in 1807, "had made a mistake in voting for an embargo without limit of time." He also blamed his grandfather, privately, for attending the Republican presidential caucus in 1808; for jumping at the Russian mission in 1809, thus "deserting his self-evident duty in Massachusetts at a time of the utmost difficulty . . . , avowedly because he wanted to escape attack"; and for dawdling in Russia when no longer useful there, against the prayers of his father and mother that he return. He nevertheless formed the peculiar judgment that his grandfather was the most important figure of American politics in the first half of the nineteenth century, and he admired his achievements after 1830, "which redeemed everything, and caused the world to forget the crushing failures of the Senate and the Presidency." It is his criticism of his ancestor that raises his praise above adulation.[52]

A clue to what John Quincy Adams meant to his grandson appeared in a letter Henry wrote from Paris in 1891 to his intimate friend Mrs. Elizabeth Cameron. His words exhibited that slightly mocking attitude of urbane deference with which formerly he had disguised some of his feelings towards his own parents:

[This evening I] hurried off to the Opéra Comique to perform an act of piety to the memory of my revered grandfather. . . . A century ago, more or less, Grétry produced his opera: Richard Coeur de Lion. A century ago, more or less, President Washington sent my grandfather, before he was thirty years old, as minister to the Hague. . . . [My grandfather] was so much attached to Grétry's music that when he was turned out of the Presidency he could think of nothing for days together, but "Oh Richard! oh, mon roy, l'univers t'abandonne. . . ." I thought I would see . . . [the opera] now that it has been revived at the Opéra Comique. . . . I tried to imagine myself as I was then—and you know what an awfully handsome young fellow Copley made me—with full dress and powdered hair, talking to Mme Chose in the boxes, and stopping to applaud "un regard de ma belle."[53]

As Henry here witnessed the operatic spectacle through his grandfather's eyes, so during the preceding decade he seems to have surveyed the political world of 1801–17 through the same medium: He did not always accept his grandfather's judgments, but they offered him a point of departure.

He could not understand, for example, why John Quincy Adams voted for Jefferson's embargo, and near the end of his life was still trying to account for the behavior of his ancestor: "If he started with a sentimental ideal of patriotism, and let himself fall into every trap . . . that lay in his path, merely because his sentimental weakness blinded him, I am worse off than before. . . . Is it possible that I could have acted in that way?" Yet Henry showed in 1874, at the outset of his study of American history, how John Quincy Adams could affect his judgment. Henry was trying to form an opinion of the Boston revolutionist Sam Adams. As for Sam Adams's anti-federalism, he wrote, "In these days I think I am rapidly coming to the conclusion that he was right, and J. Q. Adams certainly went over to his party." A hundred instances might be given of John Quincy Adams's influence on the *History*—his estimate of the Massachusetts Federalist Harrison Gray Otis, his opinion of the constitutionality of the Louisiana Purchase, his judgment of Napoleon's Continental System—but a single case may illustrate how Henry progressed beyond his grandfather's view. John Quincy Adams once noted, discussing the inconsistency between the Declaration of Independence and the institution of slavery, that Jefferson "is one of the great men whom this country has produced, one of the men who has contributed largely to the formation of our national character—to much that is good and to not a little that is evil in our sentiments and manners."[54] The question lying behind this comment was the right one to ask, but Adams's answer was embryonic. His grandson transformed the observation in both content and style:

No one questioned the force or the scope of an emotion which caused the poorest peasant in Europe to see what was invisible to poet and philosopher,—the dim outline of a mountain-summit across the ocean, rising high above the mist and mud of American democracy. As though to call attention to some such difficulty, European and American critics, while affirming that Americans were a race without illusions or enlarged ideas, declared in the same breath that Jefferson was a visionary whose theories would cause the heavens to fall upon them. Year after year, with endless iteration, in every accent of contempt, rage, and despair, they repeated this charge against Jefferson. Every foreigner and Federalist agreed that he was a man of illusions, dangerous to society and unbounded in power of evil; but if this view of his character was right, the same visionary qualities seemed also to be a national trait, for every one admitted that Jefferson's opinions, in one form or another, were shared by a majority of the American people.

. . . . .

. . . This sandy face, with hazel eyes and sunny aspect; this loose, shackling person; this rambling and often brilliant conversation, belonged to the controlling influences of American history, more necessary to the story than three-fourths of the official papers, which only hid the truth. Jefferson's personality during these eight years appeared to be the government, and impressed itself, like that of Bonaparte, although by a different process, on the mind of the nation.[55]

Adam's procedure of starting with a contemporary's reflections and moving on from there was neither rare nor culpable. The best history always exhibits the coherent viewpoint of its author, and if the author has examined the world through the eyes of an intelligent, independent contemporary, this can incite him to his own work of interpretation. The *History* profited from Adams's luck in starting so well.

Henry's feeling toward his grandfather changed radically during the years after he finished his main work. By 1909 he was seventy-one years old, and, for reasons which will appear later, had renounced most of his earlier aims and values. This filled him with ambivalence toward the grandfather so closely associated with his own earlier thinking. When Henry's younger brother, Brooks Adams, composed a long-winded, never-published biography of John Quincy Adams, he asked for Henry's judgment; and in his lengthy "Critique" Henry delivered himself of a caustic commentary upon his grandfather's accomplishments. Imagining his own life before 1890 to have been a failure, Henry saw his grandfather's career in the same terms: He "in 1830 found his whole life a sentimental folly,—a bitter absurdity,—and . . . he went on deliberately to make another, which was founded on opposite ideas. . . . [The climax of the biography ought to be] the tragic failure of the early life, with its theories, culminating in the Presidency and the triumph of Andrew Jackson. . . . The failure was turned into triumph by reversing every method and practice of the past."[56] Henry knew that, of all his progenitors, John Quincy Adams was the one most nearly touched by genius; but Henry had fallen painfully short, in his chosen profession, of the plaudits won by his grandfather in politics—the fame of a Macaulay was certainly not his—and the compensation of a happy private life had long been torn from his grasp. He never lost his admiration for his grandfather's later career nor for his earlier diplomatic work; but by 1909 Henry had lived out a quarter century of disappointment since his wife's death, and although his criticisms of John Quincy Adams were trenchant, the balanced rationality of the *History* and the warm admiration of the *Education* have been overwhelmed by the green-eyed monster. John Quincy Adams's "whole behavior," Henry alleged,

shows that he loathed and hated America. . . . He never thought of going home [from Russia] without nausea, but he, and his son, and his grandchildren, had to be trained to profess a passionate patriotism which very strongly resembled cant.

. . . Though he was brought up in Paris, London and Berlin, he seems to have been indifferent to art. I do not remember that he ever mentions interest in architecture, sculpture or painting. His taste in literature was wholly didactic.

. . . . .

I knew that the old man was in a high degree obnoxious to me . . . ; but I had no idea how acute the antipathy would be. . . . The picture of this slovenly German Gelehrte whose highest delight is to lecture boys about a rhetoric of which he never could practice either the style or the action or the voice or the art, and then gloating over his own foolish production in print, instead of rolling on the ground with mortification as his grandchildren would do,—this picture grinds the colors into my aesophagus. . . .

. . . . .

[In Adams's poetry] you will see the same vein of feeble and commonplace sentiment [as he showed in politics in 1809 and 1829], mixed with a strange burlesque of Walter Scott and Lord Byron, calculated to turn me green with shame. Literally I groan with mortification at the thought of it.[57]

This splenetic outburst of an embittered old man against an ancestor with whom he had once identified himself may not be so puzzling as it appears. Before 1868 Henry had lived many years abroad, in circles where the career of an artist ranked higher than in America, and after 1890 he spent summer after summer in France. Like Gilbert Osmond in *The Portrait of a Lady*, he was an American who seemed to value taste more than the Europeans did. He had married into a Boston family to whom art meant more than to the Adamses, and he increasingly associated himself with that family rather than with his own. In the 1870s, consciously rejecting the example of his grandfather's political career, he had staked his ambition upon artistic success; he regarded his *History* as a work of art and not simply as a piece of scholarship. In contrast to Henry James, he had gambled before 1890 that an artistic career could be pursued in his native land, and he had affirmed that earlier American writers were unjust to complain of an indifferent public.[58]

But after 1890, with the lack of public recognition of his *History*, Adams felt his race for acclaim a failure: "Like a horse that wears out, he quitted the race-course. . . . As far as Adams knew, he had but three serious readers— Abram Hewitt, Wayne McVeagh, and [John] Hay himself. He was amply satisfied with their consideration, and could dispense with that of the other fifty-nine million, nine hundred and ninety-nine thousand, nine hundred and ninety-seven."[59] Ostentatious defiance seemed appropriate when Adams discussed publicly his failure to gain "consideration." But the worm gnawed at his heart, and, in his jealous private outburst to Brooks (the disintegration of Henry's personal life magnifying many times the force of his bitterness), he directed against the philistinism of John Quincy Adams his own developing antagonism to a country that awarded nearly all of its laurels to politicians rather than artists.

Henry's assault upon John Quincy Adams in 1909 was no reliable guide to his judgment of his grandfather when, decades earlier, he had composed the *History*, but it was at least a clue to his vigorous identification with his family. As a young man Henry had once demanded of his brother Charles, "What do you mean by asserting now principles against which every Adams yet has protested and resisted." He then supposed, believing in the family's corporate unity, that a failure by one member could be redeemed by another: "My aim [as to a career] is now so indefinite that all my time may prove to have been wasted. . . . I should care the less for all this if I could see your path any clearer." In 1909, still thinking of family honor, he rejoiced to Brooks that John Quincy had broken with the South after 1830; thus we "have not to defend a sentimental Union-saver as one of our tasks."[60]

Family solidarity threatened Adams with that most ungenial of passions, resentment. He could on occasion treat criticism without rancor, as when he wrote to Gaskell, "I would like to show you some of the attacks I have met in the press here. They are usually based on my great-grandfather." But he was driven to bravado in discussing the presidential election of 1876: "The tendency to blackguard the Adamses generally is . . . irresistible to the average American politician and as we shall catch it equally whether we vote for Hayes or Tilden or not at all, we can afford to grin at it."[61] Grave danger lurked near his writing when, as in certain fastidious circumlocutions about Jefferson's inaugural addresses, he attempted to disguise resentment against an old family foe. The family passions lying beneath the surface of the *History* lend it much of its zest and piquancy but contribute also to that occasional ill-humor which was the historian's failing.

Yet Henry's identification with his family had the curious effect of strengthening his allegiance to democracy. The family came to be regarded in the North as American aristocrats, but Henry knew that in European, or even Virginian, eyes, the Adamses were upstarts. To John Randolph of Virginia, it would have seemed that John Adams "had neither family, wealth, nor land, but was a mere shoot of a psalm-singing democracy." Adams's pride in his great-grandfather culminated in his striking chapter "American Ideals," where he estimated the value of his country's experiment in egalitarianism. The United States in 1800, he declared, was "a nation as yet in swaddling-clothes, which had neither literature, arts, sciences, nor history. . . ."

Yet even then one part of the American social system was proving itself to be rich in results. The average American was more intelligent than the average European, and was becoming every year still more active-minded as the new movement of society caught him up and swept him through a life of more varied experiences. On all sides the national mind responded to its stimulants. . . . [Some of the American's] triumphs were famous throughout the world; for Benjamin Franklin had raised high the reputation of American printers, and the actual President of the United States, who signed with Franklin the treaty of peace with Great Britain, was the son of a small farmer, and had himself kept a school in his youth.

Similarly, Henry exulted that in the St. Petersburg of 1810 John Quincy

Adams could thwart the French ambassador to Russia despite his being "far too poor to enter upon the most modest social rivalry."[62]

Better training for a historian than that provided by Henry Adams's family could scarcely be imagined. His father offered Henry opportunity from the earliest age to eavesdrop on serious political discussions, and Henry was soon privy to his father's confidential negotiations in Washington and London. Charles Francis Adams's scholarly activities and his lively interest in English literature exerted direct influence on his son. The father's independence from New England sectionalism and from narrow American patriotism, combined with his dedication to the American republican experiment, prefigured qualities that distinguished Henry Adams's *History* from the sentimentality, jingoism, or narrow partisanship of most nineteenth-century American histories.

Henry's elder brother Charles, for years his closest companion, was at once Henry's greatest admirer and his roughest critic. The two young men, unlike their eldest brother John, who was something of a "society man," pursued their political and literary education with deadly seriousness. Charles also acted as a buffer between Henry and their father: He fulfilled the course of strict filial duty, getting down to "business" as soon as he finished college and serving in the army during the Civil War, while Henry spent two years after college in Europe and developed in a "feminine" direction complementing Charles's aggressive "masculinity." Henry was free to cultivate himself intellectually and aesthetically in London at the moment Charles was campaigning on Virginia battlefields.

The figure of John Quincy Adams cast a long shadow over his grandson's life. Henry admired him for his diplomatic victories, his stand against slavery, his independence from party, and his veracity as a diarist. But the grandfather's failings were increasingly irritating to Henry Adams after 1890, when Henry felt he could cherish only that aesthetic side of life where John Quincy Adams was weakest.

Henry's mother, more than anyone else, prepared him to apprehend failure. Although she provided Henry a certain relief from Charles Francis Adams's austerity, her tendency toward lamentation and self-distrust infected the young man who had always been thrown into closest contact with her. The combination of an undemonstrative father, an incapable mother, a trio of socially adept brothers and sister, and a certain physical underdevelopment attacked Henry Adams's self-confidence and led him to crave the world's applause. But the tendency was subterranean, and for years positive forces predominated. If Henry Adams profited more than do most children of illustrious families from being born in extraordinary circumstances, this was partly because his experiences in England during his twenties and his marriage to an unusual Bostonian developed much further those talents nurtured within the family.

CHAPTER 2 · *England*

BEYOND FAMILY gifts, Henry Adams possessed the benefits of training at Harvard and close personal acquaintance with most of the leading New England historians. Yet, like other unusual "New Englanders" of the era—Henry James, George Santayana, W. E. B. DuBois—he needed to cross his native culture with an alien one before he could flourish. The fusion was made possible by the stroke of fortune that in 1861 sent his father to London.

Years later he wrote of Jefferson that "his instincts were those of a liberal European nobleman, like the Duc de Liancourt. . . . With all his extraordinary versatility of character and opinions, he seemed during his entire life to breathe with perfect satisfaction nowhere except in the liberal, literary, and scientific air of Paris in 1789."[1] The thought grew from Adams's own experience, for he himself in his whole life had been in some ways easiest during his long sojourn in England, from 1861 to 1868. The first four of these years were filled with mixed joys and humiliations, but life was more uniformly pleasant from 1865 to 1868 when British passions over the American Civil War were exhausted and when Adams found himself admitted via the Gaskell family into a congenial literary and scholarly society. His stay in England "was a golden time for me," he later reminisced; it "altered my whole life." To Charles Milnes Gaskell himself, after nearly half a century, Adams's judgment on his sailing for England was not less emphatic: "I rather fancy it was the biggest piece of luck I ever had."[2]

When the twenty-three-year-old private secretary checked his possessions through the Liverpool customs office, he did not submit for examination the trunkload of presumptions with which he entered the country: that England would furnish firm support for the American antislavery cause; that America's republican political and social arrangements were far more progressive than Britain's; but that his Bostonian admiration for the British elite would be enough to make him socially accepted within the charmed circle. Two years' experience exposed the presumptuousness of the first and third theories, and

Adams's republicanism then led him toward an increasingly sharp critique of Britain. "The idea that the upper class alone was hostile [to the North], is a total mistake," he claimed years later. "It was the hostility of the middle-class which broke our hearts, and turned me into a life-long enemy of everything English."[3]

Yet Adams became permeated through and through by what he considered an English manner—a power of expressing ridicule "with a patronizing air of great good-humor"[4]—and he learned to turn this British weapon against Britain itself. He experienced, furthermore, moments of such intellectual stimulation—and he later led with Gaskell a life of such freedom from social constraint—that he could never efface the memory of happy days in England.

The young man soon recognized the futility of his hope that disapproval of slavery would prompt England to befriend the North. Two months after Sumter he still alleged that "the sympathies and the policy of England are undoubtedly with us, as has been already shown"; but Bull Run and the Mason-Slidell affair dispelled this illusion. "My own Anglicism is somewhat wilted," he confessed to J. G. Palfrey early in 1862, and to his brother Charles he was more outspoken: "They are a nasty set . . . in this country, and I have lost my respect for them entirely. . . . The tone of people here is insufferable to me. I lose my temper, or get sulky."[5]

Henry's greatest shock came on the morning of January 10, 1862, when, turning to the editorial page of the London *Times*, he read with palpitating heart and a spreading blush of mortification a full-length leader about Mr. H. Adams. The *Times*, cheerily confident in the inevitability of southern independence, was delighted at the alarm Englishmen's northern American cousins felt at the possibility of Britain's wielding her power to secure that end; and the editor was smugly certain that provincial Bostonians would always be made to feel outsiders upon the sacred ground of a truly metropolitan society. Adams had dared to intrude on a closed world, and the *Times* administered one of its set-downs with zest:

"Mr. H. Adams, son of the American Minister in London," seems to have been deputed, in November last, to report on the feelings of Manchester towards the Federal States, and the results of this delicate inquiry are published in the *Boston Daily Courier*. We had certainly not fancied that the great capital of the English cotton trade was so much out of the world as to need a Special Commissioner to bring its hidden opinions to light. . . .

We are sorry to disappoint our readers, but it really does not appear that the Manchester men interrogated by Mr. Adams disclosed any views materially differing from those which the rest of us have long entertained. . . .

Mr. Adams's diary would not have been deemed complete by those for whose eyes it was intended had it not contained a little of that gossip which our cousins import into their most serious transactions. Accordingly, a document which evidently purports to be in the nature of a State paper contains a smart comparison between London and Manchester society, greatly to the disadvantage of the former. . . . The truth is, that what is called "society" is as inscrutable to a stranger as individual character. Even though we speak the same language and belong to a kindred stock he must ever be an outsider in this kind of intercourse. . . . [Mr. Adams] will profess to know less of us when he really knows more. Let him but persevere in frequenting the *soirées* and admiring the "family pictures," which make London society "a distinct thing" from that of a provincial town, and we shall not despair of reading some day a new diary in the *Boston Daily Courier*, wherein the *amende honorable* will be made to the gay world of the Metropolis.[6]

Adams never forget this humiliation at the hands of the world's leading newspaper. At first "he felt little or no hope of repaying these attentions"— the *Times*'s derision and its hostility to the North during the Civil War. But years later, discussing in his *History of the United States* the War of 1812, he found the opportunity for retaliation. He brought to light the *Times*'s protests at American naval victories in 1812 and 1813, and he joyfully quoted another London paper on the *Times*'s "tone of whining lamentation, of affected sensibility, and puerile grief."[7] Deeply as the British literary tradition came to influence Adams, he could never overlook the evidence of British contempt for America. He made British attitudes to America, their causes and their effects, a central theme of the *History*.

In 1862 and 1863 Adams was maddened by the indifference of the British government and most members of high society to the news which arrived periodically from the American battlefields. The tone of society was no less galling: "The belief in poor Mr. Lincoln's brutality and [Secretary of State] Seward's ferocity became a dogma of popular faith. . . . Thackeray's voice trembled and his eyes filled with tears [at] the coarse cruelty of Lincoln and his hirelings. . . . At that moment Thackeray, and all London society with him, needed the nervous relief of expressing emotion; for if Mr. Lincoln was not what they said he was—what were they?"[8]

Adams's politics in the 1860s were very different from the "Conservative Christian Anarchism" of his old age. He wrote a year before Sumter that northern antislavery republicans—like his family—stood "so far on the extreme left that all European parties and party fights seem matters of the last century." John Bright, the most effective agitator in Great Britain for a second Reform Bill, was to Adams in 1862 "my favourite Englishman"; and as early as April of that year the young American envisaged an informal alliance between the North and the British working classes: "I hope before long," he wrote to Seward's son, "we may be able to begin a popular agitation to force this Government out of its belligerent ideas."[9]

Adams knew that the North would never stir popular sympathy in England until it placed antislavery principles upon its banners. "Our cry now must be emancipation and arming the slaves," he wrote only seven months after Sumter. "If some real emancipation step could be taken," he urged Frederick Seward two months later, "it would be the next best thing to taking Richmond for us here. . . . There is great difficulty felt here in supporting our Government on anti-slavery grounds. Even a small step would, I think, be of great use, especially if taken with sufficient noise and flourish of trumpets." A well-publicized granting of citizenship rights to Negroes traveling abroad would be one such step; "the sight of an effective black army" would be a greater; while the Emancipation Proclamation itself was "a Godsend."[10]

Once the proclamation was issued, certain workingmen's meetings in England announced a connection between emancipation in America and democratic reform in Britain. Charles Francis Adams was informed of the plans for the most important of these demonstrations—at St. James's Hall, London, on March 26, 1863—and he conferred upon his son the grateful role of conveyor of glad tidings to Secretary of State Seward. Benjamin Moran, the American assistant secretary of the legation, referred contemptuously to the "proceedings of a lot of English tinkers and tailors at St. James' Hall"; but to the supposedly aristocratic Henry Adams, the "radicalism" of the speakers was their merit. "The speech of Prof. Beesley of the London University [was] . . . perhaps the most effective and radical of all. . . . The meeting was a demonstration of democratic strength," he continued enthusiastically to Seward: "Every hostile allusion to the aristocracy, the Church, the opinions of the 'privileged classes,' was received with warm cheers. Every allusion to the republican institutions of America; the right of suffrage; the right of self-taxation; the 'sunlight' of republican influence, was caught up by the audience with vehement applause."[11] Henry's relish at the discomfiture of Britain's rulers and his identification with the democratic movement were expressed even more clearly in his private dispatch to his brother Charles:

I went last night to a . . . democratic and socialist meeting, my boy; most threatening and dangerous to the established state of things; and assuming a tone and proportions that are quite novel and alarming in this capital. . . . I can assure you this sort of movement is as alarming here as a slave-insurrection would be in the South, and we [in the American Legation] have our hands on the springs that can raise or pacify such agitators. . . . I never quite appreciated the "moral influence" of American democracy, nor the cause that the privileged classes in Europe have to fear us, until I saw how directly it works. . . . [Our great republic] though wounded itself almost desperately, can yet threaten to tear down the rulers of the civilised world, by merely assuming her place at the head of the march of democracy.[12]

Adams was conscious, to be sure, of "the contemptible tone politics takes with us" in America.[13] The proper role of New Englanders like the Adamses in American politics, he believed, was to inculcate morality and diffuse education among the masses. "I dread the continuance of this war and its demoralizing effects," he ruminated to Charles in 1862:

It's likely to be hard enough work to keep our people educated and honest, anyway, and the accounts that reach us of the whole-sale demoralization in the army of the West, from camp-life, and of their dirt, and whiskey and general repulsiveness, are not encouraging to one who wants to see them taught to give up that blackguard habit of drinking liquor in bar-rooms, to brush their teeth and hands and wear clean clothes, and to believe that they have a duty in life besides that of getting ahead, and a responsibility for other people's acts as well as their own.[14]

The duties of the private secretaryship were usually not taxing, and Adams's London years were a halcyon time for wide reading and apprentice efforts at writing. Searching out legal and historical precedents to strengthen his father's hand in diplomacy, the young man wandered far afield, and his light often burned until two o'clock in the morning. For years he had meant to become a lawyer as a step toward public life, but the London environment encouraged him to contemplate a literary career. Living in a foreign country spurred him to take notice of the distinctive development of his native land. Like Tocqueville, he could study and write about the democratic movement without tempering his expression to the wind of popular approval, as a full-time politician must do:

I pass my intervals from official work, in studying De Tocqueville and John Stuart Mill, the two high priests of our faith. So I jump from International Law to our foreign history, and am led by that to study the philosophic standing of our republic, which brings me to reflection over the advance of the democratic principle in European civilization. . . . I have learned to think De Tocqueville my model, and I study his life and works as the Gospel of my private religion. The great principle of democracy is still capable of rewarding a conscientious servant.[15]

It was Adams's nature to rail against the status quo wherever he was—"tell me if he cusses everything as liberally as he used," his elder brother John inquired with elder-brotherly condescension in 1864—and this made it natural for him to criticize the workings of democracy in America while inveighing against monarchy and aristocracy in Europe; but the liberalism behind his critique of European institutions was not the less genuinely felt. Thus he looked forward to the growth of a "great, reforming, liberal party" in England, and he alluded with scorn to the festivities associated with the wedding of the Comte de Paris—"the old friends of a fallen dynasty, three times proven unequal to the wants of the age, raked together with a painful observance of royal forms."[16] A trip to Italy in 1865 prompted speculations that mingled a young man's uncertain posturing with a farsighted prophecy of America's position a century later. "Like many Americans who have lived long in Europe," he began sententiously,

I have become much more radical in my convictions than is usual in America, where you exist in amusing ignorance of the fact that you are rapidly being caught up with and will soon be left behind by Europe. . . . Since 1788 we [Americans] have with difficulty sustained our position, while Europe has made enormous strides forward. At present there are two great influences holding Europe back. One is the English aristocracy, the other the Roman Church. Both of these will go down as sure as fate. I can't tell you when or how the change will take place, but whether it's ten or whether it's a hundred years, it will come, and when all the world stands on the American principle, where will be our old boasts unless we do something more?[17]

This was the concern that led to Adams's well-known query in the *History*: Could American society "transmute its social power into the higher forms of thought?"[18] Adams was slowly persuading himself that the career of a writer might be no less socially responsible than that of a politician. His historical writing would illustrate the conflicts between American democrats and conservatives early in the nineteenth century, and it would explore American-British relations during that period, interpreting British conduct by the light of Adams's experiences of the 1860s.

When he composed the *History* after 1877, Adams retained many of his earlier judgments of English politics. "We have nothing quite so bad as Disraeli or Salisbury," he insisted to the Liberal M.P. Sir Robert Cunliffe in 1882, "and no party so idiotic as the English Tories." But he was no admirer of the Liberal leadership either: "I never was much of a Gladstonian," he assured Gaskell. "He showed us what he was worth during our civil war, and I never got over the impression he then made on me." With the Conservatives dismissed and most Liberal leaders too timid to institute radical reform, to whom could Britain look for leadership? One such person was an old Radical acquaintance: W. E. Forster, Adams predicted hopefully, "will yet live to bring in my bill for reorganising that preposterous body, the House of Lords." Adams revered the monarchy no more than the Lords, his objections being social as well as political: "I wish the Prince of Wales were hung, or drowned, or any way got rid of," he expostulated in 1878. "He is, to all our pretentious and semi-vulgar people, the successor of Louis Napoleon, and his court has the same influence here that the Tuileries used to have, before the republican broom cleaned out that harpies' den."[19]

Holding such opinions, Adams naturally judged English politicians from 1801 to 1815 more severely than most British historians can yet bear to do. The Whig Charles James Fox, like most Liberals later in the century, was in Adams's view too cautious to effect an enlightened policy, but the historian's imagination was most challenged by the illiberal Tory Foreign Minister George Canning, who did much to precipitate the War of 1812 and who also practiced that art of ridiculing Americans which had scourged Adams in London. When Canning became foreign secretary in 1807 Jefferson was still president, and Adams's vignette of the British minister betrayed an unwonted sympathy for the American chief of state; for Jefferson, like Adams, was a republican, and Canning, like Napoleon, was the enemy of their cause.

Adams had perfected the historian's art of introducing and later commenting upon a quotation, as a jeweler devises the setting that will most heighten the qualities of a gem:

Canning's contempt was unbounded for everything that savored of liberal principles. . . . [Bonaparte's coup d'état of the 18th Brumaire, in 1799] threw Canning into paroxysms of delight.

"Huzza! huzza! huzza!" he [Canning] wrote on hearing the news; "for no language but that of violent and tumultuous and triumphant exclamation can sufficiently describe the joy and satisfaction which I feel at this complete overthrow and extinction of all the hopes of the proselytes to new principles. . . . It is the lasting ridicule thrown upon all systems of democratic equality,—it is the galling conviction carried home to the minds of all the brawlers for freedom in this and every other country,—that there never was, nor will be, nor can be, a leader of a mob faction who does not mean to be the lord and not the servant of the people. . . ."

. . . After the 18th Brumaire the world contained but one leader of a mob faction, brawling for liberty; but he was President of the United States. No miraculous sagacity was needed to foretell what treatment he was likely to receive at the hands of two men like Canning and Bonaparte.[20]

The strange concomitant of Henry Adams's republican sympathies and his antislavery principles was his hope in 1861 that he would be accepted into British society. The battering to which this hope was subjected for four years helps to explain Adams's later ambivalence toward England. Charles Sumner was, in Adams's pungent phrase, "rarely without a pocket-full of letters from duchesses or noblemen in England,"[21] but Adams's description of his own eagerness for social success in England and his desire to insinuate himself into the company of the great would read as equally strong satire directed against himself were the tone not deadly earnest. "Society in London certainly has its pleasures," he exclaimed breathlessly early in 1863. The Duke of Argyll had given a dinner for the Adamses, and the other guests had been asked on purpose to meet them:

There was Lord Clyde. . . .; Charles P. Villiers, a friendly member of the Cabinet; Charles Howard, a brother of Lord Carlisle; John Stuart Mill the logician and economist, a curious looking man with a sharp nose, a wen on his forehead and a black cravat, to whom I took particular pains to be introduced, as I think him about the ablest man in England; very retiring and embarrassed in his manner, and a mighty weapon of defence for our cause in this country. . . . Then came Lord Frederick Cavendish. . . . I confess that I always feel a little self-satisfied in such society. I feel my self-respect increased by the fact of standing beside, and feeding with such men.[22]

Self-satisfaction mushroomed with Adams's election to a London club; he believed his sponsor to be Cavendish himself—"I am glad to have a Duke's son to back me," he pronounced smugly—and forty years later he still had not recovered equipoise. In *The Education of Henry Adams* he disfigured the captivating account of his first meeting Swinburne by adding an egregious allusion to a minor social success: "The only record of his [Henry Adams's] wonderful visit to Fryston may perhaps still exist in the registers of the St. James's Club, for immediately afterwards [Monckton] Milnes proposed Henry Adams for membership. . . . On the whole it [the list of his seconders] suggested that the private secretary was getting on."[23] But the St. James's was merely a club for foreign diplomats of a junior rank, and Adams clung thus to outward symbols of social success because he knew that in London society in general his first years were a failure. In mid-1863 he acknowledged the distance still separating him from people of real position. If he could not touch the hems of the mighty, he could at least spit upon his own provincial background. "The atmosphere is exciting," the twenty-five-year-old boasted with much exaggeration:

One does every day and without a second thought, what at another time would be the event of a year; perhaps of a life. For instance, the other day we were asked out to a little garden party by the old Duchess of Sutherland. . . . Half the best blood in England was there, and were cutting through country-dances and turning somersets and playing leap-frog in a way that knocked into a heap all my preconceived ideas of their manners. . . . You may be certain that I took no share in it. A stranger had better not assume to be one of the Gods. . . . How much of this sort of thing could one do at Boston![24]

Fortunately these exhilarating moments were so rare that they did not utterly destroy Adams's judgment. He envied the conversational prowess of his two elder brothers. "What would I give to be able to say one good thing," he complained wretchedly a few weeks before the leap-frog party; "nowadays I feel the curse of sterility light upon my brain wherever I go. . . . I dread society because I know that I am as dull as the people I see about me." His disabilities were twofold: He still could not overcome his shyness, even after four years at Harvard and four more in Europe; and his identification with democratic America was certain to alienate the fashionable world. He was repeating his experiences of 1859 in Germany: "The [Berlin] aristocracy all belong to the Court and hate everything that smells of America," he had then grumbled. Even his habit of bearing his own traveling gear had caused the raising of well-bred eyebrows: "I suppose in Germany no gentleman carries his own carpet bag."[25]

In England the few friendships Adams succeeded in establishing before 1864 were nearly always with people twice his age; and the happy consequence of his general social failure was that most days he had many hours, for years at a time, to pursue a liberal education. He showed a characteristic nineteenth-century seriousness about independent study. "I write and read;

41

read and write," he enthusiastically told Charles in 1863, mentioning studies in history, economics, political theory, philosophy, and literature, and specifying in one letter Mill, Hobbes, Spinoza, and the poems of Arthur Hugh Clough. Charles soon came to England, briefly furloughed from the army, and was alarmed at Henry's transformation. As befitted a soldier experiencing the benefits of outdoor life, Charles was quick to blame his brother's alleged troubles upon his diminutive stature and indoor habits: "Henry! Well, Henry is a nondescript!. . . . I think he had much better, as soon as he can, go back to America. He is of immense service to the Minister here and evidently does all the confidential work. . . . But he is wizening up physically, is 123 years old mentally, and is becoming a regular recluse. He evidently feels pitiably the want of physical presence, and has just given up under it." "Henry philosophizes, and seeks the society of the profound."[26]

To mix with the intelligentsia of London was Henry's avowed object. "My most sought acquaintances," he had written early in 1863, "are men like [Tom] Hughes, and his associates, the cultivated radicals of England." Although Adams's opinions continued to fluctuate, he was beginning to make proper discriminations. He tried to persuade himself that he valued only "a few dinners and a few visits to country houses with clever people. . . . But as for fashionable society here, I say clearly that in my opinion it is a vast social nuisance and evil."[27] These may have been sour grapes, but Henry was fortunate that his lack of social skills led him to a certain clarity of vision.

While he was thus discovering his likes and dislikes in England, Adams had the excellent luck in 1863 to fall in with Milnes Gaskell, four years his junior, who graduated that year from Cambridge. A traveler often profits most from a foreign country when he establishes intimate relations with a person born and bred there—someone to open sanctuaries normally closed against strangers, to interpret the objects cherished there, and to comment on the peculiarities of his native customs. Gaskell was the person who played this role in Adams's life, and his family was the medium through which English cultural life most strongly wrought its deep influence upon the young American.

The friendship developed gradually, but by 1865 Gaskell's family had opened their hearts to Adams, and from then until 1868 he spent his happiest days in England within this cultivated circle. Gaskell's father, a Conservative member of Parliament from 1832 to 1868, owned estates in Yorkshire and Shropshire. His mother and her sister, born Wynn, followed literary interests. Gaskell's elder sister was married to Frank Palgrave, son of a distinguished historian, who himself later became Professor of Poetry at Oxford; while an uncle of Gaskell's was Sir Francis Doyle, the Professor of Poetry from 1867 to 1877. Gaskell's second cousin Sir Robert Cunliffe, grandson of a noted British general in India, later became a Liberal M.P., as did Gaskell himself. Another of Adams's intimates was Ralph Palmer, cousin of Palmerston's attorney general, Sir Roundell Palmer. Adams was much influenced by several of these individuals (he paid tribute to Palgrave in the *Education*) and the group exercised a decisive influence upon his life, for they gave him courage to pursue a literary career on principles rather different from those of American friends such as his brother Charles.

In the *Education* Adams admitted that his intimacy with Milnes Gaskell "affected his whole life"; with his usual reticence he characterized only Gaskell's father, his mother, and his local habitat, but dropped scarcely a hint about Gaskell himself. This was because a deep affection had subsisted between the two men that Adams would no more expose to public scrutiny than his early intimacy with Charles Adams or his later marriage to Marian Hooper. As in the letters to his brother, Henry's salutations to Gaskell rang the changes of attachment: "My dear Carlo," "Oh my beloved," or—five weeks after Henry's wedding—"My beloved C.G.M.G." In the nineteenth century a young man was free to address this kind of language to a male friend without being misunderstood. A letter might be signed "ever affectionately," and true feeling informed the words. In 1880, returning with Marian to America after a year's research in Europe, Adams spent the last few days before departure at Wenlock Abbey, Gaskell's Shropshire home. Like Charles Francis Adams, Henry found difficulty in expressing his feelings, but he attempted to do so in a letter mailed back to Wenlock just before the vessel steamed away:

Between ourselves, though I have not cared to dwell on it, I have little doubt that we are now bidding good-bye to Europe forever. If we wander again, it will be when the doctors send us for health.

We send you our last good wishes for happiness and contentment. . . .

This is the fourth time I have left your house to sail; rather an unusual thing in this queer world. . . .

Good-bye, which means, I believe, God be with you.

The four years when Adams took leave of Europe from Wenlock Abbey were 1868, 1870, 1873, and 1880, and the pattern was repeated in the 1890s. Gaskell was an even more devoted friend than Henry was, and he loaded presents and hospitality upon Henry and Marian. He seems to have given them as a wedding present the copy of Viollet-le-Duc that Adams later made the principal source for *Mont-Saint-Michel and Chartres*, and he turned over to them for three months in 1873, as a much more material wedding present, the exclusive use of his fashionable house on Park Lane overlooking Hyde Park, along with a new carriage. When Henry and Marian returned to Europe in 1879, Gaskell, who by then had sold his London residence, rented a house there specifically in order to furnish them entertainment in the metropolis. As years passed something of the bittersweet entered the relation.

In 1890 Adams, the *History* complete and his life a ruin, recalled and destroyed most of his own private letters and returned to the senders the letters he had received; having consigned to oblivion these vestiges of his old life, he set off for Samoa. Gaskell could not enter into the spirit of this arrangement: "I have as you know all yours [letters], and value them deeply":

> My poor old letters! I shall not open them and I shall not burn them, as I should look upon the latter act as a sort of burial of the past, and it has given me too many pleasures and enjoyments to be so badly treated. . . .
> Good bye, my dear Henry, and good luck attend you in your travels.
> Your ever affect[ionate]
Charles Milnes Gaskell

In 1909, embittered and aged, Henry did "not know that I care to live over again any part of my life, but if I did, the part connected with Wenlock and you would be it,—the most pleasure and the least pain."[28]

The outward life of Adams's friend was the unremarkable chronicle of a liberal English squire born to wealth, cultivation, and ease. With his mother's death in 1869 Gaskell inherited Wenlock Abbey, a 1,200-acre estate near Shrewsbury with an annual rent-roll of £3,000; and four years later the demise of his father, James Milnes Gaskell, brought him the house on Park Lane and a large fortune, together with another big house near Wakefield, in West Yorkshire.[29] Charles Milnes Gaskell had attended the ranking public school—"the Duke of Portland was in my division at Eton and was a great bully"[30]—and obtained at Trinity College, Cambridge, a most undistinguished third-class degree in Classics. Gaskell's father had entered the House of Commons at twenty-two, and the son, after becoming a member of the bar, sought election to Parliament in 1868 at the age of twenty-six; but he was defeated. For a time he was unhappily in love with Lady Mary Hervey, the sister of the Marquess of Bristol, whose family obliged her to break off the engagement; she never married. Although he wrote occasionally for the reviews, he led for some years—like his father before him—the inactive life of a cultivated gentleman. Recovering at least partially from his disappointment in love, he married the eldest daughter of the Earl of Portsmouth in 1876, and from 1885 he spent a quarter of a century in politics. For seven years he was a Liberal M.P. and thereafter, for nearly two decades, served as chairman of the county council of West Yorkshire, where his best efforts were devoted to fighting pollution of the rivers and supporting the work of a local insane asylum. He died in 1919, a year later than Adams.

What this man offered Henry, when their real friendship began in 1865, was not primarily a grounding in literature and art; for at first it was Gaskell, twenty-three when Adams was twenty-seven, who accepted instruction at Adams's hands—though a more equal relation quickly developed—while Adams in turn sat at the feet of the forty-one-year-old Frank Palgrave, Gaskell's brother-in-law. Nor was it an education in the principles of politics, for Adams's dissatisfaction with the aristocracy, the Tories, and most Liberal leaders went beyond the moderate Whiggery of Gaskell's conviction. Rather, he tendered unconstrained companionship to a young man stifled by the anti-American tone of London society, and membership in a richly culti-vated family, whose cultural values infused themselves into Adams's way of being. "In England," Adams reminisced, "the family is a serious fact; once admitted to it, one is there for life." The Gaskell family had weight in its part of the country. Like Lord Warburton in *The Portrait of a Lady*, Gaskell became something of a "personage" and was to be regarded not only "on the basis of character and wit—of what one might like in a gentleman's mind and in his talk—. . . .[but] as a collection of attributes and powers which were not to be measured by this simple rule, but which demanded a different sort of appreciation."[31]

Adams was fully prepared to appreciate visits to country estates after his painful first year in London, but the squirearchy did not hasten to flood the young man with invitations. His first country visit in 1862, to the Yorkshire estate of Richard Monckton Milnes, the future Lord Houghton, when Adams was overwhelmed by the genius of Swinburne, has its memorial in the *Education*; but Adams's earliest visit to Wenlock Abbey in 1864 proved more important to him. He sought to impress his hostess with his philosophy of despair, and he later rhapsodized to Charles Adams that "the youth Gaskell," Gaskell's mother, and Henry had dined in a

hall on whose timber roof, and great oak rafters, the wood fire threw a red shadow forty feet above our heads. . . . In the evening we sat in the dusk in the Abbot's own room of state, and there I held forth in grand after-dinner eloquence, all my social, religious and philosophical theories, even in the holy-of-holies of what was once the heart of a religious community. . . . We excavated tiles bearing coats of arms five hundred years old, and we laid bare the passages and floors that had been three cen-turies under ground. . . . We drove through the most fascinating parks and long an-cient avenues. . . . My visit to Shropshire was . . . curiously different from the usual stiffness of English society. . . . [The Gaskells, relatives of Lord Houghton, were] if anything, a little in his rather sensual and intellectual style.

Henry's visits to Wenlock were repeated, and in 1870, after two years of journalism in Washington, he was bursting to return to England for a sum-mer's companionship with Gaskell. His proposal was that of Jaques to Or-lando: "I will wander with you to every old house in Shropshire if you like, and swing on all the styles in the midland counties wherever there's a church with a tomb or good Gothic. We will rail in set terms at anyone we choose." Two years later, after Adams's wedding and honeymoon in Massachusetts, he introduced his bride immediately to Gaskell and Robert Cunliffe at Wen-lock Abbey. Like Henry, Marian Adams was delighted by the fifteenth-century prior's house, which she described to her father with a mixture of vivacity and exact terminology: One room, for example, had "eight mullioned windows with stone pedestal brackets to sit or rather perch on." She found that Wenlock relaxed her husband's constraint: Henry and Robert Cunliffe, "with Gaskell, behave like young colts in a pasture. They scour the hills on foot."[32]

A strong element of young-men's learned tomfoolery informed Adams's relation to Gaskell. Their friend Cunliffe's marriage in 1869 to Sophia Leigh had offered the two bachelors endless scope for transatlantic merriment. When Adams wrote to Gaskell in August 1869, he was already experimenting with the phrase whose final version appeared in the *History* as "a nation as yet in swaddling-clothes":

[Aug. 27, 1869:] After much despair I have got a present for the Baronet. It is silver, for I did not know what else to find in this land where arts are in the cradle. So I got him a little piece of American workmanship, a cheese-dish in fact, and on the lower rim of it I have had a line from Ovid inscribed. . . . [If] you can cap my motto by another more apposite, embracing not only friendship and cheese, but mice also (since two mice look over the edge and serve as handles) let some silversmith put it on, before you send it to Robert.

[Sept. 13:] Rub up your classics and cover my dish with quotations. . . .

[Oct. 5:] Why not a motto for mice? . . . Go to! You have all winter. . . .

[Nov. 7:] Confound your majesty's laziness! Aren't you a some-class-or-other in classics, and can't you bother me enough with Greek when I don't want it? And now you deny me a verse which you can invent if you like. Who says there's no analogy between cheese and Leighs! The rhyme alone is worth a permanent monument *aere perennius*. . . . But my amiable one, you *baisse*, evidently. . . . I shall pass the rustic mouse as your portrait and have your name in Gothic capitals carved under it, unless you provide my inscription.[33]

Gaskell's personality is best apprehended through the words of Henry James, who paid a four-day visit to Wenlock Abbey in the summer of 1877. James had come across the channel from Paris to settle in London during the preceding winter, and his most valuable notes of introduction proved to be those from Henry Adams to Gaskell, Lord Houghton, and other friends. James's first country visit was to Wenlock Abbey—the novelist postponed a trip to the Continent in order to accept the coveted invitation—and Gaskell seems then to have secured for James membership in the Travellers' and the St. James's clubs. James spent the Christmas holidays at Gaskell's Yorkshire estate in 1878 and 1879 (the latter was his sole country visit during the winter of 1879–80), and he had to decline another invitation a few weeks later so as to get to Florence to start the first installments of *The Portrait of a Lady*. "I am rather sorry to be going abroad," James wrote to his mother, "as Gaskell has asked me to come down to see the scrimmage in Yorkshire [a Parliamentary election was coming up]. He is not going to stand, but he is very much in it."[34] It is well known that the novelist filled his books with characters compounded from the features of his acquaintances. "Look out for my next big novel [*The Portrait of a Lady*]," he exclaimed disingenuously in 1879 to Mrs. Isabella Gardner, who perhaps was a model for Mrs. Touchett. "It will immortalize me. After that, some day, I will immortalize you."[35] It seems probable that Molyneux, Lord Warburton, the master of Lockleigh, was modeled mainly upon Milnes Gaskell, master of Wenlock Abbey.[36] What other member of the landed classes had James had such ample opportunity to observe?

James reported Gaskell to be "an excellent fellow, an entertaining companion and the prince of hosts"; but, with more than a tinge of envy, he characterized him to his mother as "an originally good fellow, depraved by snobbishness, over-many possessions and a position giving him all sorts of opportunities for taking himself and his luxuriant appurtenances with praeternatural seriousness." Of Gaskell it could certainly be said, as of Warburton, that he "pretends to be bored. . . ., [is] very intelligent and cultivated. . ., knowing almost everything in the world. . . . [He thinks] a great deal of . . . [his] position. . . . He has elegant tastes—cares for literature, for art, for science. . . . [His is] the first position in this part of the county. . . . 'Some people don't like a moat, you know' "[37] —a likeable but unexciting, slightly limited man of excellent manners, conscious of his own position yet with a great capacity for kindliness and affection. With so many points in common, it is likely that Gaskell also shared other qualities of Warburton's: gentleness, a curious mixture of diffidence and affability, a personal delicacy and sense of privacy which would naturally oppose thick walls of impenetrable civility to the thrusts of excessive familiarity—"Won't you have a potato? . . . Ah, we can be dull when we try!" Probably Gaskell's "quality was a mixture of the effect of rich experience—oh, so easily come by!—with a modesty at times almost boyish; the sweet and wholesome savour of which—it was as agreeable as something tasted—lost nothing from the addition of a tone of responsible kindness." Like Warburton, Adams's friend could offer to a restless American "peace, . . . kindness, . . . honour, . . . possessions, a deep security and a great exclusion."[38]

Thus, after Marian's breakdown and death in 1885 and the miserable years that ensued, Adams again found his way to Wenlock Abbey late in 1891. "Nothing has changed here since I first came in the year '64," he wrote to Elizabeth Cameron. "For once I find perfect stability and repose. . . . I think my true source of repose here is not so much in her [Lady Catherine Gaskell] or in her husband as in the place itself. An atmosphere of seclusion and peace certainly lingers in these stones."[39]

Two months later Gaskell accompanied his restless American friend to

London, where Henry found comfort in feeling himself to be a part of the family: "We dined with May Lacaita, the daughter of our old uncle Sir Francis Doyle, a favorite cousin of ours." With Gaskell as companion Adams revisited old English friends from the memory-laden years of the late 1860s, and was solaced by London itself: "Queer sensation, this coming to life again in a dead world. People are rather glad to see one; ask no questions; slide silently over all that has come between, as though all the ghosts were taking tea with us, and needed no introductions; and so we rattle on about today and tomorrow, with just a word thrown in from time to time to explain some chasm too broad to be jumped. . . . [I] have felt a sense of rest such as I have not known for seven years."[40]

One of the old friends Adams and Gaskell sought out was Augusta Hervey, now living in reduced circumstances, and this encounter recalled one of the closest ties between the two men—their joint courting twenty-five years earlier of young women of an aristocratic family: Lady Mary Hervey and Wilhelmina Hervey, the sister and the first cousin of the Marquess of Bristol. Adams was moved a fortnight later to tell part of the tale to Henry James, who promptly made notes of the possible plot for another story:

Poor Lady M[ary] H[ervey], who broke off her engagement with X.Y.Z. [Charles Milnes Gaskell] on the eve of marriage and now trails about at the tail of her mother—or some other fine lady—a dreary old maid. Then the situation of two other girls of the same noble house, one of whom, Augusta, now gives music lessons for a living. The other, the elder sister, was the daughter of a French mistress—dancer or someone—and of Lord A.B. [Lord William Hervey] (before his marriage) and was adopted by him and by his wife—it was a clause of the contract—as his own daughter and grew up on this footing.[41]

Lady Mary Hervey's family evidently objected to Gaskell's lack of a title and his not being a sound Trinitarian, but they seem also to have believed his conduct, and that of his American friend, discreditable. Possibly Gaskell, with Adams's knowledge, had persuaded Lady Mary to enter into a secret engagement without her family's consent. Three years after Lady Mary broke the engagement, Gaskell's brother-in-law, Palgrave, still worried that Gaskell had not recovered: "I fear he will not marry . . . until Lady M.H.——is disposed of: and (so far as I can learn) there is no thought of that neither this season. . . . [Gaskell had finished a bit of work but] unfortunately he will, I fear, now resume that otiose *nihil agendo* life which has been his father's ruin. He talks of a visit to what we call the 'Continent' . . . till next spring, and then—trying to reconcile himself to the odious task of marriage and generation."[42]

Adams probably did not acknowledge to Henry James the feeling he had once cherished for Lady Mary's cousin, Wilhelmina Hervey—the daughter, according to Adams, of Lord William Hervey's French mistress. "I have begun to be tired of having stupid people with titles sit upon me habitually," Adams had complained in 1867 to Gaskell. "You and I . . . have carried the war at times into the enemies' country and harried their young women. . . . I've no faith in any of those that we have chosen." Wilhelmina's younger sister, Augusta Hervey, may have lost her heart to Adams, but it was "Mina" in whom, despite his disavowal, Adams was interested. Soon after returning to America in 1868, he commissoned an English friend to tell Mina "that her water-colors of Cannes form a conspicuous ornament to my room here. They are really very pretty now that I have had them framed with about two inches of gold margin. As for Augusta, you can assure her of my highest consideration. But for God's sake, don't allude to my departure last summer, for we were all mixed very deep in Gaskell's affair, and in their minds I am probably always remembered in connection with the sore subject of that engagement."[43] Adams learned in February 1871—three months before he decided to pursue Marian Hooper—that Mina had become engaged to Sidney Bouverie-Pusey, and he pretended not to bat an eyelash. Marian knew better, for when Henry took her two years later to visit the Bouverie-Puseys, she had a sick headache the whole evening, and she took trouble to invent reasons not to see too much of Augusta Hervey, who pursued the recently wed Adamses with kind invitations.

The pains and pleasures of their relations with the Herveys formed one of the permanent bonds between Adams and Gaskell. In 1884 Adams observed with relish that now "a younger generation is doing very much what you and I did, twenty years ago, and finds it still exciting." Mina died the next year, and the tale was complete in 1892, when Adams wrote from London to Elizabeth Cameron. Gaskell and he, Henry reported, "sat an hour yesterday with Augusta Hervey who now gives music lessons; but is, I think, rather better off than her cousins the Bristols who are obliged to let Ickworth as well as the house in St. James's Square, and live on husks in the dark.[44]

When Adams edited the *North American Review*, he published four reviews by Gaskell which, together with private letters, a piece in the *Saturday Review*, and two suggestive articles in the *Nineteenth Century*, revealed the author's cast of mind. Gaskell was interested in the primary sources from which the social history of his century could be read. He was filled with a spirit of satire and criticism certain to encourage the further development of those propensities in Adams himself. The Englishman's constant attendance upon the nuances of literary style and his voracious appetite for curious scraps of scattered information that might augment the encyclopedic range of his allusion were bound also to affect his American friend.

To Gaskell's fastidious sense it seemed that an excessive number of unnecessary books were brought squalling into the world, and he felt a mild eugenic calling toward inhibiting their further propagation. Thus, privately, he wrote of Henry's old teacher at Harvard: "How stupid the first volume of

[James Russell] Lowell's letters is! There are one or two good things in the two volumes, but the book was not worth publishing."[45] Of the Princess Liechtenstein's *Holland House*, Gaskell unleashed fourteen pages of public satire:

The Princess, in enumerating Lady Holland's guests, endeavors to add interest to the list by short notices of their distinctions. . . . It adds but little to our information to be given a catalogue of the following kind: "Sir Philip Francis, whose supposed authorship of 'Junius' places him in historical interest on a level with the wearer of the iron mask. Byron, who dedicated to Lord Holland the 'Bride of Abydos.' Lord Jeffrey, of the 'Edinburgh Review.' Lord Thurlow, who died in the same year as Pitt and Fox. . . ."
It would be just as satisfactory if it ran thus. Byron, who kept a tame bear at the University. Sheridan, who always breakfasted in bed, and who hated metaphysics to such an extent that when his son asked him, "What is it, my dear father, that you can do with total, entire, thorough indifference?" he replied, "Why, listen to you, Tom." Lord Eldon, who was a very bad shot.[46]

While Gaskell was still an undergraduate, Adams had enunciated his first judgment, that his future friend's Cambridge set were "not very brilliant or noisy, but great scholars and pleasant fellows."[47] Gaskell's writings regularly exhibited marks of his scholarship. He threw a Latin phrase into his review of LaBouchère's *Diary of the Besieged Resident in Paris*, ended with some words in Italian, caught the author up in an error in a classical allusion, suggested that one tale in the book was in fact a paraphrase of a story from Rabelais, and played unobtrusively upon Hamlet's faith in special providence. Gaskell had a certain taste for graphic imagery, and he was not embarrassed to indulge in archaic sentence construction or hyperbole: "[During the siege of Paris] news became scarcer than food. Did a sparrow fall to the ground, there were fifty correspondents ready to welcome its fall." Gaskell's example doubtless encouraged Adams, writing of New England's Congregational clergymen in 1800, to use an archaism of his own: "In country parishes they were still autocratic. Did an individual defy their authority, the minister put his three-cornered hat on his head, took his silver-topped cane in his hand." Gaskell's metaphorical habit of mind stimulated Adams's literary imagination. A metaphor of Gaskell's might be laboriously contrived from Saint Matthew: "Charles Greville expressed surprise at the views of the Whigs in 1834, and was astonished that, after swallowing the camel of the Reform Bill, they should strain at the gnats which were perched upon the camel's back. Since 1832 they have not been given any camel to swallow until the present year [1881], when they have had a dromedary and a camel to interfere with their digestion."[48] Adams's metaphors, though more subtly devised than Gaskell's, grew from a similar disposition to convert airy abstraction into something sensible to the eye. A British frigate's attack upon the American warship *Chesapeake* in peacetime and almost within eyeshot of Norfolk, Va., spurred Adams to depict insensate rage:

For the first time in their history the people of the United States learned, in June, 1807, the feeling of a true national emotion. Hitherto every public passion had been more or less partial and one-sided; even the death of Washington had been ostentatiously mourned in the interests and to the profit of party: but the outrage committed on the "Chesapeake" stung through hide-bound prejudices, and made democrat and aristocrat writhe alike. The brand seethed and hissed like the glowing olive-stake of Ulysses in the Cyclops' eye, until the whole American people, like Cyclops, roared with pain and stood frantic on the shore, hurling abuse at their enemy, who taunted them from his safe ships.[49]

In one other respect Gaskell exerted an influence, unintended and unfortunate, upon Adams's literary practice: In noticing Edward Denison's *Letters*, Gaskell observed with distaste that "the private issue of a book seems often a tentative mode of testing the interest of the public; if it is limited to a few copies, the work becomes a literary curiosity, and in proportion to the difficulty in obtaining it is the interest excited by it."[50] Here was a clue to Adams's guileful practice, thirty years later, with the *Education* and *Mont-Saint-Michel and Chartres*.

The titles of Gaskell's two most successful articles—"The Position of the Whigs" and "The Country Gentleman"—looked toward his situation in politics and society. A "moderate Liberal" whose affections lay with the old Whig party, Gaskell sought to dissuade the Whigs from abandoning their "Radical" associates and going over to the Conservatives. In the agricultural depression of the late nineteenth century, Gaskell, like other country squires, opposed the tenant farmers' demands for lower rents; he was also hostile to a "single tax" upon land, and he defended, against suggestions of fixity of tenure, the landlord's right to replace his own tenant. But to Gaskell's Liberal eye the possibility of some form of expropriation made it the more sensible for Whigs to hasten the extension of suffrage rights. The country gentleman ought "to aid the attainment of the franchise at as early a date as possible by the people at large, so that neither Conservative nor Liberal leaders may be led into the temptation . . . of winning the suffrages of one body of men by the spoliation of another."[51]

Believing that the Radicals would not push the land question, Gaskell urged Whigs to remain loyal to the Liberal party, and he looked forward with composure to the extinction of his own political and social class. In time "there will be found no place for the old Whig. . . . Years, no doubt, would be required to bring about such a result, but the end would at least be a happy one, involving no recriminations or reproaches." The diffusion of education since the Education Act of 1870 might perhaps destroy society's need for country gentlemen as a class supposed to maintain centers of culture throughout the land, but the squires ought to be free to make a voluntary cession of their position rather than be expelled from it. A conservative like Henry James might have alleged of Gaskell, as Ralph Touchett declared of Lord Warburton, that "he's all in a muddle about . . . his position. . . . He has ceased to believe in himself. . . . [He] can neither abolish himself as a nuisance nor maintain himself as an institution."[52]

Loyal to Whig traditions, Gaskell was scathing about the hypocrisy of some of his Whig associates. "The use of the House of Lords in some [Whig] eyes is to enable Whig members of Parliament to vote with the Radicals, and to support large measures of reform, with the comfortable assurance that their labours will be useless, and that what has been spun on Monday will be unpicked on Tuesday. These assumptions, however, are dangerous."[53] Gaskell was no less critical of the failure of most squires to live up to their social responsibilities. He felt deep sympathy for the landlords' economic plight; but to him it was

humiliating to be obliged to acknowledge that . . . the average Englishman's conception of a leisured life is undoubtedly a life spent in the enjoyment of sport. . . . It would probably be found that the majority of those who spent their time in more cultivated occupations were unfitted by physical incapacity for active pursuits. Shortsightedness and lameness are the elder brothers of literature. . . .

. . . . .

. . . No race of men were ever so ignorant of the beauties of what they possessed as the English landowners; one exquisite example of mediaeval architecture after another has perished.[54]

Gaskell was sharply conscious of that much abused ideal noblesse oblige. To his mind the privileges of a squire were balanced by social duties: the jealous defense of political independence; the cultivation of high literary standards; the commissioning, restoration, or preservation of fine architecture; and the provision of hospitality. This last was not the least of a landowner's obligations: "Of late years there has been a growing tendency on the part of the upper classes . . . to shirk the responsibility and duties of their position."[55]

Gaskell's greatest contribution to Henry Adams's development was that, however imperfectly, he embodied in a vital form a tradition from which Adams needed to draw sustenance. "Do what he might, he [Adams] drew breath only in the atmosphere of English methods and thoughts; he could breathe none other."[56] Adams's life and ideals in Washington later in the century were an Americanized, urbanized version of what he found in England. The intellectual and political salon he and Marian established was such as Washington had never before seen, and the noontime "breakfasts" he later instituted were obviously modeled on those of Lord Houghton. His commissioning the foremost American architect of the time, Henry Hobson

Richardson, to build his house in Washington, was consonant with Gaskell's ideal. When he set himself an unattainably high literary standard in place of the popular ones that, in different ways and to a different degree, vitiated the histories of Bancroft and Parkman, Gaskell's cultural traditions supported him. For Adams the balance between privilege and responsibility was always perilously fragile, and when his personal life went awry, he displayed conspicuously the worst faces of his privileged position: snobbishness, self-esteem, a sense of futility. These devils were never far from the surface, but for the two rich decades of his life after his return from England, Adams held them at bay. Whatever his achievements, he owed a permanent debt to the peculiarly English virtues and limitations of Milnes Gaskell.

Two principal results of Adams's years in England may be distinguished, corresponding to the opposite poles of his feelings toward that nation. His exposure to British hostility during the Civil War strengthened his allegiance to his own country's democratic republican experiment. But his association with Gaskell encouraged him to pursue a literary career upon principles somewhat different from those he found in America.

How these influences should be interpreted depends on one's view of Adams's later life. *The Education of Henry Adams* might suggest that his allegiance to democracy was a fragile plant, quickly destroyed when President Grant demonstrated that no political role remained for the Adamses. But in fact Henry's loyalty to the American democratic experiment colored his work for years after 1869, and the deepest effects of his stay in England probably appeared during the time between 1877 and 1890, when he was writing his *History*. In composing these volumes he hoped to give evidence that American democracy could produce great works of art.[57] Yet in challenging the old British taunt that America had never produced a great historian, Adams worked on British principles; he fought against being drawn into the American main current.[58] His challenge to his brother Charles—"You like roughness and strength; I like taste and dexterity. For God's sake, let us go our ways"[59]—was the outburst of an aspiring artist who had found sustenance in England. But in 1877, as he began work on his *History*, Adams believed that the United States, after another century, would be at the center of civilization, and he hoped he and a few contemporaries might dimly foreshadow that flowering of creative genius that was to be expected.[60] Adams's years in England helped to shape the social purpose that informed the earlier part of his literary career, and they strengthened his artistic integrity.[61] These reasons perhaps best explain why his sailing for England was, in his opinion, "the biggest piece of luck I ever had."

CHAPTER 3 · *Clover*

THE MOST important person in Henry Adams's life was Marian Hooper, his wife for thirteen years until her death in 1885. Born in 1843, she was nearly twenty-nine when she married the thirty-four-year-old professor and had already developed a strong streak of individuality—she "has a certain vein of personality which approaches eccentricity," wrote Adams.[1] Harvard ran in her family, for her sister was married to Professor Whitman Gurney, one of the three strong candidates for Harvard's presidency in 1869, whom the successful Charles Eliot promptly appointed to be the first dean in Harvard's history; and her brother Edward, a connoisseur of art, held from 1876 to 1898 the key post of treasurer, thus serving twenty-two years on the university's seven-man governing committee. It was at the Gurneys' comfortable house, a mile west of Harvard Square on Fayerweather Street, that during 1871 and 1872 Adams conducted his discreet courtship of Marian Hooper. Something about "Clover," for so Marian's friends addressed her, exercised a peculiar power over the brilliant young men of her neighborhood. Henry Adams, Henry James, and the jurist Oliver Wendell Holmes, Jr., all found her fascinating.

A woman who attracted such men must have had unusual qualities, and the evidence that these three cared for her is worth a moment's examination. Holmes was an old family friend of Marian's, their fathers having studied medicine together as young men in Paris.[2] By the time Marian was about twenty, Wendell Holmes had started an annual Christmas custom of celebrating that day by going walking with her,[3] and his scanty journal mentions nine visits with her during the winter of 1866–67. But the inference about his feelings comes from a scrap of evidence in his record book.

A notation has survived of twenty books Holmes read in 1872 and of two or three important events in his life that year. He read two novels during June, one of them entitled *Goodbye, Sweetheart*. He married Fanny Dixwell, with whom he had been friends for many years, on June 17.[4] Four weeks later he noted the completion of Heineccius' *Recitationes*, and then or a little later he entered the name of the novel, postdating it, so that the record reads thus:

July 14   Heinecii Recitationes
June 27 — Goodbye Sweetheart—
July 3   Kant's Doctrine du Droit[5]

The stroke of the pen immediately after "June 27"—no other date on the page is so distinguished—suggests a moment's reflection by the young lawyer. Marian Hooper married Henry Adams on June 27.

The inverted chronology makes it impossible to suppose the extraordinary coincidence to have been mere coincidence. If Holmes here used his reading list for an unobtrusive personal reference, this was not without parallel: The well-known final entry of his reading list, written in 1935, the last year of his life, was *Heaven's My Destination*.[6] It seems likely that the newly married lawyer chose this quiet way of placing in his "strictly private" record book an allusion to a poignant moment.

If Marian stirred the self-sufficient Holmes, she also excited the imagination of Henry James. The future novelist, who was just her own age, knew Marian as early as 1866, and by 1870 associated her with his adored cousin Minny Temple. Seeking health at a British spa, James was dismayed by the young Englishwomen at the bathing establishment: "I revolt from their dreary deathly want of—what shall I call it?—Clover Hooper has it—intellectual grace—Minny Temple has it—moral spontaneity."[7]

Although Henry James was not himself prepared to marry, he betrayed pique at Marian's match with Henry Adams. James saw the bridal couple in Rome on their return from a trip to Egypt in 1873, and thought Adams the gainer from the union: "In the way of old friends we have been having Henry Adams and his wife. . . . [They] asked me to dinner with Miss Lowe (beautiful and sad) . . . and showed me specimens of their (of course) crop of bric-a-brac and Adams's Egyptian photos (by himself—very pretty)—and were very pleasant and friendly and (as to A.) improved. Mrs. Clover has had her wit clipped a little I think—but I suppose has expanded in the 'affections.'" James visited the Adamses frequently at their house on Marlborough Street, Boston, during the last two months of 1874, and doubtless he saw them during their summer residence at Beverly Farms, north of Boston, a few months later, but his subsequent return to Europe postponed further meetings for four years. Feeling his debt for the valuable introductions Henry Adams gave him when he first settled in England, James hastened to reciprocate when in 1879 the Adamses arrived for Henry's year of research in the European archives. The novelist's first impressions—though expressed guardedly even to his brother William—were those of 1873: "Henry A. can never be in the nature of things a very spacious or sympathetic companion, and Mrs. A. strikes me as toned down and bedimmed from her ancient brilliancy, but they are both very ~~brilliant~~ pleasant and doubtless when they get into lodgings will be more animated." To correspondents less confidential than his brother, James characterized Marian Adams's husband yet more cautiously: "Henry is very sensible, though a trifle dry, and Clover has a touch of genius (I mean as compared with the usual British Female)."[8]

James's letters to his feminine friends were habitually satiated, even cloyed, with professions of tender regard, but in addressing Marian he surpassed himself. In 1880 she and her husband had been replenishing her wardrobe in Paris: "If you cross to Dover," James wrote from that seaside town,

[I] shall look out for you at the ships side on that day. Why won't you stop here and see me? I will go up to London with you. . . . I shall at any rate see you in London, and see also I trust the seraphic robe, as well as the more terrestial ones. But an angel in a *walking-costume?* I didn't know angels ever walked: you will be the first! . . . [A widow James knows has announced the fact of her being about to remarry] with an abruptness which stunned me. Frailty, thy name! — — is NOT H.J. Jr.

Do decide to stop here!![9]

When in 1881 James came to America from the England Marian had "so cruelly deserted," he found in her invitation to render him social services in Washington "a pledge of delightful *intimate* weeks. . . . I remember so well your last charming words to me: 'It will be over there that we shall really meet *familiarly!*' I must tell you that I am prepared to be intensely familiar!. . . . Ever dear Mrs. Adams, impatiently and irrepressibly yours, H. James Jr."[10] Twenty years after Marian's death James was still affected by her memory. "The one thing he wanted to see in Washington," he told a friend, "was the St. Gaudens monument in Rock Creek Cemetery where Mrs. Adams was buried." At Marian's grave James stood bareheaded a long while and "seemed deeply moved. . . . Mr. James abounded in her praises. . . . [He described her as] a brilliant and charming woman, so brilliant that the circle of intimates considered her the more interesting of the two."[11]

That the Adamses figure in James's stories "Pandora" and "The Point of View" is well established,[12] but they probably affected other writings as well. Marian and Henry Adams can scarcely have been absent from James's mind when he published (a year before Adams's *History* began to appear) "The Lesson of the Master." In this story a young writer loses his "Marian" to an older author, "Henry," but fears that the older man, inspired by this intellectual woman, may achieve greater artistic success than the bachelor has done. Her intellectuality, her indulgent widowed father, and probably her un-English independence in entertaining during her father's absence were those of Marian Hooper. In *Roderick Hudson* Christina Light's persiflage, though few other aspects of her personality, resembles Marian Hooper's so strikingly as to have been drawn from life: "You have something in the expression of your face," Christina observes to an eligible young man,

> that particularly provokes me to make the remarks my mother so inconsolably deplores. I noticed it the first time I saw you. I think it's because your face is so broad. For some reason or other broad faces exasperate me; they fill me with a kind of *rabbia*. Last summer at Carlsbad there was an Austrian count with enormous estates and some great office at court. He was very attentive—seriously so; he was really very far gone. *Cela ne tenait qu'à moi!* But I could n't; he was impossible. He must have measured from ear to ear at least a yard and a half. And he was tow-coloured too, which made it worse—almost as fair as Stenterello [Christina's white poodle]—though of course Stenterello's face, like his conversation, is full of point. So I said to him frankly: "Many thanks, Herr Graf; your uniform's magnificent, but your face is too fat."[13]

The Portrait of a Lady is the novel of James's most closely interwoven with the Adamses' life. Here it is Marian Hooper's situation, rather than features of her personality, that seems to have caught James's fancy. The novelist perhaps conceived the idea of *The Portrait of a Lady* at the Roman dinner of April 1873, when the Adamses' guests were Henry James and Adams's old Boston friend Nelly Lowe.[14] In his novels James fashioned more than one character like Serena Merle after Elena Lowe, a woman supposed to have breached the social proprieties.[15] The impression of her sitting sadly side-by-side the clipped Marian and her fastidious, bric-a-brac-collecting husband was likely to be deep. By 1876 James had read *Daniel Deronda* and was shaping the outline of an American version of the story—the tale of an attractive but willful young woman's throwing herself away upon a heartless, conceited husband who fancied himself a fastidious gentleman. James planned to write the novel in 1877 but did not really set to work until April 1880, after he had had months of renewed observation of the Adamses in London and Paris. One can feel Henry Adams reacting to James, on a dull afternoon in London, with something of the distaste that Gilbert Osmond felt for the assiduous male worshipers of his wife. "London has not the material for a letter," Adams complained to Henry Cabot Lodge. "It is Sunday afternoon. Harry James is standing on the hearthrug, with his hands under his coat-tails talking with my wife exactly as though we were in Marlborough Street. I am going out in five minutes to make some calls on perfectly interesting people."[16]

Marian Hooper was more vivacious and sophisticated than Isabel Archer, whose personality seems to have been modeled largely on that of Minny Temple, but James endowed Isabel with certain of Marian's attributes. Like Isabel Archer, Marian Hooper—the image of a bent strip of wood held under pressure is the same—was the youngest of the three offspring of a well-to-do gentleman, early a widower, who gave his children the best of everything and, in addition, a somewhat unconventional upbringing. Like Isabel, Marian could have been accused of self-esteem. James said of her, as he did of Isabel, that she "chatters."[17] She took Isabel's pleasure in using her modest fortune generously.[18] It is certain that at first Marian was overawed by the knowledge-ability and connoisseurship of her much-traveled husband.[19]

Socially Marian Hooper need not have been awed by Henry Adams, for her mother was a twig upon the outspread tree of Boston's prominent Sturgis family, a neighboring branch of which has been gilded for posterity by the mild light of Santayana's *Persons and Places*. Her uncle Samuel Hooper, from 1861 to 1875 a Republican congressman from eastern Massachusetts, was chairman of the House Committee on Banking and Currency; her father, the bookish son of a rich Marblehead banker, lived in leisure as a nonpracticing medical doctor on Beacon Street not far from his friend Dr. Oliver Wendell Holmes; her brother Edward, an important member of the philanthropic band which during the Civil War tried to assist South Carolina's Sea Island blacks in their transition to freedom, became treasurer of the New England Freedmen's Aid Society before entering his long career as treasurer of Harvard College;[20] and her sister Ellen was a "clever Bostonian" destined to be one of the principal founders of Radcliffe College.

Marian's personality, which so fired the imaginations of some of her contemporaries, seemed to reflect the qualities of her mother's family. "The young woman," Adams declared of his fiancée, "belongs to a sort of clan, as all Bostonians do. Through her mother, who is not living, she is half Sturgis, and Russell Sturgis of the Barings is a fourth cousin or thereabouts. Socially the match is supposed to be unexceptionable."[21] Marian's mother, née Ellen Sturgis, who died of consumption in 1848 at the age of thirty-six, was a minor light of the Transcendentalist movement. The indiscriminate T. W. Higginson called her "a woman of genius." Emerson seems to have thought well of her poetic talent, and Margaret Fuller effused from Rome that "I have seen in Europe no woman more gifted by nature than she." Thirteen pages in an anthology of Transcendentalist poetry are devoted to Ellen Sturgis Hooper's abstract creations, mostly reprinted from the *Dial*.[22] While these cast a too searching light upon the critical judgment of her enthusiastic friends, they tell something of New England preoccupations around 1840 as Unitarianism melted into deism.

The Sturgises were known both for religious unorthodoxy and for a tendency toward self-destruction. When Marian was nine, a Sturgis aunt to whom she was close committed suicide with arsenic, and the event was believed by Henry Adams's brother Charles to have made "a dangerous impression on her mind."[23] Early in 1872 Henry's mother suggested that he marry Marian, but Charles burst out, "Heavens!—no!—they're all crazy as coots. She'll kill herself, just like her aunt!" This idea of a family propensity to suicide seemed substantiated by later events, for both Marian's sister and her brother had nervous breakdowns and both apparently ended their own lives, the one in 1887 and the other in 1901.[24] A year before her engagement Marian was already jesting to a close friend, characteristically lamenting the constraints of womanhood, "Eleanor I am only kept from self slaughter by the fact that I've lost the only 'bare bodkin' that I possessed and that a worsted needle is too *feminine* an instrument for giving a quietus." Forewarned by Charles Adams's outburst, Henry wed Marian with open eyes. "I know better than anyone, the risks I run," he confided to his brother Brooks. "But I have weighed them carefully and accept them."[25]

A dissenter from nineteenth-century notions of hereditary mental illness would doubt that the Sturgis family affected Marian as much as her father, Robert Hooper, with whom she lived until she was nearly twenty-nine. Clues to the personality of this gentleman of leisure are scarce. It seems likely that, during a trip home while he was studying medicine in Paris, and three years before marrying Ellen Sturgis, he engaged in a duel about another woman and was obliged to flee Boston temporarily to avoid prosecution.[26] This woman, Marian Marshall—later briefly engaged to Dr. Samuel Gridley Howe—was said to be beautiful, flirtatious, and spoiled; it was her first name that Robert Hooper gave nine years later to his daughter. The event did not destroy his social respectability. He had a good address on Beacon Street (114), was made a member of the Somerset Club, and built a summer residence in the superior seaside resort of Beverly Farms, with Mrs. J. Elliot Cabot as his nearest neighbor. In 1885 Henry Adams was "touched by the quiet and general respect which the society of Boston and Cambridge showed at his funeral."[27]

Toward the Adamses he evinced a marked sense of his own dignity. After Henry had lived a whole month in the same house with him in 1872, the younger man continued to address his father-in-law with the utmost formality and consciousness of distance; and when in later years Henry's parents paid a rare four-day visit to Henry and Marian's "cottage" at Beverly Farms, the nearby Dr. Hooper did not trouble to see them. He may have felt Mrs. Adams a bore, and Charles Francis Adams was already in decline. But the coolness between the Hoopers and most of the Adamses had deeper roots. Beverly Farms lay in the fashionable "north of Boston" area, while Quincy, toward the south, was declining in prestige; and the Hoopers came to represent to Henry—as Marian's distant cousins, the Russell Sturgises, had done during his London days—the aesthetic and luxurious side of life. Henry understood that to some literary people "all Adamses were minds of dust and emptiness, devoid of feeling, poetry, or imagination; little higher than the common scourings of State Street; politicians of doubtful honesty; natures of narrow scope."[28] The Hoopers' seemed a more "spacious" life than the Adamses knew, and they were more "sympathetic" to Cambridge intellectuals like Henry James's family than most of the Adamses could be. Henry

Adams was attracted ever nearer to his wife's family and away from the narrower political traditions of the Adamses; his diatribe against John Quincy Adams's philistinism marked the culmination of this development.

In addition Dr. Hooper doubtless sensed that his claim upon his daughter's love would best be preserved by his drawing Henry and Marian into his own circle and away from the Adamses. Thus the young people's honeymoon was at the seaside mansion of Congressman Samuel Hooper, Dr. Hooper's brother; and after they returned from a year's wedding trip in Europe, they settled only a short walk away from Dr. Hooper's residence, on Marlborough Street, Boston, where the sumptuousness of their household furnishings seemed remarkable to the less openhanded Charles Francis Adams. They spent their first summers mainly with Dr. Hooper, rather than with the Adamses at Quincy, and they soon built their own summer house at Beverly Farms near Dr. Hooper's. Years later Charles Adams grieved that Henry had turned away from his blood relations. The historian was about to set off to Scotland with his five Hooper nieces, and he came into Charles's Boston office "showing with almost insulting aggressiveness that he had quite outgrown his own poor mundane family and that the etherialized intercourse of the Hoopers, LaFarge [Edward Hooper's artist friend], and Mrs. Cameron alone satisfied his lofty soul!—too bad,—one more gone!"[29] This was in 1892, and Henry's one-sided identification with the Hoopers, his violent rejection of the Adams tradition, marked his *Mont-Saint-Michel and Chartres* and the latter part of the *Education*; but before 1890, when he was writing the *History*, the two strains coexisted.

Toward his daughters Robert Hooper was an indulgent father, providing them with the best schooling then available for girls—at the Agassiz school in Cambridge, forerunner of Radcliffe College—and arranging family trips to Europe in 1844–45, 1866, and 1867. His gaiety, displayed even during his last illness, was doubtless a major source of Marian's usually effervescent spirits. She wrote to him easily of books and art. From Rome, Marian reported seeing at the Ludovisi Villa "the Mars you like so much," and she and Henry assiduously searched out bronze reproductions to send to her father. After giving Marian a large cash gift, Robert Hooper would have appreciated her reference to the Book of Proverbs: "Your most welcome Christmas present came on Friday," Marian wrote: "I protest—feebly—against being pampered to such an extent, but shall enjoy it none the less. If the horseleech's daughters had called you father their importunity would have had no *raison d'être*; probably the horseleech kept them very short."[30]

If, as Adams proudly asserted, Marian knew her own mind uncommon well, it was because Robert Hooper had long given her a measure of independence, treating her as other men might treat their boys. When she was twenty-five, he and his son made a three-month trip to Europe, leaving her to "reign here [at 114 Beacon Street] in solitary grandeur." She had responsibility for decorating the house at Beverly Farms, and her father let her bring Henry to live with them there for several weeks before the marriage ceremony. Henry promised Gaskell in a letter before he left for Beverly Farms that by the time he and Marian arrived in England, "I shall have been nearly a month married . . . so that there will be no occasion for blushes, and my young woman is not at all an infant."[31] He implied that Marian's attitude to sexual relations was down-to-earth but probably did not mean that they slept together before the wedding day. Loathing conventional ceremony, they determined that there should be no more than eleven other people at their informal marriage. "When you know my young woman," he informed Gaskell four days before the event,

you will understand why the world thinks we must be allowed to do what we think best. From having had no mother to take responsibility off her shoulders, she has grown up to look after herself. . . .

The world, for all that I know, may think it peculiar that I should calmly come down here and live with my fiancée for a month before our marriage. But my father-in-law, who was educated as a physician and only gave up his profession because he was rich enough not to care for the income, is a sensible man in such matters, and a good deal of a slave to his two daughters.[32]

Although he gave Marian physical freedom, Robert Hooper bound his youngest child with other chains. After his wife's death he was so nervous about Marian's starting a cough that when at the age of thirty-five she and Henry traveled during a wintry January from Washington to Niagara Falls, she dared not notify him of the trip until it was a fait accompli. His profession did not occupy his energies, and it was as though he were the anxious, underemployed wife, staying at home and placing emotional demands upon his absent spouse. The personal upheaval Marian experienced after Robert Hooper's death might suggest not the traditional devotion of daughter to father but a more problematic and complicated interchange whose dissatisfactions color bereavement with remorse. At least once she had felt hopelessly inadequate in expressing love to Robert Hooper, her sense of guilt approaching a climax at Venice in 1872, when she had been married only four months: "I miss you very, very much, and think so often of your love and tenderness to me all my life, and wish I had been nicer to you. But I'll try to make up my shortcomings when I come home." In the succeeding weeks Marian's sense of incompetence had increased as a riverboat transported her and Henry farther and farther up the Nile, away from her father: "I long to see you and Egypt seems so far off. . . . Please don't show my letters to anyone; they sound so silly and homesick. . . . I can only say how much I love you and miss you."[33] This was a voice of pathos, the more desperate and lonely by contrast to Marian's usual ebullience, as she entered the first severe depression of her married life. Perhaps Robert Hooper's need for his daughters' love had been so violent after his wife's death, that, like a whirlpool, it drew the two—both daughters died childless—struggling pitifully, into its vortex.

Marian's sister Ellen was a different version of the type of the clever Boston woman. The two girls both studied Greek, then the ultimate sign of women's emancipation, and, like Marian, Ellen "loved books . . . , the sea and the skies, and delighted in walking and riding on horseback in the woods." Like Marian too, Ellen Gurney was troubled by insomnia and the thought of mental illness; a few months before her husband's death, and less than a year before her own nervous breakdown, Ellen confided to her intimate friend E. L. Godkin, "I have always been under a brave outside such an arrant coward—and expected if the tap-root alias Gurney was touched to collapse like a bladder and wind up in a lunatic asylum—but I am less scared as to this by far [than ten months ago]—and rarely if I sleep."[34]

It was in Ellen Gurney's library on Fayerweather Street that the first four students graduated from Radcliffe College, then called "Harvard Annex," in 1883. This was not simply the result of Ellen's being Dean Gurney's wife, for she was in her own right second only to Mrs. Agassiz as a leader in establishing the college. When Professor William Goodwin delivered the commemoration tribute to Mrs. Agassiz in 1907, he could not refrain from speaking of Ellen Gurney, then twenty years dead: She "was a brilliant example, in the second generation, of the scholarly company of ladies into which she was born. Her coming to Cambridge made an era in our intellectual life. She brought into it a fresh vitality which I shall never forget. I never undertook any important work in connection with my professorship without consulting her as well as her husband. She became at once most devoted to our new women's college, and Mrs. Agassiz always depended upon her in every forward step which was taken."[35] Ellen furnished Henry Adams a different model from his mother's of what wedded life could offer, and her manner of living with Whitman Gurney helped to spur him and Marian, who were meeting frequently at their house, to marriage.

When Henry first described Marian to Gaskell, he found it difficult to disguise his pride. "She reads German," he fairly glowed, "—also Latin— also, I fear, a little Greek, but very little. She talks garrulously, but on the whole pretty sensibly. She is very open to instruction. *We* shall improve her. She dresses badly. She decidedly has humor and will appreciate *our* wit. She has enough money to be quite independent. She rules me as only American women rule men, and I cower before her. Lord! how she would lash me if she read the above description of her!" As years passed, Adams continued to spoof his wife about her acquaintance with foreign languages; he was not quite equal to being proud of her mind at the expense of her appearance: "I have become bored with the idea of getting any new gowns," Marian wrote to her father from Paris, "but Henry says 'People who study Greek must take pains with their dress.' "[36]

German of course played a more important role in the Adamses' married life than Greek or Latin. "We have begun to read together now that the evenings close in early," she wrote during her wedding trip in Europe, "and have begun Schiller's *Thirty Years' War*, reading it aloud in German, which is hard to me but good fun. On the Nile we hope really to study, as there will be many long days with no ruins to fill them up." Marian's impatience with conventional wifely submissiveness was stronger than her spoken German; thus when the American minister in Berlin, George Bancroft (a distant cousin of hers) invited Henry to a dinner for males only, the latter "said he must go back to dine with his wife. . . . George was very much excited," Marian continued, "and pretended I was his dearest friend and insisted that I must come too." Marian ended as the only woman in a dinner for eight including Mommsen, the historian of Rome, Ernst Curtius, and Hermann Grimm. "There was much good talk, but unhappily for me it was chiefly in German and so rapid that most of it was lost on me."[37]

She affected to deprecate the money Robert Hooper had spent on her linguistic education, but abstract pedagogical method, not education itself, was what she scorned. At a diplomatic dinner in Washington in 1882 a friend of Marian's, the daughter of the secretary of state, tried to use her own language training to speak to the German and the Italian flanking her at the table. Marian dashingly satirized foreign language primers to her father: Miss Frelinghuysen

half swooned in my arms after dinner. We deplored to each other the vast sums our respective and respected parents had vainly "fooled away" on our education, the dem'd total being useless. "Have you the apricot of my aunt?" "Has the baker the coat of the tailor?" though excellent exercise in themselves, are as useless in the sea of real life as a dory without oars—the sexes of my nouns are as undecided as that of Oscar Wilde or Dr. Mary Walker [the prototype of Dr. Prance in *The Bostonians?*]. Never mind, you meant well.[38]

No sense of incompetence had deterred Marian from getting up Italian so that she could bargain for bric-a-brac in Naples, or Spanish to help Henry on a research trip to Seville. Her quickness and her identification with Henry's work appeared in an incident of the Spanish journey. Adams's research in the archives of England, France, and Spain was more easily planned than executed: In each country he had to wage a patient diplomatic campaign to extract from its reluctant government permission to examine secret files. Despite an introduction to the French prime minister, he had not yet succeeded after five weeks in gaining access to the main body of papers in Paris, and he and Marian departed temporarily to try their luck in Spain. The Duke of Tetuan, the Spanish foreign minister, exuded promises, but after another week's delay "his Chief of Archives reported he had found the papers but that they were of 'too reserved a character to be shown,' was very sorry, etc. etc.—so that our object in this long journey is utterly defeated." Fleeing southwards from Madrid, the Adamses found themselves in the compartment of a train with a well-to-do Spanish merchant and his family. Marian's linguistic ability now came into its own, and she reported the scene to Robert Hooper with the verve of a feminist Eve:

We soon fell to prattling. They were on their way home from a journey in Italy of several months, had bought jewelry at Castellani's which I was called on to admire, and became quite confiding. I muttered to Henry that perhaps the Señor might know the Chief of Archives in Seville, and why didn't he make a shot in the dark and see what he could bring down. Henry, true to the characteristics of his first ancestor, wished me to "bite first." So, with an assumed air of casual curiosity, I bit deep into the core, and asked if by any chance he was acquainted, etc., etc. He said no, but that he could give us a card of introduction to a gentleman in Granada who would pass us on to the Chief of Archives in Seville. My heart jumped at the faint hope of circumventing Tetuan and creeping between the meshes of his red tape.

This lighthearted punning on Henry's surname contrasted with the self-conscious version of the same joke attempted twenty-five years later by Adams himself. No one in the 1840s, he alleged heavy-handedly in *The Education of Henry Adams*, had suggested "a doubt whether a system of society which had lasted since Adam would outlast one Adams more." Marian's mental distinction did not stop at her flair for foreign languages.[39]

Part of her charm arose from an irreverence, which took the form of self-satire, toward conventional religious practices. When a suitor of Miss Hooper's, Dr. Fred Shattuck, once managed to get her to accompany him to church, she reported her own deportment to his absent sister: "I was ever so good and only whispered once and sat very still and liked the singing very much indeed." But churchgoing did not suit her, and a month later, on a Sunday morning, Marian's pleasures were more pagan than Christian. "It seems a fitting time for a friendly chat," she wrote to the same friend, "when the gay church bells have rung the good white sheep into their respective folds and left the naughty black ones to outer sunshine and quiet. I'm so happy sitting on the floor with my back against the window and hot sun going through me bringing a prophecy of spring and summer and green things."[40]

Disregard of the Puritan principle of self-denial dictated one of Marian's most generous acts. Miss Catharine Howard, an esteemed former teacher of hers, suffered ill health, and the twenty-five-year-old Miss Hooper wished to give her $5,000 for a year's holiday in Europe. Her tone was at once tactful and imperious. "Three years ago," she began,

I made a will and left you five thousand dollars—but, you see, I don't die, but only "wax fat and kick," and so not wishing to be balked by destiny, in my lawful pleasures, I told my brother, the other day, that I meant to ask you to take it now, when I might have the pleasure of seeing you get some fun out of it. . . . With five thousand dollars, even at present rate of exchange, you could go abroad and stay a good while and come back with *no head* and a good backbone and lots of new ideas to innoculate young victims with. . . . Switzerland in the summer and Italy in the winter! Does not that move your hard heart? You may think me interfering, if you like, but that, I consider, one of the perquisites of a spinster friend.

She had trouble injecting hedonism into Miss Howard's self-abnegation. She tried to persuade her that to accept would be to shoulder her benefactress's guilt in gratifying her own desires: "I am not making any sacrifice," she assured Miss Howard, "nor entailing any degree of self-denial on myself. I am ashamed to get the credit of it. I often think, with a prophetic shudder, of the old man who, when he was dying, devoutly said, 'Thank God, I have never denied myself anything.' Now if you will give in simply and go away and get strong, it will be a pleasure to me that you will have to share the responsibility of, if it comes under the head of self-indulgence." By good fortune a suitable friend soon turned up who could accompany Miss Howard to Europe. "I had heard of your good luck from Miss Lucinda before I got your most satisfactory letter the other day," Marian affectionately teased her friend. "I think it would be a pleasing illustration of the reward attending submission to the will of others, valuable to the American Tract Society. . . . What wearisome traveler's yarns you'll spin in future years! If you ever dare mention to me the charms of the Coliseum by moonlight, all further intercourse between us will cease."[41]

Miss Hooper exhibited no more reverence for the great men of Boston than for the religious scruples of the community. At the time of the Franco-Prussian War she found herself at a dinner with the best-known scientist in America, the French-Swiss geologist Louis Agassiz: "Mr. Ag thinks the cause of civilization is set back thirty years by the triumph of Prussia," she reported to Eleanor Shattuck. "I think that his judgment in many things is as valuable as a pussy cat's." John Lothrop Motley, a successor of Charles Francis Adams's as American minister in London but soon sacked by the Grant administration, did not inspire greater awe. "It seems to me," she opined to Eleanor Shattuck, "that Mr. Motley acted as any one might have seen a man of his temperament and want of tact would and his incapacity to feel himself snubbed when he was most emphatically shows a pathetic self confidence. . . . What a nice piece of gossip the whole thing is! and no one thinks that they are gossipy in discussing *men's* affairs, but only 'showing a proper interest in public questions of the day'!"[42]

Conventional ideas of what was or was not "feminine" always made Marian restive. Not only did she challenge the notions that gossip is "feminine" and using bodkins "masculine"—that she should knit in a Berlin hotel while Henry attended an all-male dinner or that Adam was less interested in the apple than Eve—but she inverted the stereotype that indiscretion is a female attribute. E. L. Godkin, editor of the weekly *Nation*, was one of the three people in whom the Adamses originally confided Henry's plan to publish an anonymous novel, *Democracy*; but Marian feared that, when pressed, Godkin would fail to maintain his reserve: "As to that 'Dead Secret,'" she admonished him, "if it ever is born—you must puff it and praise it and perjure your soul as friend and editor—let me at least believe that *one* man can keep a secret."[43]

"If I were a boy," she once wrote from England, "I should say that we are having a 'bully' time." She loved outdoor activity and characteristically the only good extant photograph of her, taken when she was twenty-five, finds her on horseback. "Yesterday I goaded Henry into a ride," she exulted in a letter to her father from Washington one wintry January day in 1881, "the thermometer saying 40°—and such a ride! The horses not sharpened, and the roads proved solid ice under the mud. The beasties balanced themselves on their tails, and when Georgetown Cemetery was reached it seemed wiser and more economical to dismount and save future transport, but curiosity led us on to see if we could get home. We slid gaily down a long hill and crawled over horsecar tracks, frozen and penitent, to our stable." Marian relished casting her husband as the weaker vessel: "I chaperon no one but Henry," she wrote of their Washington social life. She once purchased a melancholy watercolor for Robert Hooper—"so sad that my sensitive half wouldn't have it, though he was fascinated by it"; and when a newly plastered ceiling fell down in their Washington house, at the same moment that their main sewer was blocked and their water supply cut off, she assured her father that "the patience and amiability of my better half never fail in these crises."[44]

This satirical, critical, strong-minded, physically active woman possessed exactly the attributes Henry Adams required. When only twenty-one years old he was already expressing admiration for a German girl who reminded him of Nelly Lowe: "She's a will of her own and gives me the most immense delight. A perfect little Tartar, and smooth as a cat." But Adams's wretched years of chaperoning his mother and sister Mary around Europe furthered a disinclination to marry; in 1865, acting in Rome once again as the head of the family, he had just experienced the horrors of a week's shopping when the news arrived of his brother Charles's engagement: "You, my envied brother, whose acquaintance with women in domestic relations, has yet to begin, and that too, under a form exceptionally agreeable, know little of the meaning of a week's shopping. . . . Freedom is still sweet," he sighed, "even though I do not deny that a bondage more pleasing than mine, may be still sweeter. The Minister writes as though he expected me to marry at once, but

I have tried it at the wrong end, and having once learned what the duties are, without the pleasures, I shall have to wait long before trying either duties or pleasures again, if I've got to take them together." For sexual pleasures Henry Adams resorted to prostitutes—"a necessity for me as for everyone"—yet life was often stale to this epicurean bachelor. If he was ever to renew his faculty of enjoyment, Henry knew what sort of a wife he needed: "Only a great passion could finish me now," he speculated in 1865 to Charles, "and though I can imagine a great passion, I do not think I could ever feel it. When I marry, too, I want a woman who will take care of me, and keep me out of mischief, a good, masculine female, to make me work, and be blind to Burgundy and French cooking."[45]

During Adams's first hectic year of teaching at Harvard he was intimate at only one house, the Gurneys', and it was there he found Marian Hooper. "I have had the design ever since last May," he wrote to his younger brother early in 1872,

and have driven it very steadily. On coming to know Clover Hooper, I found her so far away superior to any woman I had ever met, that I did not think it worth while to resist. I threw myself head over heels into the pursuit, and succeeded in conducting the affair so quietly that this last week we became engaged without a single soul outside her immediate family suspecting it. . . . I'm afraid she has completely got the upper hand of me, for I am a weak-minded cuss with women, and the devil and all his imps couldn't resist the fascination of a clever woman who chooses to be loved.

. . . . .

I shall expect you to be very kind to Clover, and not rough, for that is not her style.

On the afternoon of Tuesday, February 27, 1872, Adams brought his suit to a successful conclusion by outstaying his rival, Dr. Fred Shattuck, of whose disappointment Marian made light in a letter to his sister, herself recently married, "I love you more because I love Henry Adams very much and it seems to be returned. And you needn't try to think how happy I am but look at yourself. . . . I've been engaged since Feb 27th. . . . Tell your family for me and Fred that he nearly stopped all this and that if he had sat one hour longer that fatal Tuesday P.M. this might never have come to pass—so I like him better than ever—Henry outstayed him and vows he will never go away." "Absurdly in love," Adams attempted nevertheless to preserve the image of a man of the world unruffled by "this new complication." Believing that passion was only one phase of married life, he wrote to Gaskell two months after his engagement a sentence the Englishman must have read and reread after Marian's death: "If it weren't that I am such a sceptical bird, I should say that we two were a perfectly matched pair and that we were sure to paddle along through life with all the fine weather and sunshine there is in it, but perhaps when one is in the lover's stage, it is safest not to look at the future."[46]

Years later Adams expressed his disbelief in ceremony as the sanction of love: "It is but a vain form. . . . Nature shows no trace of a marriage ceremony even among the doves, and it is so much purer and loftier an ideal to pair without permission." Some such conception, shared by both Henry and Marian, dictated the informal nature of their own wedding at Robert Hooper's house in Beverly Farms. Henry's brothers Charles and John were his only blood relations present for the occasion, and Charles could not believe his eyes. "The wedding was like the engagement," he wrote to Charles Francis Adams, who was abroad at the Geneva arbitration,

—peculiar. The only persons present were . . . thirteen human beings in all, including the unfortunate victims themselves. The ceremony lasted in the neighborhood of two minutes, after which we all bundled into luncheon and sat down anywhere and the bride, at the head of the table, proceeded to calm her agitation by carving a pair of cold roast chickens. John and I dashed into the breach and labored hard to stimulate an aspect of gaiety, but the champagne wasn't iced and made its appearance only in very inadequate quantities, and the aspect of affairs continually tended towards the commonplace.

Charles's chagrin at the loss of his brother, and his sense of exclusion from a (possibly superior?) world where certain social conventions mattered little, colored his report of the festivities. "After lunch the happy pair went off," he continued, "and we sat on the piazza and talked—Harvard College. Why it is necessary or desirable to thus keep the world at arm's length and to carefully remove what little of form and sparkle comes in one's way in life, is 'not perfectly clear' to my mind, but everyone to his taste. . . . [As the parties] do not seem to care to have any interest taken in their matters, I suppose I may as well dismiss them here."[47]

Having started married life somewhat inauspiciously by alienating his brother, Henry made a terrible miscalculation in planning the European wedding journey. The visit with Gaskell at Wenlock Abbey was a happy one, and in Switzerland Marian was delighted to find her old friends from Boston, Henry James and Lizzie Boott. Perhaps a summer in Switzerland and a winter's residence in Italy, as Marian had proposed for Miss Howard, would have suited her as well, but the constant moving from one place to another and the wrench from the familiar associations of Switzerland and Italy to the strange land of Egypt, at a moment when she was coming to terms with a new life away from her father in Massachusetts, shook her bright but fragile spirit.

The depression that soon overcame Marian is worth attention because it foreshadowed her fatal but less well-documented depression in 1885: Clues to her mental state in 1872–73 throw light on the later collapse. Surprisingly, for a well-traveled woman who had nevertheless always traveled with her own family, Marian was dreadfully homesick in 1872. Adams crowded too much into the schedule and did not get his wife south of the Alps before the rainy season began. Her spirits, crushed by the bad weather and the upsetting preparations for three months on an Egyptian riverboat, sank progressively from September. Travel became a series of frustrations. "It is not right to be in smoky stuffy cities through these pleasant summer days," she wrote from Dresden to her father at Beverly Farms. "When you answer this do enclose a bright red maple leaf so that I may feel that I have had a glimpse of autumn. . . . I miss you all the time, and love you very much." The rain set in at Berlin: "In gloomy Germany," Marian later recalled, "[we regretted] we had not died when we were babies." The Swiss and Italian lakes did not cheer her: "Alas! our stay at Cadenabbia [on Lake Como] was not a success. It rained every day." By the time Marian reached Venice she was bitter: "[I] ignore the painful fact of savage mosquitoes who make nights hideous. . . . Today, of course, is very rainy, as all our Sundays are, and there is no fun in a gondola in the rain and no light for seeing pictures." At Florence preparations for the next stage of the journey preyed upon her mind.[48]

Marian castigated herself for dull senses and lack of spontaneity. She had given up waltzing before reaching her twenty-ninth birthday, and she felt herself, by contrast to an Italian acquaintance, to be an "undemonstrative New Englander." She hated sightseeing, especially in Egypt, where she was ignorant of what she was viewing; in letters to her father she contrasted "enthusiastic Egyptologists" such as Henry with "people so painfully wanting in enthusiasm as I am. . . . It is useless to try and tell you how it all looks. I never seem to get impressions that are worth anything, and feel as if I were blind and deaf and dumb too."[49]

Incompetence seemed to stare her in the face. Becoming depressed after marriage is no rare thing for a bright, spirited woman: Marian had to get used to the loss of her previous somewhat masculine independence, and she was transformed abruptly from the bright star of an illuminated circle into the small fish of a large pool. She could not help feeling eclipsed. She would never be able to attain the standard of letterwriting set in an earlier generation by her husband's illustrious great-grandmother. "Life is such a jumble of impressions just now," she despaired to her father, "that I cannot unravel the skein in practical, quiet fashion. Oh, for the pen of Abigail Adams!" On the Nile she and Henry joined forces with Samuel Ward, a power in the Metropolitan Museum of New York, and his wife; Mrs. Ward was a consolation to Marian in her depression. Henry, while attentive and infinitely patient—"Dr. Bethune would feel more sadly than ever if he could see how Henry spoils me," Marian had written earlier in the journey—was not deflected from his other purposes. His knowledge and energy overwhelmed his wife: "I confess that temples do begin to pall. . . . How true it is that the mind sees what it has means of seeing. I get so little, while others about me are so intelligent and cultivated that everything appeals to them." "Henry has been working like a beaver at photographing."[50]

In this crisis Marian mortified herself. It seems possible that she would have appreciated the pyramids more had she enjoyed married life more. She feared that Henry would cease to love her. He would have liked her to be more Oriental, and he purchased for her a Bedouin necklace which "he vows I shall wear, though no one less Egyptian than Alice Sumner could carry it off." But Henry at the same time wondered whether he himself were a mere desiccated Casaubon—he and Marian both read *Middlemarch* on their five-day sea voyage from Egypt to Italy—pursuing his own researches to her exclusion and plunging another devoted but bewildered Dorothea into experiences yet more alien than those of Rome. They witnessed groups of spinning and howling dervishes in Cairo, and Marian was unnerved: "It was the most extraordinary spectacle and by no means a pleasant one," she reported to Robert Hooper. "It gave one the feeling of being surrounded by maniacs." In Boston twelve months earlier Henry's mother had seemed on the verge of nervous collapse, but Henry had been unflappable and all had turned out well; in Egypt patient, affectionate attentiveness was again his resource as he entered the unsettling realm of matrimony, and eventually his calm was again justified. "One has a very helpless feeling," he wrote to young Henry Cabot Lodge in a different connection, "the first time one plunges into a new existence, no matter what the medium is. . . . I have found by turn the same sense of helplessness in entering on each new stage of life, both in Europe and at home. Patience is the salvation of men at all such emergencies."[51]

Marian had languished for want of contact with home and friends. "[I] like to think of you and Whitman [Gurney] in my dear room [at Beverly Farms]," she had written her sister Ellen after two months of marriage, "though I'd like to skip back every night." Egypt had seemed, even in anticipation, a long way from Boston. "We shall be so utterly cut off on the Nile," she warned her father, "that I rather cling to any little American gossip which to you may seem not worth sending."[52] It was not astonishing that Marian's heart leapt as she and Henry boarded ship to depart from Egypt. From the moment she set foot upon the familiar soil of Italy her usual ebullience returned. The visit to Sorrento was a joy, seeing Henry James in Rome was just like home, and not even a bout of suspected typhus fever could deflect her usual torrent of high spirits and irony; in her letter to her father from her sickbed in Rome she was as voluble and irrepressible as ever:

We went back to Naples Saturday because the Empress of Russia was coming that day and we thought one distinguished party enough for such a small town as Sorrento. . . . [In Naples] we stumbled on an antiquity shop kept by a French archangel; I really care more for him than I do for Henry, but don't tell Mrs Adams. . . . Henry is sitting by my side drawing a plan for an immense library for Harvard College, which is to be built with our united fortunes after ten years' accumulation, in case we both die of Naples fever, which at present does not seem probable. The plan is thrilling!—and if Mr. Eliot had even a squinting at it, he would at once despatch emissaries abroad with prussic acid to slay us. . . . We forgive [Ellen and Whitman Gurney for not writing recently] . . . because their example goaded us on to matrimony and we like it when it doesn't rain and we don't have dyspepsia.[53]

Having completely recovered her spirits, Marian only once again fell into a serious depression during the dozen years from March 1873 to March 1885,[54] possibly at the end of Adams's European research trip in 1880, when he doubted whether they would ever venture across the ocean again. The dread of another relapse was always present. When Henry published the second of his anonymous novels with Marian as heroine—"Esther," she was called this time—and when at Niagara Esther refused the suit of the man she loved, Adams knew his heroine ought to jump into the Falls as Marian would have done: "Certainly she would," he later told his confidante, Clarence King, "but I could not suggest it." He dared not leave her even for twenty-four hours at a time, so that at the death of her sister-in-law, Fanny Hooper, early in 1881, she wrote to her father from Washington, "I want to go on and see all of you, but . . . Henry flatly refuses to let me go alone and I am not willing to pull him up from his work."[55] Only once during their married life before March 1885 did Henry risk the separation, when Marian went for a five-day trip to New York in 1883.

Marian's two depressions before 1885 marred what was otherwise exceptional happiness. "For twelve years I had everything I most wanted on earth," Adams cried in anguish after her death. To the woman he later loved, Mrs. Cameron, he was frank: "In forty years of search, I have never met but one woman who met me all round so as to be a real companion"; and Elizabeth Cameron, who wanted to name her only child "Marian" after Adams's dead wife, knew of course who was meant. "Life has for me no more interest or meaning," Adams continued; "and never had any except in marriage." These words echoed his last letter to Marian herself, a few months before her death. She was in Cambridge at the bedside of her dying father, and in her desperation was at her most imperious and unapproachable. Henry had at this crisis the conviction of closeness with his wife rather than the sensation of it. His uncertainty how to reach her heightened the awkwardly impersonal tone in which he attempted to express, without sentimentality, his loneliness and dependence. His scientific metaphor transmuted Goethe's in *The Elective Affinities*, yet anyone knowing this man would recognize the feeling struggling behind his words—when he referred to his own emotions, "craving" and "satisfaction" were not terms he dropped lightly: "How did I ever hit on the only woman in the world who fits my cravings and never sounds hollow? Social chemistry—the mutual attraction of equivalent human molecules—is a science yet to be created, for the fact is my daily study and only satisfaction in life."[56]

To the Adamses' acquaintance the marriage was obviously a good one. Clarence King, their hyperactive geologist friend, whose own domestic arrangements were in serious disarray, found it "awfully comfortable and regulating to the mind to stay with you. I feel calmer and more like marrying for a week afterward." Three years later King declined to purchase a house in Washington adjacent to the Adamses and the John Hays: "If I were only married how I should delight in buying the house. . . . But I am human and could not bear the exasperating spectacle of your and Hays domestic happiness." Mrs. Anne Proctor, a social leader in London, reported that Lady Petty, from whom the Adamses had rented an elegant residence there in 1880 had "found an atmosphere of married happiness pervading her house." Henry's brother Charles knew Marian had never liked him, "nor can I blame her much for that;—I trod all over her, offending her in every way"; yet he conceded that she and Henry "were a well matched pair; and when the fit was not on her . . . he and she lived very happily. . . . Him, she adored; and well she might, for his patience and gentleness seemed inexhaustible. She, in return, entered into all his pursuits and made his house just what he most liked." One of those nieces of Marian's to whom Henry later addressed the preface of *Mont-Saint-Michel and Chartres*, fourteen years old when she last saw the Adamses together, never forgot the summers at Beverly Farms: "Often in the afternoons, the nieces would watch—almost enviously—the two figures on horseback vanishing into the flickering sunlight of the woods. An impression of oneness of life and mind, of perfect companionship, left an ideal never to be effaced."[57]

Although horseback riding and collecting objets d'art were cherished recreations of the Adamses, their companionship was built upon a common interest in politics, a joint involvement in Henry's work, and upon Henry's admiration for the intellectual vivacity of his articulate wife. Marian did not much regret their childlessness, and while Henry grieved at the fact, he acknowledged that it brought him and Clover even closer together. "One consequence of having no children," he told Gaskell, "is that husband and wife become very dependent on each other and live very much together. This is our case."[58]

Marian's passion for politics had been nourished by youthful visits to the Washington house of her uncle, Congressman Samuel Hooper. When she became engaged in 1872, Charles Francis Adams's prospects for the Liberal Republican presidential nomination were excellent, and she was quivering with excitement at the chance of becoming a president's daughter-in-law. Her satisfaction with Washington instead of Boston as a place of residence after 1877 acknowledged the political pull of the capital. One of her successful dinner parties in 1882, with Carl Schurz and former Attorney General Wayne MacVeagh among the guests, occasioned her jubilant outburst: "Kept it up till twelve, very amusing and interesting, not *one* word but of politics from 7 to 12."[59] It was to Marian rather than Henry that Republican Secretary of the Interior Schurz brought a copy of his report on Indian affairs, and to her he talked about the experiment of educating young Indians at Hampton Institute.[60] Similarly, Marian was the one to whom the estimable Democratic Congressman Abram Hewitt sent a copy of his correspondence in the "Morey" imbroglio. So interested was Henry Adams by his wife's response to Washington politics that he wrote a widely read novel, *Democracy*, about this reaction. Their distaste for James Blaine, the Senator Ratcliffe of the novel, impelled them with other Mugwumps to support Grover Cleveland in the presidential election of 1884, and this joint political interest appeared in their correspondence the next spring: "Dear Mugwump," Henry addressed his wife; and he chortled to her after a month of Cleveland's presidency that so far "our" gamble seemed to be turning out well.[61]

Seeking an active-minded woman to make him work, Adams found just that. Marian was intensely ambitious for her husband and showed her conception of wifely duty in her scorn for the spouse of an American painter in Rome: Mrs. Vedder was "an ordinary little girl and won't push him up to anything great." Marian told a former graduate student of Adams's that "she had once stirred Henry into a spasm of work by reporting to him the number of candles Mr. George Bancroft consumed while writing before breakfast." When Adams was editor of the *North American Review*, he read aloud to his wife essays that had been submitted for publication; and he wrote to Gaskell, after his first hard winter's research for the *History*, that she had been helping him. Five years later, as the *History* began to take shape, Marian was her husband's most valued critic. When he explained this to John Hay, Adams was still playing the role of man of the world, pretending not to be unduly impressed by his quick-witted spouse: "I make it a rule to strike out ruthlessly in my writings whatever my wife criticises, on the theory that she is the average reader, and that her decisions are, in fact if not in reason, absolute." That the first volume of the *History* was immaculate owed something to Marian's vigilant eye.[62]

Naturally Henry's wife was ecstatic at the stir caused by his novel *Democracy*, in which she was protagonist, but her interest in his historical writing was also great. "I am glad to have evidence up to Dec 9th that you live," she accosted E. L. Godkin in macabre vein on Christmas Day 1879, writing from Paris soon after he had published Charles Adams's vitriolic, unsigned review of *Gallatin*, "for as most of our friends die nowadays and 'The Nation' ceased coming weeks ago we supposed you and it had perished from the earth. If as you say a genial and suave notice of the Life of Galln. was intended to 'do Henry good' I've no doubt it will and that future works will be full of what Mary Mabel Dodge calls 'Sparkling Sallies' but why should an organ cease playing when moral improvement is included." Godkin, a year later, still had not assuaged his guilt at publishing Charles's blast, and again he addressed Marian with self-reproach. "My wife got your letter of the 19th yesterday," Adams promptly replied, "and . . . we laughed consumedly over your wail."[63] So far did Marian identify with Henry's work[64] and so sharp was her mind that Wayne MacVeagh professed to believe her, not Henry, the true author of the first two volumes of the *History*: "I sought for some real defect as with a lighted candle" MacVeagh reported to Henry after reading the early, privately printed version of these volumes, "but whoever wrote it for you, and I suspect I know, it is extremely well done. The more work of the kind you can publish as if your own, the better for your reputation." When Marian died a year later she was widely believed to be the author, or at least the coauthor with her husband, of *Democracy*, and the rumor of her authorship was printed in her newspaper obituaries. The impression of her literary power had arisen from the Adamses' dinner parties, where the flow of Marian's conversation cascaded about her quieter husband and the brilliance of her satire relegated him to the shadows. "We never knew how delightful Henry was until he lost her," Henry James averred rather disingenuously; "he was so proud of her that he let her shine as he sat back and enjoyed listening to what she said and what others let her say."[65]

However far Marian's interest in politics and her intelligent involvement in Henry's work may have created an atmosphere conducive to his writing good history, her greatest gift was undoubtedly the effervescence that so delighted her husband. Marian "takes malicious pleasure in shocking the prejudices of the wise and good," Henry reported with satisfaction in 1878, fashioning thus early the sardonic phraseology with which in the *History* he gibbeted the self-satisfied upholders of conservative orthodoxy.[66] In marriage, as during her spinster days, Marian found an inexhaustible source of such pleasure in satirizing the church: She termed her regular Sunday evening tea party the "vesper service," and she designated the building style of her good friend, Henry Hobson Richardson, the foremost American architect of his day, "neo-Agnostic." She gaily reported of another friend, a well-known political journalist, that "Nordhoff is out in a new line—sent me yesterday his last book— 'God and a Future life'—to me it is incomprehensible stuff— but life passed between Mrs Nordhoff and the New York Herald office may account for a good deal." Yet when in 1880 Marian attended a London dinner at W. E. H. Lecky's house, sitting beside Ernest Renan, the guest of honor, the noted French freethinker exercised over her a power of transmuting scornful satire into something verging on affection; the words of her report were accompanied at the left-hand margin by Marian's sketch of a jovial face arising from behind a hill: "Renan is charming—most sympathetic and chatty—as big as a whale, no neck and a jolly round face rising directly from his shoulders—you can think of nothing but a full harvest moon rising above a mountain and a curious survival of the Jesuit in his expression." Other guests at this dinner, Robert Browning and Herbert Spencer, did not escape so lightly: Browning "has the intellectual apathy in his face of a chronic diner out. . . . Herbert Spencer—looks like a complacent—crimson owl in spectacles—with an assumption of omniscience in his manner which is reassuring in this age of unbelief—You are led to believe that his very first principle of all is belief in himself."[67]

Among those unable to sympathize with her irony, Marian gained a terrible reputation. Her contempt for the Stalwart faction of Republican politicians was lost upon the wealthy banker Levi Morton, a favorite of Stalwart Senator Roscoe Conkling, who was chairman of the finance committee of the Republican party in 1880 and later became vice president of the United States. Dining at Morton's sumptuous Washington establishment, Marian sat at his left: "He is a light-weight," she opined to Robert Hooper, "and very ordinary; if he can be a successful public man, none need despair. He asked my political opinions. I told him I was a boss-Stalwart, believed in the machine, and the chaff spread; but he is too dull to catch chaff." But this same sharp manner, directed vigorously and gaily against a man who relished being challenged, could be a joy. Thus Marian's reprimand from Paris was bound to tickle the British-born E. L. Godkin: "Pleasant as our seven months abroad have been we want to be at home which suits our tastes and tempers and age better than your effete monarchies—the unfeeling taunts in your letter about roving habits and nomadic tastes are cruel to homesick Americans—did you when a youth pull off fly's wings—or is wanton cruelty a product of ripening years?"[68]

The principal victim of Marian's chaff, of course, was her husband. Henry Adams was short and prematurely bald. It was said of his family that "the Adamses have a genius for saying even a gracious thing in an ungracious way." Thus when Marian received an invitation to be the hostess at a ball given by the Bachelors Club in Washington, she suggested that had she accepted the invitation the popular press would have written up the event somewhat as follows: "The guests were received by Mrs. Henry Adams. . . . By her side stood her husband, a man of superb physical proportions, two well-set eyes surmounted by a brow of great height and lustre; he ably supported his lady by his genial bonhommie—hereditary it may be, but none the less his own." Two weeks later Marian returned to the attack. She and Henry had examined two portraits by Sir Joshua Reynolds with a view toward possible purchase, but their tastes differed. Marian, with an independent income, bought them and was impenitent: "I prefer the woman; Henry, the man," she informed Robert Hooper, but Henry wished neither and "hates portraits."

> Jack Sprat dislikes portraits,
> His wife dislikes paysages,
> and so betwixt them both
> The choice is very large.

I mean to . . . hang these two between the library windows, side by side; Henry can look the other way.

Marian was as quick to mock her husband's literary style as he to profess belief that she was an "average reader." Robert Hooper guessed that his daughter was connected with *Democracy*, but Marian sought to mislead him in such manner that Henry would enjoy the joke. "I am much amused but not surprised at your suspecting me of having written *Democracy*," she protested solemnly. "*I* did not write it. Deny it from me if anyone defames me absent, and say to them, as Pickering Dodge of his parrot: 'if she could n't *write* better than that I'd cut her ——— head off.'" '69

Henry learned from his life with Marian the delight of being satirized by a loving companion. "My wife and I have been reading the dolorous letters of Mrs. Carlyle," he once wrote joyfully to Gaskell, "and it seems to us that we too live in that literary wilderness. In fact she commonly addresses me as 'man of genius,' after the example of that painfully droll couple, and I call her Mrs. C." Adams referred cheerily to Marian's "impudence" and repeatedly quoted her critical remarks and mots with pride of possession. Thus at the end of a none-too-successful missive to Gaskell he concluded, "My wife says this is a *clammy* letter so she adds a Postscript." Marian's satirical remarks upon the rural preoccupations of the British gentry once permitted Adams to make a roundabout thrust at Henry James. In London society, he told one of his closest English landowning friends, "as usual, the weather is the chief topic of conversation, always followed by that of American cattle, until my wife says that herds of those beasts pursue her in her dreams and she hears nothing but their mournful bellowing. I think Henry James is regarded as one of them, for—again according to my wife's experience—he is always brought forward as a topic of conversation with these." '70

Adams's enjoyment of his wife's barbs and his appreciation of her astuteness explain some of the strengths of the *History*. No other work of an American historian is so funny. *The Taming of the Shrew* was written in a society where constant clash of wit sharpened the author's invention, and the deliciously ironic spirit of Adams's *History* proceeded from the ceaseless testing of his wit against that of his nearest companion. Yet it is impossible to convey by means of extracts the character of Adams's humor. In the famous

early chapter on New England, his mockery of American poetical pretensions depends upon his building higher and higher a mass of illustration—
for a dozen pages he deflates his countrymen's bombast—and brief excerpts
do no justice to the satirical method: "In Connecticut," he began,

the Muses were most obstinately wooed; and there, after the Revolutionary War, a
persistent effort was made to give prose the form of poetry. The chief of the movement was Timothy Dwight, a man of extraordinary qualities, but one on whom
almost every other mental gift had been conferred in fuller measure than poetical
genius.

. . . . .

[Joel Barlow's] "Vision of Columbus," magnified afterward into the "Colum-
biad," with a magnificence of typography and illustration new to the United States,
remained a monument of his ambition. In this vision Columbus was shown a variety
of coming celebrities, including all the heroes of the Revolutionary War:—

> "Here stood stern Putnam, scored with ancient scars,
> The living records of his country's wars;
> Wayne, like a moving tower, assumes his post,
> Fires the whole field, and is himself a host;
> Undaunted Stirling, prompt to meet his foes,
> And Gates and Sullivan for action rose;
> Macdougal, Clinton, guardians of the State,
> Stretch the nerved arm to pierce the depth of fate;"
> [Ten further lines are reproduced.]

More than seven thousand lines like these furnished constant pleasure to the
reader. . . . The Hartford wits, who were bitter Federalists, looked upon Barlow as
an outcast from their fold, a Jacobin. . . . [But they could not] without great in-
gratitude repudiate his poetry as they did his politics, for they themselves figured
with Manco Capac, Montezuma, Raleigh, and Pocahontas before the eyes of Columbus; and the world bore witness that Timothy Dwight, "Heaven in his eye and
rapture on his tongue," tuned his "high harp" in Barlow's inspired verses.[71]

Although Adams's tone was sardonic, his thought complex, and the ornamentation of his literary edifice immensely elaborate, the spirit of his satire
resembled that of Marian's. A constant, vigorous challenging of conventional
pieties was an essential element of Marian's psychological makeup, to be
dispensed with only at her own great peril. Her delight in satire, and Henry's,
was their strongest intellectual bond.

The Adamses liked to go riding together, sharing a love of nature. Their
schedule varied according to the season: "Every morning at nine o'clock my
wife and I set out on horseback," Adams wrote one autumn from Washington, "and only get back to breakfast at half-past eleven," but their normal
routine was a long ride after Henry had worked five hours on the *History*.

Fine spring weather extended the tours. Thus in late April "the temptations of riding till sunset have broken up five o'clock tea"; at that season the Adamses' daily three to four hours in the saddle led them occasionally across the Potomac into Virginia, other times along the old Bladensburg road: Henry's biting account of the American humiliation in 1814 at Bladensburg grew from his ever-renewed familiarity with the battleground. If Marian were not able to take a ride, Henry would bring her back a bunch of hepaticas from the woods; and when she was attending her father's deathbed in Cambridge, Henry reported how he managed in her absence: Yesterday "I took my first three-hour spring excursion round by the dog-tooth violets. . . . A few maples show a faint flush here and there, but not a sign of leaf is to be seen, and even the blood-root and hepatica hid themselves from my eyes. . . . No sign of a peach-blossom yet, and not even the magnolias and *Pyrus Japonica* have started. . . . I have not even seen the yellow Forsythia in flower." [72]

Like other childless couples, the Adamses sometimes expressed affection for each other through their animals, their three Skye-terriers; thus Henry once wrote that "the dogs and I have just come in from picking some violets for you, which we have put in your little Hizan tea-pot on our desk." At the beginning of Marian's stay at her father's bedside, Henry mourned that "the dogs and I try to be gay, but Possum is in very low spirits." Marian sent a rubber ball by express; when it arrived, Henry attempted to maintain his reserve, pretending to curb Possum: "No sooner did he see the address with his name than he began jumping and screaming till I had to reprove him severely. He kept up a wild dance while I opened the package; and then seized his ball and retired to the entry to munch it." By the next day Adams's stiff upper lip had softened: "Possum has eaten up most of his ball, and is hunting for the remnant, which I hide and he seeks. Love, love, love! " [73]

The most affectionate stroke of Adams's *History*—in his vignette of John Marshall—touches the chief justice as he carries clover seed on horseback. [74] In a passage of *Gallatin* Adams also briefly bordered on expressing his feelings for Clover Hooper. Just as his most esteemed professor at Harvard was the Swiss Louis Agassiz, so his greatest admiration in the *History* was reserved for the Swiss-born Albert Gallatin. When Adams published Gallatin's biography in 1879, his literary style was still stiff and unformed, but the tribute to Gallatin's marriage seemed to project Adams's feelings about his own. Gallatin wrote to a friend—rather as Adams had written to Gaskell in 1872—that he had become engaged to

"a girl about twenty-five years old, who is neither handsome nor rich, but sensible, well-informed, good-natured, and belonging to a respectable and very amiable family". . . . The characteristic self-restraint of Mr. Gallatin's language in describing her to his friend is in striking contrast with the warmth of affection which he then felt, and ever retained, towards one whose affection and devotion to him during more than half a century were unbounded. . . . His temper, his tastes, and his moral convictions combined to make him thoroughly dependent on his wife and his children. He was never happy when separated from them.[75]

Yet Marian combined with her numerous virtues certain glaring faults. The details of furnishing the new house Richardson was building for her and Henry proved to be too much for her, and Henry obviously found her exasperatingly exacting: "Do you want more than one bell in dining-room? I see no good in the stupid floor-bells. I hate the one at Beverly. Do you want a bell to ring up-stairs? If so *from* what room, and *to* what room?" Furthermore, Marian's irony was often savagely misplaced when she was dealing with those of a different social class: "The cabmen [in Paris] are fresh from the country," she once complained to Robert Hooper, from the French capital, "and know nothing. I said to one the other day who couldn't find any place, 'I advise you to study a map of Paris; you'll find it interesting.' "[76] But her greatest failing, one suspects, was an inability to free herself from her father's bonds, so that she could accept the intimacy of love.

Adams's fiction reflects this side of Marian's personality. She was the prototype for the heroines of both his anonymous novels. *Democracy* narrates Madeleine Lee's liberation from her sense of duty to a plausible but maleficent older man, and Adams defines the heroine's "tendency towards asceticism, self-extinction, self-abnegation," her "painful efforts to understand and follow out her duty," her "saint's capacity for self-torment." Possibly behind Carrington's struggle to save Madeleine Lee from her feeling of "her duty and her responsibility to Ratcliffe" lay Adams's effort to preserve Marian from her sense of responsibility to Robert Hooper.[77]

Esther, whose heroine finally rejects the love of a young cleric to whom she is strongly attached, approaches closer to the Adamses' situation. The details of the story grew from Marian's and Henry's own experience. The church in *Esther* is patently Trinity Church in Boston, five minutes' walk from the Adamses' house on Marlborough Street. When they lived in Boston this building was being raised and ornamented by their close friends Richardson and John LaFarge. The Episcopalian rector, Esther's suitor, initially suggests Phillips Brooks of Trinity Church, whom Marian knew before she became engaged to Adams. The death of Esther's father anticipates that of Marian's. The incompatibility between Esther and the Rev. Stephen Hazard is, in the novel, explained by Esther's agnosticism, and this certainly resembled that of Marian Adams.

Yet the psychological currents of the novel run deeper. The chief symbolic passages—echoed in the contrast between Henry Brooks Adams's middle name and that of his female pseudonym, Frances Snow Compton—set the rush of Niagara Falls against the wintry coldness of the Upper New York State countryside, where Esther finally freezes the flow of Stephen Hazard's impassioned suit. A clerical disguise would not seem inappropriate to a scholar who "always felt [himself] . . . like Casaubon in *Middlemarch*" and who sometimes pretended to think himself fitted for ecclesiastical life.[78] The vowel sounds and rhythm of syllables of the suitor's name likened those of Marian's husband as closely as the decorating of the church resembled the painstakingly elaborate ornamentation of the artistic edifice of the *History*, which Marian's husband (who later referred to another piece of nonfiction as "a work of art . . . like Rheims or Amiens Cathedral")[79] was constructing in their study. *Esther* seems to express, with characteristic indirection, Adams's hurt at an obscure rejection by his fascinating wife—who perhaps at times was sexually chilly, "painfully wanting in enthusiasm,"[80] and who yet so obviously cared for him.

Earlier, when Marian was entering her first severe depression in 1872, she gave voice to her peculiar dependence upon her father at the moment her husband was most attentive: "I miss you and want to see you," she wrote Robert Hooper as she prepared to depart from Italy for Egypt, "though Henry is so utterly devoted and tender that I am sure you would wonder at my ever feeling a yearning for the old diggings, which I do very often."[81] The dynamics were the same, yet even more powerful, during Robert Hooper's last illness in the spring of 1885. Henry accompanied Marian to Cambridge at the beginning of her vigil, but she found his regular presence intolerable: His aim was to protect her from the inevitable physical and psychological strains of caring for her father; hers was to make an exhausting final atonement to Robert Hooper for not having been, in earlier years, everything to him he may have felt he required. These two motives were incompatible, and Marian soon packed Henry off to Washington.

Except for her brief trip to New York in 1883, they had not been apart in thirteen years. They wrote to each other every day. As Henry had varied his salutations to Charles Adams and to Gaskell, he now varied them to his beloved:

> Dear Clover,
> Madam,
> Dear Mistress,
> Dearest Mistress,
> Dear Aspasia,
> Dear Lady,
> Dear Angel,
> Dear Mugwump,
> Dear Clo.

After eight days Marian sent a desperate telegram of her need for Henry, which alarmed him for her stability: "Your telegram inviting me to Cambridge . . . at first frightened me out of my wits; but Richardson read it and reassured me, declaring that he would give anything in the world if his wife would send such a telegram to him." But after Henry spent four more days at Cambridge, Marian banished him again to Washington. Four nights later he was allowed to return to Boston for nearly a week, then again dispatched, protesting. The struggle approached a climax, "I want to join you tomorrow," Henry wrote, on April 10, "but dare not without permission." The next day: "I wished you had called me [in your despatches received yesterday]; but perhaps I should be in your way, and in such circumstances I must depend on your judgment." A day later: "Uneasy as I am about you, and unable to do anything here, I go on from hour to hour and make no engagements at all."[82]

Dr. Hooper, in a coma, breathed his last on the thirteenth and Adams set off for Cambridge, his fourth such long, slow rail journey within five weeks. He professed to be satisfied with Marian's state of mind: She "has come back [to Washington] in better condition than I feared," he wrote a week later; but she had no children to immunize her against grief, and the ensuing months were fearsome.[83]

The risk of malaria deterred the Adamses from summer residence in Washington, yet Marian wished to avoid the painful associations of Beverly Farms. At first they contemplated a summer's expedition to the Canadian Rockies, but she did not seem up to it and this was abandoned for six weeks in Yellowstone; these in turn shrank to a month at the mountain resorts of West Virginia. Marian's condition worsened and they had to go to Beverly Farms after all. The prospect of taking up again their architectural furnishing—Richardson's new house, opposite the White House, would be ready for them in December—worked upon her mind. Doubtless she was insomniac during the summer, and Adams later hinted at an interpretation of her state in commenting upon Spencer Perceval, the British prime minister, engulfed by disasters in 1810: "Responsibilities that might have driven him to insanity took the form of religious duties; and with the support of religious or patriotic formulas statesmen could sleep in peace amidst the wreck of nations." In September the Adamses attempted a trip to Saratoga Springs, N.Y., but it was not successful. Marian's satirical tongue was stilled, and, lacking this combative defense, she sank into a pitiably gentle and helpless condition. "Mrs. Adams has had a wretched summer," Gurney confided to Godkin in October, "in the gloomiest state of mind, and the gloom has not yet lifted. Time seems the only remedy and I hope that in the course of the winter she will return to her normal state. Her general depression has been accompanied by the greatest sweetness towards us."[84]

When Henry and Marian set off from Boston to spend their usual winter in Washington, Charles Adams chanced to be on the same train. He "tried to talk with her. . . . She sat there pale and careworn, hardly making an effort to answer me, the very picture of physical weakness and mental depression. As she was then, she had been for a long time. . . . She was engaged the whole time in introspection and self-accusation." "Physically and mentally she was . . . [for months] an object for the most profound compassion, and as irresponsible for her own act as an infant. The burden laid upon her was greater than she could bear."[85]

Twice her husband had pulled Marian through morbid spells which "though he never spoke of them, must to Henry have been periods of Hell." In autumn 1885, drawing upon his earlier experience with his mother and with Marian in Egypt, Henry followed the advice he had given James Russell Lowell in analogous circumstances:

I know that the only right course for you now is to turn yourself into a methodical machine; allot your hours; insist upon exercise; take all the distraction you can manage; and make things yield to your own needs. A little selfishness and a great deal of method is sometimes the highest altruism. You are in for a long campaign, and like a good general, should coldly make the most of your strength.

All of which is easy to say. As for doing it, I know that I should break down at the start.

Henry accepted the nineteenth-century theory that mental illness had a physical origin; as Charles stated the idea, Marian had inherited a latent tendency to depression: "It was in the Sturgis blood. . . . The tendency was organic. . . . In Clover's case any period of excitement and unnatural action was sure to be followed by a corresponding period of depression and morbid reaction. . . . Presently, when the general health of her system was restored, the morbid tendency passed away."[86] Henry thus believed that Marian would recover from depression soon after her physical condition began to improve. It was his desperate wish to carry her through this state, as he had done before, until such time as the body began again to heal itself; and by December he thought a physical change for the better had taken place: Mental improvement would soon follow. Henry did not know that in a depression like Marian's the period of incipient recovery is a dangerous time, for the patient then regains vigor to undertake enterprises previously ruled out by apathy.

The suspicion crossed Charles's mind that Marian would never really recover,[87] and this had been Marian's fear too, as the weeks passed into months. "She would interrupt her conversation to put her hand impulsively to her forehead, rubbing it back and forth, as if trying to comprehend something that was beyond her."[88] She scarcely ever was happy, and so rare were her moments of pleasure that after one of them Henry exclaimed to the friend who daily visited her in Washington, Rebecca Dodge, "I shall never forget what you've done. . . . You made Clover smile."[89] Overwhelmed, Marian felt that if life were to continue in misery, death would be better. Long ago she had shown interest in a woman "plucky enough" to poison herself,[90] and she now sought to bring her own courage to the sticking point. After lunch on Sunday, December 6, the day she had been used to write her weekly letter to

Robert Hooper, she addressed a letter to her sister Ellen. It was a cry of self-humiliation and despair. "If I had one single point of character or goodness," she said, "I would stand on that and grow back to life. Henry is more patient and loving than words can express. God might envy him—he bears and hopes and despairs hour after hour. . . . Henry is beyond all words tenderer and better than all of you even."[91] Sealing this note, she addressed a parting message to Henry and then swallowed a sufficient dose of potassium cyanide from her photographic-developing supplies.

It was her husband's turn now for self-flagellation, and remorse still beset him twenty-five years later: "Your tragedy," he wrote Brooks Adams—referring to the tragedy of John Quincy Adams's life, in Brooks's manuscript biography of their grandfather—"will be indicated, as it is in the lives of us all, by the chief failure." Henry had not succeeded in keeping alive and in good health the woman he most cared for, and a profound sense of failure dogged him for the rest of his days. He had done the intelligent and compassionate thing by keeping Marian with him instead of sending her to a mental institution, but in attempting to carry on something resembling the normal routine of life, he had left her, in a dangerously morbid state, unattended. He seemed once in a while to advert, in some different context, to the sense of his negligence that afflicted him: "Patience was the last resource of fools as well as of sages. . . . Inertia almost invariably has ended in tragedy."[92] This feeling of having let his wife down, of his having drifted instead of somehow winning her back to health—not some supposedly thwarted political ambition—was probably one of the driving forces behind his repeated cries of failure in the *Education*.

Although he sought always to maintain silence, during the earliest days of his bereavement a wail of despair occasionally found expression. "Never fear for me," he wrote Godkin ten days after the event,

I have had happiness enough to carry me over some years of misery; and even in my worst prostration I have found myself strengthened by two thoughts. One was that life could have no other experience so crushing. The other was that at least I had got out of life all the pleasure it had to give. I admit that fate at last has smashed the life out of me; but for twelve years I had everything I most wanted on earth. I own that the torture has made me groan; but, as long as any will is left, I shall try not to complain.

He turned, a broken man, to things reminiscent of Marian and to the greatest literature of the language. "He rides—" Ellen Gurney reported, "moves his books—looks out of window—is like a small child—reads Shakespeare aloud evenings—has several familiar friends of theirs—mostly Mr. Field and women just now." His Washington friends admitted him into a freemasonry of suffering; in March bitterness welled up from Adams's heart: "What a vast fraternity it is,—that of 'Hearts that Ache.' For the last three months it has seemed to me as though all society were coming to me, to drop its mask for a moment and initiate me into the mystery. How we do suffer! And we go on laughing; for, as a practical joke at our expense, life is a success."[93]

"We go on laughing": With Puritanic self-denial the remorseful widower sought to withhold from himself the release of expressing grief through conventional forms; except toward his most intimate friends and relations he cultivated an impenetrable exterior, hiding feeling behind a sardonic mask. Some of the evasions and half-truths of *The Education of Henry Adams* originated in this habit of lying to the world. But to one or two friends Adams showed himself as he was. In June he visited Boston, and Marian's sister was his resource: "I, perhaps, am his 'safety valve' for expression," Ellen wrote disconnectedly to Godkin; "at least Gurney thinks it a good sign that he has it out—know that the 'stoic' aspect is thin glaze—that the worm never dies—he is restless—hates to be alone—likes any life—especially—young life round to mark the 'human passing of the hours.'" After the escape of a summer's journey to Japan with LaFarge, Adams returned to find Whitman Gurney dead of anemia and Ellen staggering under the new blow. She knew Adams had not recovered: "The wound is not skimmed," she reported. "I hope he will stand it—he has thus far, and has got to. I could never have gone through a day, it almost seems to me, of the agony he has had to, for months and months—and to have such heavy shadows on so many of your memories would be blasting. But he may have the force—to turn from the side—on which it is madness—and vain to dwell—and there was so much— for so long—just what he wanted."[94]

In 1915 Anna Lodge died, Henry Cabot Lodge's wife and one of Adams's most intimate friends. He attempted to prophesy to Lodge what the future held:

You have got to endure what I have endured for thirty years. . . . My only comfort then was to be told, over and over, how much I had lost,—as though I did not know it better than anybody. . . . I have gone on talking, all that time, but it has been to myself—and to her. The world has no part in it. One learns to lead two lives. . . .

I can sit now for hours, quite still, with my hands before me, thinking of them, as all that is left worth a thought. . . . Meanwhile, try to go on with your daily work.

The routine of writing the *History* sustained Adams for the first four years after Marian's death. Half of the nine volumes was already complete, and he attempted in 1886 to carry on so that no reader could detect the point where the blow had fallen. "Henry Adams is pegging at his History, I rejoice to say," Ellen notified Godkin early in 1887. "Of course he has no heart for that or anything—but I long for him to get back the habit of work—and to exorcise the demon of restlessness which pursues him.[95] Adams commissioned the sculptor Saint-Gaudens to erect the Buddha figure that stands over Clover's grave and his in Rock Creek cemetery, but his *History* is the true memorial of his rich life with a woman whose intellectual ebullience, irreverence, and mockery were his joy.

During the half-dozen years following Marian's death, Adams came to feel revulsion against his former way of life and against the *History* so closely associated with his marriage. Doubtless he conceived that marriage a failure, despite its years of happiness. He probably tried to reassure himself that depression lay in Marian's nature. He had seemed to explore, in *Democracy*, Marian's self-flagellating sense of duty to a much older man, and in *Esther* her incapacity to respond warmly to a suitor for whom she deeply cared. The breakdown and apparent suicide of Marian's sister in 1887 suggested that Marian's troubles stemmed from her own family.

Yet this train of thought was not likely to stifle Adams's self-doubt after his wife's death. What was wrong with him as a husband, he must have wondered, that he could keep Marian happy neither when he took her from her father to Egypt in 1873 nor when her father died? The clerical Stephen Hazard did bear a share of responsibility for Esther's fate—his vocation separated him from her—and the more so in *Middlemarch* did the dry-as-dust Casaubon allow scholarship to separate him from Dorothea. Perhaps Adams associated his work on the *History* with failure in his marriage. Marian herself had spurred him on to his historical work, yet Adams may have felt—as many a husband has felt—that devotion to work diminished what he offered his wife. Such considerations would help to explain Adams's dismal feelings about the *History*, even before it was published, and they would account substantially for his ultimate conviction of failure.

But before Marian's death Adams was an ambitious man. His sense of vocation needs to be examined at the moment his creative energies were at full flood.

CHAPTER 4 · *Historian*

ALTHOUGH THE *Education* disguises Adams's relation to Clover, to Gaskell, and to several members of his family, its most important distortion lies in its twisting the truth about his career between 1870 and 1890. He declares of his teaching at Harvard that "as a professor he regarded himself as a failure. . . . He had accomplished nothing that he tried to do";[1] and he pretends that he went to Washington in 1877 chiefly because he believed he had no function in life except that of associating with politicians. All of the evidence points in a different direction.

Adams was undoubtedly an excellent teacher, his success arising from his informality with students, high standards and thoroughness, objectivity, and constant challenging of accepted views. His graduate students and his more active undergraduates experienced something of his manner with his intimate friends. "His smile had in it fellowship, welcome, and heartiness," one of them recalled, "but his laugh was infectious." He invited his advanced students to his apartment in Wadsworth House—a yellow wooden dwelling still standing at the side of Harvard Square—or later to his study at Marlborough Street and there conducted informal seminar discussions in an intimate atmosphere. "He was the first teacher of history at Harvard to discard the textbook, and put his students to work for themselves," said one former student, later a well-known medievalist. "'Research' courses they were in fact. . . . They afforded me more training than all the rest, and I worked hardest on them."[2]

Adams's bête noire was the dilettantism of merely amateur gentleman-scholars; his method of stalking the beast was to oblige his students to criticize first-rate histories and to study sources with Germanic care. "I have again this year taken a class through your *Ancient Law*," he wrote Sir Henry Maine in 1875, "encouraging them to dispute, and overthrow if they could, every individual proposition in it. Then we read Germania and are now half way through the Lex Salica, translating and commenting on every sentence."

He moved increasingly toward United States history during his last years at Harvard, and here again his method was to challenge the students' inertia. "It was his delight to make his pupils fight over again the battles [of early American politics]," another former student recalled, "forcing Bostonians of Federalist lineage to support the Jeffersonian position, and those of the Democratic tradition to defend the most abhorred tenets of blue-light Federalism."[3]

Adams was proud that his methods did not please every scholar. "My rule in making . . . up [my examination papers] is to ask questions which I can't myself answer," he once explained; and the result of another examination "was to display a degree of ignorance in my young men, such as I had not even imagined. The result has been a row. I have caused it to be intimated to about one third of the youths that they are in a parlous state, which has naturally discomposed their serenity. You may imagine that I am not altogether popular now-a-days." But the best students throve. "His intellectual independence was his most marked characteristic," J. Lawrence Laughlin exclaimed; he wished to "shake up established complacency. . . . Adams had a genius for starting men to think. . . . His unconventional manner and his sense of humor attracted the students. . . . He was so stimulating . . . that he conveyed to one unconsciously the true concept of education as the power to think in a subject. . . . [His was] the first true seminar in this country." These judgments were not isolated; to Edward Channing, later a professor at Harvard and a prolific writer in the field of American history, Adams was "the greatest teacher that I ever encountered."[4]

Although he worked assiduously to reform curriculum, teaching methods, and library practices for the benefit of undergraduates and to import German standards and methods for graduate students, Adams found the collegiate atmosphere of Harvard stultifying. He was exasperated that "the teacher assumes that teaching is his end in life, and that he has no time to work for original results."[5] He did not concede that his years at Harvard contributed to his subsequent career as historian. But the professorship forced Adams to educate himself in German historical method; his manner of teaching gave him practice—whose result is evident on every page of the *History*—in criticising both parties to a political dispute; and college lecturing doubtless increased his capacity for clear organization. The Harvard post established Adams as a historian to whom, as happened in 1877, valuable papers like those of Albert Gallatin might readily be entrusted. Moreover, Adams's dual position as editor of the *North American Review*, conducted in the interest of political reform, and history professor gave him a bridge for gradual movement from journalistic enterprises to his true vocation.

Adams had once assumed that his career would be political: "The Irish gardener once said to the child: 'You'll be thinkin' you'll be President too!' The casualty of the remark made so strong an impression on his mind that he never forgot it. He could not remember ever to have thought on the subject; to him, that there should be a doubt of his being President was a new idea." Late in the 1860s he wished to combine literature and politics: He would establish himself with political contributions to the *Edinburgh Review*, and he hoped for a position on a New York daily. But after he became editor of the *North American Review* in 1870 his involvement in the reform movement gradually declined, and in his biography of his hero, Albert Gallatin, he hinted at the disenchantment with politics he had come to feel. He sought to avoid the scholar's curse of making everything explicit, for he understood that an artist must leave something to the reader's imagination. "The moral of [Gallatin's] . . . life," he ruminated in private, "lies a little deeper than party politics and I have tried here and there [in the biography] rather to suggest than to assert it. The inevitable isolation and disillusionment of a really strong mind—one that combines force with elevation—is to me the romance and tragedy of statesmanship. . . . [Gallatin] could and did refuse power when he found out what vanity it was, and yet became neither a cynic nor a transcendental philosopher." Sensing the vanity of power, Adams turned to a literary career with high hopes. By 1877, when he left Harvard for Washington, his mind was full of his great historical project. "I am satisfied that literature offers higher prizes than politics," he told Gaskell on the eve of departing for Washington. "A political life vulgarises and narrows intelligent people," he continued two years later to Cunliffe:

I should care less on the subject if I did not see so many acquaintances made victims to this beastly political juggernaut. Here is poor Bryce who should have been now the best historian in England; . . . and a dozen others, all the worse for trying to mind other people's business. The ground is literally strewn with such melancholy victims to a diseased appetite. I sincerely hope that you, my dear friend, may escape, and Carlo too; but if you get into Parliament, evidently it will be better for me to avoid England. I will certainly not submit to be bored. . . .

Henry misled his insensitive younger brother, Brooks, into supposing that his ambitions were principally social, but some of his acquaintance knew better. "His real ambitions were literary," declared J. Lawrence Laughlin, and this judgment was echoed by Cabot Lodge's son: Adams "wanted social acclaim [and] political influence," he told an early biographer, "but got [his] chief pleasure from his writings, although he would never admit it."[6]

Attempting in the *Education* to disguise what the writing of history had once meant to him, Adams nevertheless allowed an occasional glimpse of the truth. He pretended to have felt in 1877—when in fact his literary ambition was soaring—that "as far as he had a function in life, it was as stable-companion to statesmen"; and turf imagery recurred in the *Education*'s only extensive reference to the *History*. Adams calculated the cost of producing the work (including research expenses and an imputed salary) at $100,000: "an expenditure rather more extravagant in proportion to his means than a rac-ing-stable." These equine figures almost betrayed him, for he seemed to ad-mit that he had raced hard, spurred by the wish to elevate his country's artistic standards and to gain the glittering prize of fame: In 1890—the year he finished the *History*, though this fact is not mentioned in the *Education*— "like a horse that wears out, he quitted the race-course, left the stable, and sought pastures as far as possible from the old." Adams pictures himself in Washington as an idle onlooker, jadedly laughing at the political scene; but the ambiguous imagery refers again to his role as historian: "He gravely thought that . . . , in the long run, he was likely to be a more useful citizen without office. He could at least act as audience, and, in those days, a Wash-ington audience seldom filled even a small theatre. He felt quite well satisfied to look on, and from time to time he thought he might risk a criticism of the players." After the *History* was finished, Adams's self-portrait turns floral as he accepts the epithet of a hostile Republican senator: By 1892 he was a "thirsty and faded begonia." The closest he came in the *Education* to a cry of despair was his evocation of "the old, half-witted soldiers [contemplating the bronze figure over Clover's burial spot in Rock Creek cemetery] who denounced the wasting, on a mere grave, of money which should have been given for drink"; and his nearest admission of what the *History* had meant to him was the confession that "life was complete in 1890; the rest mattered so little!"[7]

As early as 1857 the nineteen-year-old undergraduate had protested against "the appearance of sentiment in any form in public. . . . An affectation of love where none is felt is absurd. A display where it is real, is disgusting."[8] In public he would no more explicitly concede that writing the *History* had been a labor of love than he would acknowledge his feeling for the woman in the Rock Creek grave. But in private he had not been able to conceal his passion:

I am at work again to my great joy.

. . . . .

I am living [at Beverly Farms] like a hermit in a wood. Work and read ten hours a day, till my mind is scoured like a kitchen copper.

. . . . .

[We are coming to England in June 1879.] This is some months earlier than was intended, but I wanted to be at work and to dawdle about Beverly Farms seemed absurd, after I had got my books out.[9]

. . . . .

I want to tell the whole truth, in regard to England, France and Spain, in a "History of the United States from 1801 to 1815," which I have been for years collecting material for.

. . . . .

I enjoy immensely the investigation. . . .

. . . . .

It's wildly interesting . . . to me.

. . . . .

[In ten years] I expect that my work in life will be done.[10]

. . . . .

I have worked very steadily and have felt for the first time a sort of nervous fear of losing time. . . . Life is slipping away so fast that I grudge every day which does not show progress in my work. I have but one off-spring, and am nearly forty-four while it is nothing but an embryo.

. . . . .

I am so absorbed in my own pursuits that I see nothing else. . . . I write for five hours every day, and ride two, and do society for the remainder. . . . If I felt a perfect confidence that my history would be what I would like to make it, this part of life—from forty to fifty—would be all I want. There is a summer-like repose about it; . . . a feeling that one's bed is made, and one can rest on it till it becomes necessary to go to bed for ever.

. . . . .

The world is ready enough to give one whatever one does not want and would not take. The only thing I want is that they should read my books. . . .

. . . . .

I am working very hard to get everything out of my brain that can be made useful. If my father is a test, I can count on twenty years more brain, if the physical machine holds out.[11]

. . . . .

My husband is working like a belated beaver.[12]

Although Adams never clearly avowed the social purpose impelling him to these labors, it is readily inferred. The American republican experiment was conducted, he believed, within a strong social organism—"except for Negro slavery it was sound and healthy in every part"; but he knew that as of the 1870s America's cultural attainments fell lamentably short of those of England, Germany, or France. He looked to the day when his country's social power might translate itself into artistic achievement:

The American democrat [of 1800] knew so little of art that among his popular illusions he could not then nourish artistic ambition; but leaders like Jefferson, Gallatin, and Barlow might without extravagance count upon a coming time when diffused ease and education should bring the masses into familiar contact with higher forms of human achievement, and their vast creative power, turned toward a nobler culture, might rise to the level of that democratic genius which found expression in the Parthenon; might revel in the delights of a new Buonarotti and a richer Titian; might create for five hundred million people the America of thought and art which alone could satisfy their omnivorous ambition.

Artistic ambition: Might not Adams himself hope to join others beginning by 1880 to create an America of thought and art worthy of its founders' aspirations? While Adams could express his hopes for his native land, he felt obliged even with Gaskell to conceal behind a curtain of self-mockery his own personal stake: "I belong to the class of people," he wrote in 1877, "who have great faith in this country and who believe that in another century it will be saying in its turn the last word of civilisation. . . . [I] try to imagine that I am myself, with my fellow *gelehrte* here, the first faint rays of that great light which is to dazzle and set the world on fire hereafter." Six years' labors did not alter Adams's aspirations. "I am always at work," he told his English friend in 1883; "it amuses me and is worth quite as much as the work I see of other people. . . . I confess to thinking it [the United States] the only country now worth working for." To John Hay, traveling in England, Adams a few days later alluded scornfully to the historian Lord Acton; "Tell my Lord to come over here and live for the future, not for the middle-ages." The first volumes of Adams's *History* were by now being printed in a private edition, and he came the nearest ever to avowing his passion: "As it gets into type I cower before it in hope and fear, for it is all I shall make of this droll toy called life."[13]

This hope was crushed with Clover's death on December 6, 1885. After a dazed interval Adams dragged himself reluctantly to complete his work; the weariness of his spirit found expression in his visual condition: "I work near ten hours a day," he wrote in 1887 from his father's stone library at Quincy; "I work frantically. If my eyes hold out, they will really do themselves credit. As yet they grumble but march." Adams's determination to complete the *History* made his close friend Clarence King uneasy. "Whenever I think of you," King admitted, "and the splendid work you are carrying through with such silences of purpose and conscientiousness of effort, I feel that you must regard me with disfavor and be amazed at the barrenness of my poor life." To carry on writing was a desperate act for Adams, a Puritanic triumph of will over the inclination to cease struggle. King pretended it was better never to have tried at all than to experience the completion of such a labor. He confided to John Hay: "Generally I am low in my mind, but I am a comic opera beside Henry Adams whose grim, gray scorn of this universe seems to me very ashen and disembodied. . . . It's evidently a horrible thing to finish one's magnum opus. I, who will never begin mine, may always have the gentle tonic of perpetual gestation, the soft genial pride of an important bellyful, with none of the throes of printing and none of the ghastly hollow-ness of collapsing sides. Can a man have a second magnum opus?"[14] The thirteen-year labor of hope and despair was completed in 1890. Adams felt his life at an end.

If exceptional talent is to flourish, it usually requires the nourishment of a preexisting tradition. Henry Adams had the fortune to be born in that American city, and at that moment, when literary history was beginning to take root in New England. He was five years old when Prescott brought out his *Conquest of Mexico* (1843); during his student days Motley's *Rise of the Dutch Republic* appeared (1856); and he witnessed as an adult the publication of Parkman's volumes, culminating in *Montcalm and Wolfe* (1884). These older historians—all natives of the Boston area and all Harvard graduates—were gentlemen-scholars whose inherited wealth enabled them to spend years on research and writing. Adams was a young man when Prescott died, but he was closely associated with both Motley, as on their voyage back from England in 1868, and Parkman, to whom Henry and Marian lent a stateroom during their transatlantic wedding trip in 1872. The examples of the older men showed Adams that an American of independent income could follow the historian's calling, with profit to his country and honor to himself. But Adams's relation to Prescott, Parkman, and even Motley resembled in more than one respect the ambiguous relation of Henry James to Nathaniel Hawthorne. An examination of the older men's work may throw light on the American tradition which nourished Henry Adams but against which—to some degree—he rebelled.

Prescott thoroughly investigated Cortez's expedition and the Aztecs whom Cortez subjugated, but he shaped his historical materials into a tale of romance. He exults that "the whole story has the air of fable, rather than of history! a legend of romance—a tale of the genii!"[15] Not infrequently his story seems like an old-time Hollywood spectacular: Fanatical Indians swarm about beleaguered white men whose leaders, in this case, have "the generous hearts of the Spanish cavaliers" (2:81). Meteorological imagery is meant to enhance the awesomeness of the scene—stones and arrows "fell every moment faster and more furious, till they thickened into a terrible tempest. . . . The Spaniards pushed steadily on through this arrowy sleet" (2:78). The din of the Mexican battlefield might be that of the Trojan plain: "Above the combatants rose a wild and discordant clamour, in which horrid shouts of vengeance were mingled with groans of agony" (2:80).[16]

Concerned with the grandeur of the spectacle, Prescott attends perhaps excessively to the sound of words. Alliteration sometimes is ostentatious: "That this should have been done, not to a drivelling dotard in the decay of his fortunes, but to a proud monarch in the plenitude of his power . . . is a thing too extravagant, altogether too improbable, for the pages of romance!" (1:353). Adjectives selected for sonority suggest stereotypes rather than individual character: "Such was the *crafty* policy of the Mexican priests. . . . [Reverence for religion] maintained its hold on the *iron* nature of the warrior, long after every other vestige of education had been effaced by the *rough* trade to which he was devoted" (1:43–44).[17] The ruins of a temple are "massy"; Herodotus is "the Father of History"; and the opportunity to generalize calls forth Prescott's most ponderous imagery: "Thus it happens in those great political convulsions which shake the foundations of society—the mighty events that cast their shadows before them in their coming. Then it is that the atmosphere is agitated with the low, prophetic murmurs with which nature, in the moral as in the physical world, announces the march of the hurricane" (1:38, 35, 171–2). The Aztecs' best-known religious ceremony elicits adjectives of conventional sentiment: "the dreadful stone of sacrifice . . . the dismal rites of sacrifice . . . the dread ministers . . . this cruel abomination . . . the fatal day of sacrifice . . . the sad procession . . . the unhappy victim . . . the minister of death . . . the indignant eyes of the Europeans" (1:45–47). Prescott is confident in God's desire that these Europeans should liberate a benighted land from superstition: "In this state of things, it was beneficently ordered by Providence that the land should be delivered over to another race, who would rescue it from the brutish superstitions that daily extended wider and wider. . . . [The conquerors] brought Christianity, whose benign radiance would still survive when the fierce flames of fanaticism [the Inquisition] should be extinguished; dispelling those dark forms of horror which had so long brooded over the fair regions of Anahuac" (1:51–52).

Prescott's subject is the dramatic confrontation between Spanish and Indian civilizations. He renders this conflict vivid and conveys in easily digested form a mass of accurate information. Yet his rhetoric is often lifeless and his thought unoriginal.

From Prescott's melodramatic pages a reader may turn with zest to Motley's *Rise of the Dutch Republic*. Little known to students of American history and literature, Motley's study of the first thirty years of the Netherlands' struggle against Philip II is yet the strongest of the early New England histories. No less than Prescott did Motley see God's hand in history; no less did he exhibit his own moral judgments; no less was he enamored of the striking spectacle—he describes minutely the scene of William the Silent's assassination, and even the clothes he wore, while he dwells with loving care upon the torture and execution of the assassin.[18] Motley's superiority to Prescott lies in the way he handles these elements: in the acuity of many of his perceptions, in the vitality of much of his language.

In describing Philip II's religious enthusiasm, Motley does not use the well-worn phrase "overriding purpose"; instead he pauses a moment to explore the power of Philip's conviction: "To one great purpose, formed early, he adhered inflexibly. . . . The idea seemed to express itself through him, to master him, rather than to form one of a stock of sentiments which a free agent might be expected to possess" (1:133). Motley sometimes presents psychological observations with aphoristic terseness: Philip "was prolix with his pen, not from affluence, but from paucity of ideas" (1:133). Motley defines the Duke of Saxony's attitudes toward war, peace, and truce with admirable brevity: "War was not only his passion, but his trade. Every one of his campaigns was a speculation. . . . War being his element, he considered peace as undesirable, although he could recognize its existence. A truce he held, however, to be a senseless paradox, unworthy of the slightest regard"

(1:140–1). A cynical intelligence and a succinct manner of expression produce flashes of humor not to be found in Prescott. Viglius, the president of
Philip's privy council at Brussels, was "already anxious to retire. . . . He was
a scholar, and could find more agreeable employment among his books. He
had accumulated vast wealth, and was desirous to retain it as long as possible.
He had a learned head, and was anxious to keep it upon his shoulders. These
simple objects could be better attained in a life of privacy. . . . If it had ever
been possible to find the exact path between right and wrong, the President
would have found it, and walked it with respectability and complacency"
(1:321–22). Motley can also control a complex syntax. He condenses into a
single sentence a memorable portrait of the Emperor Charles V in monastic
retirement:

He had neither the taste nor talents which make a man great in retirement. . . . Bitter
regrets that he should have kept his word to Luther, as if he had not broken faith
enough to reflect upon in his retirement; stern self-reproach for omitting to put to
death, while he had him in his power, the man who had caused all the mischief of the
age; fierce instructions thundered from his retreat to the inquisitors to hasten the
execution of all heretics,—including particularly his ancient friends, preachers, and
almoners, Cazalla and Constantine de Fuente; furious exhortations to Philip—as if
Philip needed a prompter in such a work—that he should set himself to "cutting out
the root of heresy with rigour and rude chastisement;"—such explosions of savage
bigotry as these, alternating with exhibitions of revolting gluttony, with surfeits of
sardine omelettes, Estramadura sausages, eel pies, pickled partridges, fat capons,
quince syrups, iced beer, and flagons of Rhenish, relieved by copious draughts of
senna and rhubarb, to which his horror-stricken doctor doomed him as he ate—
compose a spectacle less attractive to the imagination than the ancient portrait of the
cloistered Charles. Unfortunately it is the one which was painted from life. [1:123]

But the quality of Motley's prose is uneven. If sometimes he utters his
judgment of the Inquisition with fine terseness—"However classified or entitled, it was a machine for inquiring into a man's thoughts, and for burning
him if the result was not satisfactory" (1:295)—he descends at other moments to tiresome rhetorical questions, flat replies to these same questions,
and the uninspired alliteration of "darker doom." An otherwise effective
description of Charles V's edict of 1550 is blotted by a paragraph of un-
bridled indignation: "What was the penalty," Motley cries,

inflicted upon . . . the parent, not being a Roman Catholic doctor of divinity, who
should read Christ's Sermon on the Mount to his children in his own parlour or
shop? How were crimes like these to be visited upon the transgressor? Was it by
reprimand, fine, imprisonment, banishment, or by branding on the forehead, by the
cropping of the ears or the slitting of nostrils, as was practised upon the Puritan
fathers of New England for *their* nonconformity? It was by a sharper chastisement

than any of these methods. The Puritan fathers of the Dutch Republic had to struggle against a darker doom. [1:240]

Rampant moralism is not Motley's only failing. Although his craftsmanship is often skilled, it is frequently defective. Chapter titles contain stale metaphors: "Tyranny's Tide Begins to Ebb." Portentous sentences are meant to stimulate the readers appetite: "The reward reserved for the victor was to be recorded on a later page of history" (1:170). The introduction to a quotation often repeats the quotation itself: "These rhetoricians were particularly inflamed against Granvelle. They were personally excited against him. . . . 'These rhetoricians who make farces and street plays,' wrote the Cardinal to Philip, 'are particularly angry with me'" (1:318). Repetitiousness, it has been cogently argued, was Motley's most grievous sin.[19]

Yet Motley's best passages are so lively as to redeem his faults. By comparison Parkman's is a rather unexciting mind and an often undistinguished prose. While Motley discusses the political, religious, and military history of a highly developed region at the center of European affairs, Parkman suffers—in his most mature work, *Montcalm and Wolfe*—the disadvantage of focusing on the military history of a handful of French settlers at the fringe of civilization; consequently he runs the greater risk of falling into antiquarianism. Parkman's strengths lie in his apprehension of the natural wilderness of North America and in the comparative sobriety with which he treats the opposing forces in Canada: One senses the progress of "scientific history" between 1856 and 1884.

Wishing to avoid the "pallid and emasculate scholarship" of many other New England historians,[20] Parkman strains to evoke the uncanny silence, the lurking treachery of the forests that dwarfed puny mankind:

Month after month the great continent lay wrapped in snow. Far along the edge of the western wilderness men kept watch and ward in lonely blockhouses, or scoured the forest on the track of prowling war-parties. The provincials in garrison at Forts Edward, William Henry, and Oswego dragged out the weary winter; while bands of New England rangers, muffled against the piercing cold, caps of fur on their heads, hatchets in their belts, and guns in their mittened hands, glided on skates along the gleaming ice-floor of Lake George, to spy out the secrets of Ticonderoga, or seize some careless sentry to tell them tidings of the foe. Thus the petty war went on; but the big war was frozen into torpor, ready, like a hibernating bear, to wake again with the birds, the bees, and the flowers. . . .

. . . . .

On the sixteenth, the army re-embarked. The din of ten thousand combatants, the rage, the terror, the agony, were gone; and no living thing was left but the wolves that gathered from the mountains to feast upon the dead.[21]

Against pitiless nature struggle isolated heroes: Sometimes they come to life in a brief phrase—Wolfe "was a living barometer, and his spirits rose and fell with every change of weather" (2:195)—more often through their actions in the midst of combat. If the themes of nature and the hero seem perilously romantic, Parkman often avoids the danger by his command of the sources and the quiet clarity with which he can lay his sources before the reader. Parkman's subject, like Prescott's, was picturesque, and the romantic tradition within which he worked was also Prescott's; but a clearer, cooler northern light rests upon his landscapes and his figures.

But Parkman is susceptible to several of Prescott's diseases: He indulges, especially in his earlier works, in that type of "fine writing" that was to earn the scorn of a younger generation;[22] his thought is conventional; and his passion for heroes diminishes the authority of his judgments. "Never was the soul of a hero cased in a frame so incongruous," Parkman writes of Wolfe: "His narrow shoulders, slender body, and long, thin limbs were cased in a scarlet frock. . . . A delicate and sensitive child, but an impetuous and somewhat headstrong youth, [he] had served the King since the age of fifteen" (2:192). "Cased," twice within a dozen lines, is doubtful taste, while "a delicate and sensitive child . . . served the King" suggests Macaulayesque tendencies towards stereotyped expression. "Impetuous" conferred an element of individuality upon the young Montcalm (1:397); but applied again to the second hero of *Montcalm and Wolfe*, it limits, instead of adding to, the number of drawers into which Parkman distributes human nature. Too often Parkman uses hackneyed language, and he does not flinch at flattering his New England readers: "Meanwhile, at the head of Lake George, the raw bands of ever-active New England were mustering for the fray" (1:393). One of Parkman's explanations for England's success in the New World suggests the limitations of his mind: "The Germanic race, and especially the Anglo-Saxon branch of it, is peculiarly masculine, and, therefore, peculiarly fitted for self-government. It submits its action habitually to the guidance of reason."[23]

Parkman is given to projecting human emotions onto nature. In a remarkable sentence, 36 lines long, he infuses Tennyson, Milton, perhaps Jean Paul into his observation of a New Hampshire forest:

some wild shy rivulet steals with timid music through breathless caves of verdure; gulfs where feathered crags rise like castle walls . . .; ancient trees hurled headlong by the storm, to dam the raging stream with their forlorn and savage ruin . . .; green and glistening mosses carpeting the rough ground, mantling the rocks, turning pulpy stumps to mounds of verdure, and swathing fallen rocks as, bent in the impotence of rottenness, they lie outstretched over knoll and hollow . . .; mountains basking in the glory of the summer noon, flecked by the shadows of passing clouds that sail on snowy wings across the transparent azure.[24]

Although Parkman had reduced his stylistic excesses by the time he wrote

Montcalm and Wolfe, his "trite, inconsistent imagery and shoddy diction" plagued even that work.[25]

Thus Henry Adams's New England heritage mingled disparate elements. The art of history was earnestly cultivated, and works of power had been, or were being, written. Prescott, Motley, and Parkman had conducted thorough, and increasingly critical, research, and the products of their labors merited the respect of scholars. Prescott had used history to create romantic art; Parkman had continued in this tradition, but more soberly, closer to the documentary sources; while Motley's analytic mind and rhetorical skill pointed toward a more sophisticated art. The challenge to a historian reared in New England was to bring his work even closer to the sources than Parkman had done; to avoid the simplistic reductions of Prescott and Parkman, the blatant moralizing of Motley; and to refine their literary craftsmanship.

The culture that Henry Adams brought to his career as historian was literary. In college he neglected prescribed course work for extracurricular reading, and his own habits may be inferred from his strictures in the *Harvard Magazine* upon those of his classmates. Harvard students of the 1850s felt obliged to define their tastes and to develop literary manner; and sophomores, Adams observed skeptically, loudly expressed their admiration for Macaulay or Prescott. They liked

> De Quincey and Irving, and all writers whose aim has been to amuse, without too much exciting the brain, or requiring too much attention from it. . . . [By their third year, students normally prefer Thackeray to Dickens.] Macaulay's Essays become popular, partly because they are useful in writing themes. . . . They try to form a style, commonly after Macaulay, which they practise in their letters to their fathers and mothers. They are very fond of rounding off their periods. . . . [A fourth-year student may be found studying Sartor Resartus] or, even in a few very solitary cases, it is possible we may find him striving to fix his attention on a volume of Gibbon. . . .

> Crowds graduate who never read a page of the Spectator. Not one in a dozen ever read the Paradise Lost. Not one in twenty ever read the Divine Comedy. Not one in a number that we should not dare to estimate, ever read Shakespeare's plays through. . . . [Very few like classics or foreign literature.] English literature is the bound, and even in English literature, little except the lightest and the most common portion is at all known.

The excellence of dinner-table conversation at Charles Francis Adams's house had incited Henry to wide reading during school and college days, and the habit persisted. In after-dinner political talk with Senator Sumner during the secession crisis Henry "got out Lord Bacon and read him a few lines of the Essay on Seditions and Troubles."[26]

His nine years in Germany and England furnished prolonged opportunity for reading. Certain of his studies were evident from Henry's attacking John Quincy Adams's ignorance of Goethe, Schiller, and Voltaire; and from his devotion to Tocqueville and Mill. For some time in Germany he took daily lessons in Ovid, and he worked on Kugler's history of painting; but his ostensible study of law and his getting bogged down in learning German sometimes interfered with cultural pursuits: "My pleasantest reading has been Cicero de Officiis and v. Rönne, das prussische Schulwesen," he once wrote in exasperation. "Puchta and the Institutes and Cicero will satisfy my cravings for literature."[27]

Britain was more conducive to general reading. "My burial place of ambition and law, is geology and science," he wrote early in 1863, and four years later he struggled with the study of fossils in preparation for a lengthy review of Sir Charles Lyell's *Principles of Geology*. He also spent time "in sleepy struggle with philosophers and political economists," exhorting Charles to read regularly the London *Economist* and expounding the philosophy of Comte. But literature and art were always closest to his heart. Thus he sent his soldier-brother in 1863 "my little pocket Horace. . . . Certain odes where the leaf is turned down and pencil-marked, were the ones which Charles James Fox admired most. They are certainly not the best known." He planned that year to visit the Isle of Skye and the Hebrides "in imitation of Dr. Johnson"; and his close association with Gaskell's family was further incentive to the development of his own taste.[28]

Not until 1877 did a book by Gaskell's uncle, Sir Francis Doyle, "induce . . . me to buy a complete set of Wordsworth, Prelude, Excursion and all, for the first time." But the influence of Gaskell's brother-in-law, Frank Palgrave, was more prompt. In 1861 Palgrave had already issued the most famous anthology of English lyrical poetry ever published, *The Golden Treasury*. Born in 1824, he had been in Henry James's words "the great man of his day at college and was expected to set the world on fire"; but his domineering manner and hypercritical diatribes prevented his being a social success, and his career failed to fulfill early promise. To Marian Adams, no mean conversationalist herself, he was "the fastest talker I ever imagined," and James considered him "the biggest talker in England or the world—it's a current there's no standing against." His introductory remarks in *The Golden Treasury* demonstrated the complacency which—apparently tending to justify a later age's dismissiveness toward Victorianism—has obscured the more sophisticated attitudes of such a Victorian as George Eliot. Of Jewish extraction, Palgrave seemed to wish to be more British than the British in his paean to national greatness and in his earnest devotion to moral improvement. "Like the fabled fountain of the Azores, but with more various power," ran his apotheosis of poetry, "the magic of this Art can confer on each period of life its appropriate blessing: on early years Experience, on maturity Calm, on age Youthfulness. Poetry gives treasures 'more golden than gold'. . . . [Her true accents] may be heard throughout the following pages:—wherever the Poets of England are honoured, wherever the dominant language of the world is spoken, it is hoped that they will find fit audience."²⁹

These pious tones belied the combative spirit that gave Palgrave "perhaps . . . a right to claim the much-disputed rank of being the most unpopular man in London; but he liked to teach, and asked only for a docile pupil. Adams was docile enough, for he knew nothing and liked to listen. Indeed, he had to listen, whether he liked it or not, for Palgrave's voice was strident, and nothing could stop him. Literature, painting, sculpture, architecture were open fields for his attacks, which were always intelligent if not always kind." Palgrave's influence upon Adams lay partly in the field of the fine arts: He impelled the young American to read Fergusson and Ruskin on architecture, made gifts of drawings by Flaxman, Stothard, Gainsborough, and William Blake—Blake's Ezekiel weeping over his dead wife was his eerily prophetic wedding present to Henry and Marian—acted as one of Adams's agents in making other purchases, and discussed all such matters with great authority. He also increased Adams's appreciation of English poetry, and especially of the romantic poets: Palgrave's "literary taste, condensed into the 'Golden Treasury,' helped Adams to more literary education than he ever got from any taste of his own."³⁰ But his strongest influence was to reinforce that critical spirit that Adams had inherited so plentifully from his father. Palgrave and Gaskell frequented a fashionable London park with their American friend, and "St. James Parkian contempt" was Adams's phrase for the spirit binding them together. Like Charles Francis Adams, Palgrave was no votary of the reigning Victorian deities. "Carlyle and Carlylism—treated as a windbag of the first water"—this was a project of his for a review article; another was a notice of Huxley's lay sermons, handling the collection "with a little of. . . .[its] own arrogance." Palgrave scorned "Darwin, H. Spencer and the others of the hypothesis-taken-for-proof school"; and nothing could have pleased him more than "to overhaul some modern English poets. The atheist scream of Swinburne, the crypto-brothelism of Rossetti—Moore's misonomist monotony, Browning's barbarous travesty of Euripedes—here is enough material; letting alone the overdrawn Arthurianisms of Tennyson, whose immense superiority to all his contemporaries, however, shines before me daily more and more."³¹

As was true of most of Adams's best friends, Palgrave was more conservative than Adams, and he knew it. Thus when in 1875 Adams noticed a volume of Palgrave's poems in the *North American Review*, Palgrave mentioned "how unsympathetic my Hellenism and Trinitarianism must be to you"; and Adams certainly did not accept all of Palgrave's judgments. Yet this avuncular figure, fourteen years older than Henry, performed the function of a sort of graduate-school teacher, offering him valuable criticism.

When Adams wrote his first article for a major review, "Captain John Smith" (published in January 1867), Palgrave paid him the compliment of "scoring my *North American* wildly. . . . The marginal notes made it look like a variorum edition of Plato."[32] This vigorous, opinionated, tactless, often superficial critic was immensely kind to the young American and did more than any other individual except Charles Francis Adams to set before Henry's eyes the immense riches of the English literary past.

Adams's absorption in British tradition did not exclude familiarity with American writing. When in 1869 Gaskell wanted to prepare a popular lecture on American style, Henry overflowed with suggestions: His judgments and omissions might be challenged by later connoisseurs, but there was little to scorn in the precision of his information, and his reserve toward Longfellow was not excessive. Jefferson's Declaration of Independence seemed to Adams

the best specimen of his style. . . . By all means quote the whole of Lincoln's little speech at Gettysburg and a sentence or two from his second Inaugural to show the biblical influence on American minds. In poetry you might extract from Bryant the last few lines of Thanatopsis, or the lines to a water-fowl, or the "melancholy days have come"; from Longfellow a stanza or two of the Wreck of the Hesperus or the Skeleton in Armor, both pretty ballads well adapted to a popular audience. . . . If you want a specimen of style from Hawthorne, take the description of old Pynchon sitting dead in his chair, in the *Seven Gables*, or the discovery of Zenobia's body, in the *Blithedale Romance*. Your audience will listen hard to either. . . . It is a pity you can't quote some choice lines from Walt Whitman. . . . [As you want to amuse your audience, don't dwell long on historians, essayists or critics except Irving], whose account of Bracebridge Hall might amuse, and is a good specimen of his style. A few sentences or half a page of it would do for you to point the customary allusion to Addison upon. Cooper's novels are no great [*sic*].[33]

When Adams turned professional historian, his interest in literature did not expire. Neither did his newfound admiration for Wordsworth and Shelley cause him to abandon his eighteenth-century taste in poetry: "Everyone now snubs the last century," he complained to Lodge in 1875, "and I see that [Leslie] Stephen considers Scott to be poor stuff. I confess I do think Pope a poet, and Gray, too, and Cowper, and Goldsmith. But this may be . . . prejudice contracted in youth." Gaskell and Palgrave continued to inform their American friend about a wide range of British publications: "Browning has added another volume to the Unreadable," Palgrave reported of the 1878 harvest; "Arnold writes flimsy prose criticism and what he calls politics and theology and culture. . . . You may read Wallace's Tropical Countries, and Lecky's 18th century, with pleasure. But we have no book this year so good as William Sellar's *Virgil* of 1877: a capital piece in a very difficult style." Settled temporarily in London in 1880, the Adamses "were more startled by

George Eliot's marriage to John Cross than by the elections themselves." The American couple knew Cross, and in society, Marian reported, "we declare that a woman of genius is above criticism. . . . I've written as kind a note as I could to Mr. Cross." As Adams started to write the *History*, his extracurricular interests sometimes focused more nearly upon the professional: In 1882 he requested the Harvard librarian to send him "the first volume of Thucydides: Greek text, and Latin, French or English version on the same page." But in 1885 his evening reading was far from historical: "I have laid in a cargo of French comedies for after-dinner next winter," he wrote to a Washington friend, "and have begun to read Molière through,— the toughest job I have tried since trying to read Rabelais and Hudibras."[34]

Adams wrote at the moment amateur historians were making way for professionals, and he profited from withholding full allegiance to the ideals of either. While contemptuous of dilettantish amateurs, he also scorned professionals with noses so close to the grindstone that they could not see far beyond. Thus in criticizing F. J. Jackson, an early British minister to Washington, for being too narrowly professional, Adams expressed his view of the requirements of his own calling. Late in the summer of 1809, Jackson prepared to enter a difficult negotiation with President Madison; his immediate predecessor as minister had been David Erskine, whom Canning had just recalled to England in disgrace:

> Part of Jackson's leisure was employed in reading Erskine's correspondence, although he would have done better had he neglected this customary duty. . . .
>
> . . . . .
>
> Evidently . . . [Madison's] deference pleased the British minister, who saw nothing behind it but a social triumph for himself and his wife; yet . . . had he read Shakspeare rather than Erskine's writings, he might have learned from Julius Caesar the general diplomatic law that "when love begins to sicken and decay, it useth ever an enforced ceremony." A man of tact would have seen that from the moment Madison became formal he was dangerous.[35]

Adams's early training meant that literary allusions, particularly to Shakespeare, sprang easily to his mind. In November 1810 President Madison, declaring by proclamation that France had revoked certain decrees obstructing American commerce, notified Britain that unless she made equal concession the United States would cease trading with her. France had not in fact revoked her decrees, and Adams's impatience with Madison was unconstrained. "The United States had the right to make war on England with or without notice," he fumed,

> either for her past spoliations, her actual blockades, her Orders in Council other than blockades, her Rule of 1756, her impressments, or her attack on the "Chesapeake," not yet redressed,—possibly also for other reasons less notorious; but the right to

make war did not carry with it the right to require that the world should declare to be true an assertion which the world knew to be false. Unless England were a shrew to be tamed, President Madison could hardly insist on her admitting the sun to be the moon.[36]

Beyond Shakespeare, Adams's second favored source of literary reference was classical. In May 1812, six weeks before the United States declared war on Great Britain, the war spirit in Congress faltered in the face of American unpreparedness for combat. An allusion to the gruesome demise of the aged Pelias, who let Medea persuade him that being boiled would restore him to the vigor of youth, was only one of four comparisons that started to Adams's mind as he marveled at the astonishing spectacle:

The experiment of thrusting the country into war to inflame it, as crude ore might be thrown into a furnace, was avowed by the party leaders, from President Madison downward, and was in truth the only excuse for a course otherwise resembling an attempt at suicide. Many nations have gone to war in pure gayety of heart; but perhaps the United States were the first to force themselves into a war they dreaded, in the hope that the war itself might create the spirit they lacked. One of the liveliest and most instructive discussions of the session, May 6, threw light upon the scheme by which the youthful nation was to reverse the process of Medea, and pass through the caldron of war in confidence of gaining the vigor of age.[37]

Although Adams also referred occasionally to Cervantes, to Milton, or to eighteenth-century British authors, his text was in fact but lightly spiced with such allusions—there was no parade of esoteric learning. His literary training was far less important as the supply for a few allusions than as a constant reminder that he aimed to be no mere conveyor of historical information. He was a man of letters and sought the honors of a literary artist in a country that had only the beginnings of a tradition of esteeming its own literature. His strictures to Brooks Adams upon the latter's abortive biography of John Quincy Adams made Henry's conception of his calling clear. In enumerating the artistic canons Brooks had violated, Henry urged that their grandfather's figure be left partly in the shade so that the reader would have scope to employ his own imagination: "Magni nominis umbra is an artistic secret, dead with Michael Angelo." "A literary artist ought to pose, as his test of art, the rule that the less profanity he uses, the more he will make his reader swear." "Keep your temper!. . . . Try to be a man of letters!" One of the rules to which Adams constantly recurred was that "all considerable artists make a point of compelling the public to think for itself."[38]

Considering his calling that of a literary craftsman, Adams had understood from the outset that a great proportion of the labor on the *History* must be devoted to revision. "For men like you and me," he advised Lodge, "Buffon's aphorism is the only safe guide: *Le génie, c'est une longue patience!. . . .*

Never think anything finished while you have time to improve it." As early as 1869 Henry's passion for revision had struck his father; to Charles Francis Adams "this whole subject [of style] both in speaking and writing always had a peculiar fascination," and he confessed that "in my youth, I wrote my papers over nearly as many times as you do."[39] Henry's father recommended that he merely correct details, not rewrite whole passages, and this advice of a compromiser probably affected the younger man's practice in novel writing and in his biographies of Gallatin and John Randolph. But the biographies were mere outriders for the *History*, and here Adams certainly practiced what he had preached to Lodge.

Whatever the reasons for his not publishing the first volumes of the *History* until the last were complete, the consequence was that the author had an extra five years for revision. "I doubt if there is a chapter in my history that I have written less than four or five times," he later recalled to a visitor, and his definition of his practice to Brooks Adams was even more exact. He admitted that the *History* had grown out of control and that it was less satisfactory as a whole than in its separate parts:

All my life I have labored and sweated to get Form [i.e., to avoid diffuseness], and always I have failed, because the difficulties become enormously increased with every enlargement of detail. The details themselves require only patient labor, and I could sit patiently during long years writing paragraph after paragraph, over and over again, chapter after chapter—volume after volume,—recasting, reconsidering, re-arranging, without ever quite concluding, but I could never get to the point of seeing a big work as a whole. I doubt whether I have ever published a chapter in which every paragraph has not been re-written, with my own hand, fully three times, and reconsidered, pen in hand, full thirty.

As a young man Adams was already exclaiming that "writing is only one half the art; the other being erasure"; and his later, exasperated advice to his brother Brooks suggests the kinds of revision to which he subjected his own manuscript: "'Choose his profession without hesitation.' Two shuns!" "I have a foolish antipathy to 'however,' 'moreover,' and all such superfluities." "I hate infinitives as nouns."[40]

Henry's abiding interest in the elements of literary style was partly inherited from his grandfather, who was professor of rhetoric at Harvard from 1806 to 1809. Doubtless John Quincy Adams's *Lectures on Rhetoric and Oratory*, published in two volumes in 1810, was in Charles Francis Adams's library when Henry did his lessons there; but it was an awkwardly expressed work of no great originality, and Henry probably was far more influenced by Bishop Richard Whately's *Elements of Rhetoric*, first published in Great Britain in 1828. This was the principal text for written composition in Harvard's compulsory course on rhetoric, which extended over no less than six semesters of Henry's undergraduate career.[41] Whately lucidly explained the meaning of a period as distinguished from a loose sentence; discussed how Tacitus made great use of antithesis but little of periods; and unblushingly advocated the use of repetition as the happy medium between conciseness and prolixity. He had the good sense to recommend—what few twentieth-century historians would accept—that much must be left for the reader to work out for himself. Metaphor, the Bishop argued, was always to be preferred to comparison "wherever it is sufficiently simple and plain to be immediately comprehended. . . . [If Comparison has to be used,] this is never to be done more fully than is necessary to perspicuity; because all men are more gratified at catching the Resemblance for themselves, than at having it pointed out to them." This principle was at least as old as Aristotle, and Whately's chief claim to originality lay in his attack upon the style of Samuel Johnson. While conceding that Johnson had been an exceptionally good writer, Whately attacked him for prolixity, heaviness, excessive use of antithesis, frequent faulty redundancy, and "over-attention to the roundness and majestic sound of his sentences, and a delight in balancing one clause against another. . . . To string together substantives, connected by conjunctions, . . . is the characteristic of Johnson's style"; and the Bishop regarded imitators of Johnson, destitute of his vigor of thought, as intolerable.[42]

Adams's college essays were nevertheless replete with the mannerisms predictable in a mid-nineteenth-century undergraduate consciously aiming at literary effect. An essay would begin with a couple of paragraphs of sententious, insipid generalization, in weak imitation of Macaulay, before getting down to business; and it would assume a tone of relaxed philosophy quite incongruous with the jejune observations filling out the body of the essay. Later on, when traveling in Scotland in 1863, Henry modeled his letters to Charles, most unsuccessfully, upon the style of Walter Scott, but soon he was inveighing against American imitators of Dante or Tennyson, requiring almost as one-sidedly as Emerson that American writing be original and not a mere echo of Europe. Beginning in 1867, when he was still in England, Henry practiced his literary technique in a series of long, forceful articles published in the *North American Review*, the *Edinburgh Review*, and the *Westminster Review*. "Polish be damned," he declaimed to Charles in 1869: "I never tried to polish in the sense of smoothing. All I ever wanted was to polish away my stilts and get down to firm ground, and that is precisely what I despair of doing. If you glance your eye over my last things as compared with the *Harvard Magazine* you will see how bald I have become, thinking that the first step should be to unlearn a vicious habit before hoping to start again." Two years later, fearing that his cousin Will Everett might submit an article for the *North American Review*, Adams as editor shuddered "at the prospect of having to cut out all his fine writing."[43]

Henry's reaction against the mannerisms of youth ran parallel to his admiration for German historical method and his impatience with such English historians as the medievalist Edward Freeman. "The first step seems to me to be to familiarise one's mind with thoroughly good work," he told Lodge in 1873, "to master the scientific method, and to adopt the rigid principle of subordinating everything to perfect thoroughness of study. I have therefore advised your learning German, because I think the German method so sound. . . . An ignorant, or a superficial work could hardly come from any distinguished German student. I can't say the same for other countries. Great as is Mr. Freeman's parade of knowledge, he has never written anything really solid. . . . Unless one learns beforehand to be logically accurate and habitually thorough, mere knowledge is worth very little." This phase of Adams's development culminated in his essay "Anglo-Saxon Courts of Law," published in 1876 along with those of Lodge and two other Ph.D. students of Adams's in *Anglo-Saxon Law*. J. R. Green, author of the famous *Short History of the English People*, warned his American colleague how far he had strayed. "John Green is one of my intimate friends here," Adams wrote to Lodge from London in 1880, "but how he objurgates you fellows for your German style. He says my Essay is bad enough, but you others are clean mad."[44]

Adams later came to believe there was an irreconcilable conflict between thoroughness and art. "The Frenchman [writing history] is an artist," he alleged in 1909, "and very properly refuses to sacrifice his art in order to run after what Germans call truth. The German is scientific and becomes dull and unreadable, because he is always making historical dictionaries,—trying to be true in every possible direction at once."[45] This conception affected the writing of *Mont-Saint-Michel and Chartres*, but in the 1880s Adams aspired both to have and eat his cake: Still aiming for German thoroughness, he sought nevertheless to marry this god to the British literary goddess of his youth.

Bishop Whately's influence had never entirely lapsed and in 1874, after thoroughly exposing Lodge to Germanic method, Adams set out for him his own—still primitive—canons of prose style. His creed, enshrining force and variety, was stated as explicitly as that of any textbook writer on rhetoric, and one precept might have been copied directly from the Anglican bishop: "Great effects are best produced by lowering the general tone. Follow Canon I as a rule [the subject should normally precede the predicate], and it becomes easy to make a sensation with Canon III [when accentuation is wanted, begin with the word or idea to be accentuated, even if this is the predicate]. The higher you pitch the key, the harder it is to sing up to it, and the effect no greater." From this elementary tenet Adams progressed during ensuing years to an ever clearer conception of the principles of his craft. In 1879 he still complained that "the most difficult thing to me is to vary the length of my sentences so as to relieve the attention";[46] but a decade later, recreating the battle of Bladensburg, he had learned to measure his sentences in proportion to the military force concerned:

Some Maryland regiments arrived at the same time with [Secretary of State] Monroe. About three thousand men were then on the field, and their officers were endeavoring to form them in line of battle. General Stansbury of the Baltimore brigade made such an arrangement as he thought best. Monroe, who had no military rank, altered it without Stansbury's knowledge. General Winder arrived at noon, and rode about the field. At the same time the British light brigade made its appearance, and wound down the opposite road, a mile away, a long column of redcoats, six abreast, moving with the quick regularity of old soldiers, and striking directly at the American centre.[47]

Short sentences seemed deceptively simple, but it took Adams years to learn how to round out a daringly long period, stretching tension tightly over its whole length. In a letter of 1862 to his brother Charles, as Henry was beginning to talk himself into a literary rather than a political career, he argued that his own Hamlet-like indecisiveness barred success in politics. He tottered along the tightrope of an excessively long sentence, only to fall flat on his face:

The more I see, the more I am convinced that a man whose mind is balanced like mine, in such a way that what is evil never seems unmixed with good, and what is good always streaked with evil; an object never seems important enough to call out strong energies till they are exhausted, nor necessary enough not to allow of its failure being possible to retrieve; in short, a mind which is not strongly positive and absolute, cannot be steadily successful in action, which requires quickness and perseverance.[48]

Yet practice improved Adams's technique so that, writing of Napoleon's grotesque flattery of America in 1810 at the very moment the French emperor was in fact robbing its commerce, Adams could achieve clarity in an extravagantly long period. Surrounding for variety the long by two much shorter sentences, Adams included within the centerpiece an interesting generalization, a concise summary of Napoleon's deeds contrasted to his professions, and an imaginative operatic analogy. The tension in this sentence expressed the tautness of Adams's feelings as he contemplated the stupid American fish lazily swallowing the French fisherman's deadly hook, baited with perfumed worms:

One might doubt whether Napoleon or Canning were the more deficient in good taste; but Americans whose nerves were irritated to fury by the irony of Canning, found these expressions of Napoleon's love rather absurd than insulting. So little had the mere fact of violence to do with the temper of politics, compared with the sentiments which surrounded it, that Napoleon could seize without notice ten million dollars' worth of American property, imprisoning the American crews of two or three hundred vessels in his dungeons, while at the same instant he told the Americans that he loved them, that their commerce was within the scope of his policy, and as a climax avowed a scheme to mislead the United States government, hardly troubling himself to use forms likely to conceal his object; yet the vast majority of Americans never greatly resented acts which seemed to them like the exploits of an Italian brigand on the stage. Beyond doubt, Napoleon regarded his professions of love and interest not as irony or extravagance, but as adapted to deceive.[49]

Interest in literary craftsmanship was of course no rare thing among nineteenth-century historians, for the fame of Gibbon and Macaulay still echoed in England, while in America Prescott, Motley, and Parkman wrote history as literature. The careers of these three Americans made it easier for Adams to decide to become a historian and reminded him of the importance of literary form in history. But Adams betrayed toward the Americans that tinge of condescension that a younger generation sometimes feels for elders upon whose backs they seek to climb. He believed Prescott, Motley, and Parkman to be "none of them men of extraordinary gifts." Parkman seemed to him the best American historian, but Adams—who had expressed the resolution to be "unpopular"—referred a little patronizingly to Parkman's "relatively . . . popular volumes."[50] Adams's mind was quicker, his craftsmanship finer, than those of his older Bostonian colleagues, and although he chose, unlike Henry James, to reside in America, both he and the novelist were attempting to rival Europe. Adams challenged not native standards but British: Gibbon was his standard for excellence, Macaulay his measure of worldly success.[51] Until 1890 he pursued with silent purpose and conscientious effort his aim of studying history with the scientific accuracy and thoroughness of the Germans, but of presenting the fruits of his research in artistic form. Could American society, he inquired, "transmute its social power into the higher forms of thought? . . . Could it give new life to . . . art?" Adams might have said of his own aims, as he said of Jefferson's political theories, that "the history . . . will show how these principles were applied, and what success attended the experiment."[52]

PART II · *History*

CHAPTER 5 · *History as Art*

IF THE *History* is a work of massive research and caustic criticism, its great distinction nevertheless lies in the way Adams used these materials to create art. His literary method deserves analysis, but the best way to apprehend the flavor of the *History* is to linger with its opening volume, which in any case is the most expertly written.

I. Method

Adams's is not the language of a historian intent on stating a thesis and amassing evidence sufficient to drive the reader into agreement. He wishes to stimulate the reader's imagination and delight his palate, as well as to nourish his intellect. History is for him a form of literature intended to provoke as well as to persuade.

Near the beginning, as Adams sketches the physical condition of Washington in 1800, he speculates on the nation's democratic ideal and suggests an idea contrary to his own conviction. He makes this idea seem plausible with a profusion of vivid images. Only after making the reader consider the hypothesis does he put forth his own view, and he rather implies than states it; metaphors and similes, seemingly arbitrarily devised, are the vehicles that convey his real belief. "The contrast between the immensity of the task and the paucity of means," he suggests,

seemed to challenge suspicion that the nation itself was a magnificent scheme like the federal city, which could show only a few log-cabins and negro quarters where the plan provided for the traffic of London and the elegance of Versailles. When in the summer of 1800 the government was transferred to what was regarded by most persons as a fever-stricken morass, the half-finished White House stood in a naked field overlooking the Potomac, with two awkward Department buildings near it, a single row of brick houses and a few isolated dwellings within sight, and nothing

111

more; until across a swamp, a mile and a half away, the shapeless, unfinished Capitol was seen, two wings without a body, ambitious enough in design to make more grotesque the nature of its surroundings. The conception proved that the United States understood the vastness of their task, and were willing to stake something on their faith in it. Never did hermit or saint condemn himself to solitude more consciously than Congress and the Executive in removing the government from Philadelphia to Washington: the discontented men clustered together in eight or ten boarding-houses as near as possible to the Capitol, and there lived, like a convent of monks, with no other amusement or occupation than that of going from their lodgings to the Chambers and back again. . . . Public efforts and lavish use of public money could alone make the place tolerable; but Congress doled out funds for this national and personal object with so sparing a hand, that their Capitol threatened to crumble in pieces and crush Senate and House under the ruins, long before the building was complete.

A government capable of sketching a magnificent plan, and willing to give only a half-hearted pledge for its fulfilment; a people eager to advertise a vast undertaking beyond their present powers, which when completed would become an object of jealousy and fear,—this was the impression made upon the traveller who visited Washington in 1800, and mused among the unraised columns of the Capitol upon the destiny of the United States.[1]

That the United States was a scheme, advertised with effusions to the Rights of Man but dedicated in fact to sordid avarice, was the suspicion of numerous European travelers, and they were not slow to contrast Washington's pretensions with its actual discomforts. Adams is pleased to make plausible their idea of Washington: "fever-stricken morass . . . half-finished . . . naked . . . awkward . . . isolated . . . swamp . . . shapeless, unfinished . . . two wings without a body . . . grotesque . . . discontented." Yet he believes that these European travelers misunderstood America, and his own interpretation appears in the word "faith." He thought American democrats in some ways idealists, genuinely devoted to raising the condition of the masses of mankind, and he hopes his reader may explore the character of this idealism by comparing it with the religious faith of the Middle Ages. Hence the imagery: "Never did hermit or saint condemn himself . . . ; [clustered together] like a convent of monks, with no other amusement or occupation."

Adams foresaw that the United States, feeble in 1800, was destined to become what he called an "empire," and he applauded. Deeply involved as his family had been in the fortunes of this developing empire, he was bound to wonder about its future, and as he began to write his *History*, his thoughts turned to Gibbon's famous ruminations upon the fate of another empire: "It was at Rome, on the 15th of October, 1764, as I sat musing amidst the ruins of the Capitol, while the barefooted friars were singing vespers in the Temple of Jupiter, that the idea of writing the decline and fall of the city first started to my mind."[2] Thus when Adams talks of "a convent of monks" and of the Capitol's threatening "to crumble in pieces and crush Senate and House under the ruins," he is indulging no wayward fancy. The meticulous author is preparing his reader's subconscious to respond to the allusion to the bare-footed friars and the razed columns of the Roman Capitol. He quietly sets his work against that of his idol.

In the first six chapters of the *History*, where he sketches American intellect and national character in 1800, Adams introduces certain protagonists of the later narrative. Antidemocratic leaders appear in the chapter on New England. That Adams disagrees with Fisher Ames, George Cabot, and their New York colleague Alexander Hamilton is everywhere apparent. His first work in American history had been to publish, in *New England Federalism*, his grandfather's allegations that influential Federalist leaders had countenanced secessionist activities before and during the War of 1812. "I dislike Hamilton," Henry Adams had written privately to Lodge. "From the first to the last words he wrote, I read always the same Napoleonic kind of adventuredom."[3] Adams's condemnation of Otis and Cabot, as well as Pickering, distinguishes his work from that of their modern defender, James Banner.[4]

But while disagreeing with the extreme Federalists, Adams strains to understand them, to clothe himself in their thoughts so that even their habits of expression become his own: "When in 1793 the French nation seemed mad with the frenzy of its recovered liberties, New England looked upon the bloody and blasphemous work with such horror as religious citizens could not but feel. Thenceforward the mark of a wise and good man was that he abhorred the French Revolution, and believed democracy to be its cause" (1:82). No footnote obtrudes to demonstrate that "wise and good" was current Federalist usage. Adams continues instead to draw the reader into Federalist paths of thought: "What had happened in France must sooner or later happen in America if the ignorant and vicious were to govern the wise and good. . . . So strong were the wise and good in their popular following, that every newspaper seemed to exult in denouncing the people" (1:83–84). Led thus, the reader scarcely notices when the voice changes from Adams's to that of the Federalist Dennie:

A paragraph from Dennie's "Portfolio," reprinted by all the Federalist newspapers in 1803, offered one example among a thousand of the infatuation which possessed the Federalist press, neither more extravagant nor more treasonable than the rest:—

"A democracy is scarcely tolerable at any period of national history. Its omens are always sinister, and its powers are unpropitious. It is on its trial here, and the issue will be civil war, desolation, and anarchy. No wise man but discerns its imperfections, no good man but shudders at its miseries." [1:85]

The point that Federalists employed the term "wise and good" is corroborated without a trumpeting of the evidence.

As Adams temporarily dons the New England Federalists' habits of thinking, so he shapes his metaphors to their heritage. Their English ancestors had crossed a stormy sea in frail boats, embarked on a serious enterprise with the help of God and of civil leaders imbued with an Old Testament faith; they reached a land whose rock-strewn soil and a climate whose frozen chill accentuated the more unyielding, frigid side of their Puritan faith. It was not surprising that Adams's Federalists "sat down to bide their time until the tempest of democracy should drive the frail government so near destruction that all men with one voice should call on God and the Federalist prophets for help"; nor that Ames and his friends were "resolute sons of granite and ice" (1:87), seeking in despair to protect the things they held most dear.

These efforts at understanding the Federalists accompany a serious attempt to reach balanced judgment: Adams strives to set against every exposed vice some compensating virtue, to balance every implied criticism with an extenuating circumstance. Thus, when calling attention to Hamilton's antidemocratic pronouncements, he seizes the occasion for an acute observation about the source of Hamilton's political influence:

The Philadelphia grand jury indicted Dennie for this paragraph as a seditious libel, but it was not more expressive than the single word uttered by Alexander Hamilton, who owed no small part of his supremacy to the faculty of expressing the prejudices of his followers more tersely than they themselves could do. Compressing the idea into one syllable, Hamilton, at a New York dinner, replied to some democratic sentiment by striking his hand sharply on the table and saying, "Your people, sir,—your people is a great *beast!*" [1:85][5]

On the verge of showing Fisher Ames morbid, apocalyptic, and hysterical, Adams defers to his ill health and acknowledges his intellectual stature:

The answer to every democratic suggestion ran in a set phrase, "Look at France!" This idea became a monomania with the New England leaders, and took exclusive hold of Fisher Ames, their most brilliant writer and talker, until it degenerated into a morbid illusion. During the last few months of his life, even so late as 1808, this dying man could scarcely speak of his children without expressing his fears of their future servitude to the French. He believed his alarms to be shared by his friends. "Our days," he wrote, "are made heavy with the pressure of anxiety, and our nights restless with visions of horror. We listen to the clank of chains, and overhear the whispers of assassins. We mark the barbarous dissonance of mingled rage and triumph in the yell of an infuriated mob; we see the dismal glare of their burnings, and scent the loathsome steam of human victims offered in sacrifice." [1:82–83]

But when Adams is about to pass judgment on the whole group of extreme Federalists, something beyond this balancing habit of mind seems to move him. He shows the Federalist leaders badly misjudging the social condition of America, sardonic and obstinate in their folly. Yet his tone is melancholy. The Federalists are seen almost as they saw themselves, and they are given the last word, for they are shown in their devotion to those New England institutions for which they cared most. Alliteration suggests the sighs of frustrated men:

The obstinacy of the race was never better shown than when, with the sunlight of the nineteenth century bursting upon them, these resolute sons of granite and ice turned their faces from the sight, and smiled in their sardonic way at the folly or wickedness of men who could pretend to believe the world improved because henceforth the ignorant and vicious were to rule the United States and govern the churches and schools of New England. [1:87]

The simpleminded, overpowering convictions of these serious citizens appear as the sad aberrations of once-loved members of one's own family rather than as the vices of enemies. Although Adams had, for years, repudiated the parochialism of New England, he could not extinguish the embers of affection for the region where he first perceived a yellow kitchen floor in strong sunlight, tasted a baked apple, and learned his balanced habit of mind.

When he comes to Jefferson, the central figure in half of the *History*, Adams adopts the method of a novelist. He furnishes no convenient digest of Jefferson's character and ideas to which a reader might turn as to a passage in a compendium. He scatters instead a dozen references to Jefferson over the surface of the introductory chapters, seeds that later are to sprout into vigorous plants. The first clue is dropped during Adams's discussion of the unproductive agriculture of Virginia:

Even Jefferson, the most active-minded and sanguine of all Virginians,—the inventor of the first scientific plough, the importer of the first threshing-machine known in Virginia, the experimenter with a new drilling-machine, the owner of one hundred and fifty slaves and ten thousand acres of land, whose negroes were trained to carpentry, cabinet-making, house-building, weaving, tailoring, shoe-making,—claimed to get from his land no more than six or eight bushels of wheat to an acre, and had been forced to abandon the more profitable cultivation of tobacco. [1:32]

The main theme of the *History* is that hard realities—military adventurism in France, antirepublican bigotry and commercial greed in England—drove the Jeffersonians to abandon their hopes for a pacific diplomacy. Can it be accidental that Adams shows Jefferson here, a lively and attractive theorist in agriculture, driven by harsh realities into abandoning his more sanguine hopes for success with enlightened farming practices?

The next important reference to the Virginian comes in the chapter on New England. Congregational clergymen saw Jefferson as the incarnation of Jacobin theories, the leader of speculators, scoffers, and atheists:

He had doubted the authority of revelation, and ventured to suggest that petrified shells found embedded in rocks fifteen thousand feet above sea-level could hardly have been left there by the Deluge, because if the whole atmosphere were condensed as water, its weight showed that the seas would be raised only fifty-two and a half feet. Sceptic as he was, he could not accept the scientific theory that the ocean-bed had been uplifted by natural forces; but although he had thus instantly deserted this battery raised against revelation, he had still expressed the opinion that a universal deluge was *equally* unsatisfactory as an explanation. [1:80]

A key to Jefferson's character, Adams had come to believe, was his willingness to temporize: As president he buried his constitutional scruples about the purchase of Louisiana, did little to limit the powers of the national government, and restrained the attack that had seemed imminent against the federal judiciary. That Jefferson "instantly deserted this battery raised against revelation" prefigures Adams's theme that Jefferson, in office, would quickly abandon theories he had pressed against the Federalists.

The stage being set for Jefferson's inauguration, the curtain rises in chapter 7 upon a tableau of five figures: Jefferson; Madison; Gallatin, Jefferson's secretary of the treasury; the chief justice, John Marshall; and the vice president, Aaron Burr. That Madison did not actually attend the ceremony is a fact deftly sidestepped, for Adams seeks to introduce the chief officeholders in that way which will throw most light on Jefferson himself. Incessant comparison—between the log cabins of Washington and the elegance of Versailles, between the social condition of Jefferson's America and that of Catiline's Rome—was Adams's instrument for distinguishing the character of a city, a society, or a statesman. Thus we can imagine Jefferson dining in the White House like a tall, shambling, large-boned farmer in his ill-fitting clothes, talking to his friends without pause, laxity of manner shed about him; but his personality becomes clearer when two of these friends sit beside him for comparison:

Madison had not so much as Jefferson the commanding attitude which imposed respect upon the world. . . . In deportment modest to the point of sensitive reserve, in address simple and pleasing, in feature rather thoughtful and benevolent than strong, he was such a man as Jefferson, who so much disliked contentious and self-asserting manners, loved to keep by his side. . . .

The third aristocrat in this democratic triumvirate was Albert Gallatin. . . . Like the President and the Secretary of State, Gallatin was born and bred a gentleman. . . . [He] possessed the personal force which was somewhat lacking in his two friends. . . . Three more agreeable men than Jefferson, Madison, and Gallatin were never collected round the dinner-table of the White House; and their difference in age was enough to add zest to their friendship; for Jefferson was born in 1743, Madison in 1751, and Gallatin in 1761. While the President was nearly sixty years old, his Secretary of the Treasury had the energy and liberality of forty. [1:188–91]

These glimpses of Jefferson's person and these modest reflections on life—seemingly passed off by inadvertence—arrive in a prose suitably relaxed and leisured; but when a fourth figure comes into view, Adams marks the moment with syntactical tension. A formidable sentence, the longest and most dense in the whole chapter, helps us feel the presence of a commanding force:

In this first appearance of John Marshall as Chief-Justice, to administer the oath of office, lay the dramatic climax of the inauguration. The retiring President, acting for what he supposed to be the best interests of the country, by one of his last acts of power, deliberately intended to perpetuate the principles of his administration, placed at the head of the judiciary, for life, a man as obnoxious to Jefferson as the bitterest New England Calvinist could have been; for he belonged to that class of conservative Virginians whose devotion to President Washington, and whose education in the common law, caused them to hold Jefferson and his theories in antipathy. [1:192]

Initially Adams withholds the reason for Marshall's profound aversion; he discusses instead the unaffected simplicity of the chief justice's life and the irresistible influence of his mind. This excursus completed, the author again stretches tension the length of a well-filled sentence, not to be released until the final words:

Nevertheless this great man nourished one weakness. Pure in life; broad in mind, and the despair of bench and bar for the unswerving certainty of his legal method; almost idolized by those who stood nearest him, and loving warmly in return,—this excellent and amiable man clung to one rooted prejudice: he detested Thomas Jefferson. He regarded with quiet, unspoken, but immovable antipathy the character and doings of the philosopher standing before him, about to take the oath to preserve, protect and defend the Constitution. No argument or entreaty affected his conviction that Jefferson was not an honest man. [1:194]

The force of these sentences is magnified by iteration: "Pure in life; broad in mind . . . excellent and amiable . . . quiet, unspoken, but immovable . . . preserve, protect and defend . . . No argument or entreaty." Characteristically, Adams does not flourish his judgment of this Virginian: It lies inconspicuous in the short sentence alleging Marshall's weakness. A reader, stumbling over "great," attends the opinion all the more because Adams is so sparing with words ordinarily overused—in the nine volumes of the *History* no higher praise is expressed than this simple tribute to the chief justice.

But what of Marshall's alleged weakness? Was detestation of Jefferson a failing, or is this idea another provocation—like the travelers' idea of the United States as a fraudulent scheme—meant to stimulate the reader's own thinking? To clarify his conception of a dishonest man, Adams requires a fifth figure in the tableau, Aaron Burr. He travels afield for comparisons to illustrate the vice president's character:

An aristocrat imbued in the morality of Lord Chesterfield and Napoleon Bonaparte, Colonel Burr was the chosen head of Northern democracy, idol of the wards of New York city, and aspirant to the highest offices he could reach by means legal or beyond the law. . . . Among the other party leaders who have been mentioned,—Jefferson, Madison, Gallatin, Marshall,—not one was dishonest. The exaggerations or equivocations that Jefferson allowed himself, which led to the deep-rooted conviction of Marshall that he did not tell the truth and must therefore be dangerous, amounted to nothing when compared with the dishonesty of a corrupt man. . . . The self-deception inherent in every struggle for personal power was not the kind of immorality which characterized Colonel Burr. [1:195]

The art of these passages lies in their forwarding, at each stage, the reader's acquaintance with Jefferson, while they seem simply to introduce key figures and to describe the inaugural scene.

The first person to step forward from the tableau is the president, who delivers his Inaugural Address nearly inaudibly. As Adams struggle to infer the principles of the incoming administration, a new tone is felt. Jefferson has been congratulating the country on the success of its republican experiment; to the Virginian's assertion that America's was the strongest government on earth, Adams replies,

That the government, the world's best hope, had hitherto kept the country free and firm, in the full tide of successful experiment, was a startling compliment to the Federalist party, coming as it did from a man who had not been used to compliment his political opponents; but Federalists, on the other hand, might doubt whether this government would continue to answer the same purpose when administered for no other avowed object than to curtail its powers. Clearly, Jefferson credited government with strength which belonged to society; and if he meant to practise upon this idea, by taking the tone of "the strongest government on earth" in the face of Bonaparte and Pitt, whose governments were strong in a different sense, he might properly have developed this idea at more length, for it was likely to prove deeply interesting. [1:201–2]

Adams's passions are aroused, no longer controlled by his hard-learned balance of mind. Clues to his feelings lie at the points where strain breaks through the measured prose. If Jefferson "had not been used to compliment his political opponents," one of those least frequently complimented had been Adams's great-grandfather; "no other avowed object" suggests that the historian's antipathy is stirred by lack of candor; "curtail its powers" points toward the Kentucky Resolutions; while the "deeply interesting" idea was that commercial pressure, apart from military force, would suffice to maintain the nation's dignity against England and France.

That Adams's quarrel with Jefferson did not rise from antidemocratic sources is worth emphasis.[6] As has appeared, Henry was proud that John Adams "was the son of a small farmer, and had himself kept a school in his

118

youth" (1:181),[7] and he showed power in formulating the aspirations of the democratic leaders.[8] Eli Whitney, Robert Fulton, and other quick-minded inventors were born of the poorer or middling classes. "All these men," Adams affirms, "were the outcome of typical American society, and all their inventions transmuted the democratic instinct into a practical and tangible shape. Who would undertake to say that there was a limit to the fecundity of this teeming source?" (1:182–3). Adams was an apostle of what he called "science,"[9] and he sometimes associated the antitraditional outlook of science with democracy. In bringing forth Jefferson as the most suggestive advocate of the democratic philosophy against its conservative detractors, he declares that "probably Jefferson came nearest the mark, for he represented the hopes of science as well as the prejudices of Virginia" (1:178). Adams believed Jefferson, if anything, too little attached to democratic principles, for democracy implied the end of slavery. Upon John Calhoun "was to fall the duty of attempting to find for Carolina an escape from the logical conclusions of those democratic principles which Jefferson in 1800 claimed for his own, but which in the full swing of his power, and to the last day of his life, he shrank from pressing to their results." (1:154).

Adams's hostility toward Jefferson arose principally from the historian's abhorrence of "States-rights conservatism," manifested in the Kentucky Resolutions, and from his aversion to Jefferson's conduct of American foreign policy. But Adams, like John Marshall, felt antipathy toward some of Jefferson's political ideas and his personality. Crediting the president with purity of character and fidelity to the faith of his life, the New Englander was nevertheless stung by what he regarded as Jefferson's self-deception, disingenuousness, and occasional untruthfulness. Jefferson had persuaded himself—as had self-seeking politicians like Senator Giles and eccentrics like John Randolph—that his predecessors were monarchists who had deliberately steered the republic into stormy waves "with a view to sink her";[10] and he believed these predecessors to have been subject to British influence.[11] Adams's family pride is aroused as he comments on his great-grandfather's absence from the inauguration: "Perhaps the late President was wise to retire from a stage . . . where he would have seemed, in his successor's opinion, as little in place as George III. would have appeared at the installation of President Washington" (1:191).

Adams was further goaded by what he considered the theoretic, unrigorous, overspeculative side of Jefferson's personality. Adams's practice of attenuation—his setting against every thesis its antithesis—stimulates the reader to deduce an appropriate synthesis: Thus Adams no sooner criticizes Jefferson for sloppy thinking than he remarks a corresponding virtue and makes a trust at Calvinist New England: Jefferson " was a theorist, prepared to risk the fate of mankind on the chance of reasoning far from certain in its details. His temperament was sunny and sanguine, and the atrabilious philosophy of

119

New England was intolerable to him." From such materials one hesitates to deduce Adams's position merely by eliding; yet the words here are strong and the emotion genuine. Jefferson "sometimes generalized without careful analysis. . . . He was superficial in his knowledge, and a martyr to the disease of omniscience. . . . His English was often confused, his assertions inaccurate" (1:145–46).

The author's severity with his protagonist is not wholly explained by the character and theories of Jefferson; an unexpected subjective force is at work. While Adams's picture of the president is marked by brilliant strokes and filled with accurate details, its likeness at the same time to self-portraiture suggests a strange kinship between painter and sitter.[12] Jefferson was reserved

in the face of popular familiarities . . . [not] seen at all except on horseback, or by his friends and visitors in his own house. . . . He led a life of his own, and allowed few persons to share it. His tastes were for that day excessively refined. His instincts were those of a liberal European nobleman. . . . Personal attacks made him keenly unhappy. His true delight was in an intellectual life of science and art. To read, write, speculate in new lines of thought, to keep abreast of the intellect of Europe . . . were pleasures more to his mind than any to be found in a public assembly. . . . He fairly revelled in what he believed to be beautiful, and his writings often betrayed subtle feeling for artistic form,—a sure mark of intellectual sensuousness. . . . His yearning for sympathy was almost feminine. [1:144]

Those weaknesses of Jefferson's most irritating to Adams strikingly resembled his own. If Jefferson deceived himself and was disingenuous, "Henry was never . . . ," according to his brother, "quite frank with himself or with others."[13] Jefferson undoubtedly generalized sometimes without careful analysis, but what of the man who, in his later fatigue and disappointment, relaxed into the abstractions of "A Law of Acceleration"?

Adams's emotional involvement with the Virginian, traces of jealousy not entirely suppressed, caused him to set for Jefferson the extremely high standards on which, at this period in his life, he insisted for himself. His exasperation with the president's character and theories sometimes spoils the tone of the *History*, affects the judgment, and causes failures in the reading of evidence. Yet passion can lead to unusual insight, to alertness to those nuances which escape an objective observer. Adams's critique of Jefferson's character and his assault on certain of Jefferson's principles suggest important truths about an admired American leader whose career has not always been examined with critical rigor.[14]

Those Jeffersonian policies that especially interested Adams lay, not surprisingly, in the field of diplomacy; for Adams's training was diplomatic, while Jefferson and Madison regarded the national government as preeminently an instrument for the conduct of foreign affairs. When Adams introduces the most powerful ruler of their times, Napoleon, he marks the occasion—even more than the entry of John Marshall—by extravagant grammatical construction. A Latinate or Germanic casting of the verb to the end of the sentence creates tension; every device heightens the antithesis between Napoleon's force and the mildness of the American president. "Without the mass of correspondence and of fragmentary writings collected under the Second Empire in not less than thirty-two volumes of printed works," Adams asserts,

the greatness of Napoleon's energies or the quality of his mind would be impossible to comprehend. Ambition that ground its heel into every obstacle; restlessness that often defied common-sense; selfishness that eat like a cancer into his reasoning faculties; energy such as had never before been combined with equal genius and resources; ignorance that would have amused a school-boy; and a moral sense which regarded truth and falsehood as equally useful modes of expression,—an unprovoked war or secret assassination as equally natural forms of activity,—such a combination of qualities as Europe had forgotten since the Middle Ages, and could realize only by reviving the Eccelinos and Alberics of the thirteenth century, had to be faced and overawed by the gentle optimism of President Jefferson and his Secretary of State. [1:334–35]

Adams's allusion to his primary sources is discreet, and his language exact: The original meaning of "comprehend" fits the "greatness of Napoleon's energies." Personification, simile, and hyperbole increase the vividness of the picture—ambition grinds its heel, selfishness eats like a cancer, ignorance amuses a schoolboy; while across the last of these figures rests again the squat shadow of Gibbon, whose Oxford tutor exhibited "a degree of ignorance of which a schoolboy would have been ashamed."[15] Napoleon's every quality—restlessness, energy, amorality—is a reef for mariners who seek to navigate on pacific principles.

As Jefferson has become better known through comparison with Marshall and Burr, so Napoleon must be set against Talleyrand. Adams's opinion of Marshall lies inconspicuous in a sentence alleging a fault of the chief justice's; similarly, his judgment of Napoleon occurs almost as an afterthought, in a sentence about Talleyrand and Moreau. Once again a complex sentence, verb thrown toward the rear, helps convey the difficulty the Americans will experience in understanding French policy. "As if one such character were not riddle enough for any single epoch," Adams suggests,

a figure even more sinister and almost as enigmatical stood at its side. On the famous 18th Brumaire, the 9th November, 1799, when Bonaparte turned pale before the Five Hundred, and retired in terror from the hall at St. Cloud, not so much his brother Lucien, or the facile Sieyès, or Barras, pushed him forward to destroy the republic, but rather Talleyrand, the ex-bishop of Autun, the Foreign Secretary of the Directory. Talleyrand was most active in directing the *coup d'état*, and was chiefly responsible for the ruin of France. Had he profited by his exile in America, he would have turned to

Moreau rather than to Bonaparte; and some millions of men would have gone more quietly to their graves. . . . Superior to Bonaparte in the breadth and steadiness of his purpose, Talleyrand was a theorist in his political principles; his statecraft was that of the old *régime*, and he never forgave himself for having once believed in a popular revolution.

. . . In diplomacy, a more perplexing task could scarcely be presented than to fathom the policy which might result from the contact of a mind like Talleyrand's with a mind like Bonaparte's. . . . [Napoleon's] character was misconceived even by Talleyrand at this early period; and where the keenest of observers failed to see through a mind he had helped to form, how were men like Jefferson and Madison, three thousand miles away, and receiving at best only such information as Chancellor Livingston could collect and send them every month or six weeks,—how were they, in their isolation and ignorance, to solve a riddle that depended on the influence which Talleyrand could maintain over Bonaparte, and the despotism which Bonaparte could establish over Talleyrand? [1:335–36]

The language is concrete and succinct. Hypothetically Bonaparte might have "lost his self-possession as he stood in front of the assembly, and left the legislative building unnerved and fearful"; but instead, he "turned pale before the Five Hundred, and retired in terror from the Hall at St. Cloud." Adams evades the diffuse "If Talleyrand had made good use of" his exile in America with "Had he profited by." Another author might declare, "It would be hard to imagine a more difficult problem for a diplomat to deal with." Instead Adams's ear for sound and rhythm brings this to life: "In diplomacy, a more perplexing task could scarcely be presented." As Adams had earlier written "comprehend" in lieu of the colorless "understand", so he continues here, fertile in producing the appropriate synonym: "to *fathom* the policy" ousts "to understand the policy"; and "His character was *misconceived*" replaces "His character was misunderstood." The less vivid word is used only when Adams wishes to direct attention away from a subordinate idea toward the more important one that follows: "If Talleyrand was an enigma to be *understood* only by those who lived in his confidence, Bonaparte was a freak of nature such as the world had seen too rarely to comprehend" (1:336).

The customary precision of Adams's language permits him an occasional leap of the imagination, and his usual terseness earns him the right sometimes to be profuse. Thus, in explaining (directly after the paragraphs about Napoleon and Talleyrand) how Spain affected American politics, he devises from American experience one of his well-known metaphors, at once vivid and exact in its parallel. Characteristically, the imagery is prepared before the figure finally appears: "The Government at Washington . . . never missed an opportunity to thrust its knife into the joints of its unwieldy prey. . . . To sum up the story in a single word, Spain had immense influence over the United States; but it was the influence of the whale over its captors,—the charm of a huge, helpless, and profitable victim" (1:340).

Adams's ability to understand the feelings of combatants—both the despair of Federalists at Jefferson's election and the optimism of Jefferson about democracy's prospects, both Spanish dread of America and American contempt for Spain[16]—contributes to the sophistication of his judgments; and his manner of drawing conclusions, a reaction against the bald moralizing of earlier American historians, increases the impression of subtlety. His mentor Palfrey had not been embarrassed to write of John Winthrop, the first governor of the Massachusetts Bay colony, "They who, to make up their idea of consummate excellence in a statesman, require the presence of a religious sense prompting and controlling all public conduct, will recognize with admiration the prominence of that attribute in the character of this brave, wise, unselfish, and righteous ruler."[17] Eliminating every dead formula of this sort, Adams keeps the reader alert by occasionally offering a fragment of ginger root to be chewed a moment before it is rejected: "Europe could show no two men more virtuous in their private lives than King George III. of England and King Charles IV. of Spain. If personal purity was a test of political merit, these two rulers were the best of kings" (1:341–42). When judgment is finally to be rendered, the reader may be beguiled into belief: Charles IV "held the priesthood in deep respect; his own character was open and frank; he possessed the rare quality of being true at any cost to his given word; he was even shrewd in his way, with a certain amount of common-sense; but with all this he was a nullity, and his career was that of a victim" (1:344). But the usual way of avoiding pat moralizing is to hide judgment in a passage apparently pointed quite differently. An elaborate description of Charles IV's sporting activities reminds us again of Napoleon's prodigality with human life: The more Adams seems to praise the vacuousness of the Spanish monarch, the more Bonaparte is damned. Every day "King Charles set out . . . and drove post with guards and six coaches of companions. Three hundred men drove the game toward him," Adams observes; "seven hundred men and five hundred horses were daily occupied in this task of amusing him. The expenses were enormous; but the King was one of the best shots in Europe, and his subjects had reason to be grateful that his ambition took so harmless a path as the destruction of vast swarms of game" (1:343). One carefully wrought passage after another stimulates the reader's imagination, feeds his mind, appeals to his artistic sensibility.

This glance at its first volume may suggest that the *History* is not simply a narrative of diplomatic, military, and political affairs, though that is its form. Ostensibly an account of American affairs, it tells in fact a vast amount about the rulers of Britain and France as seen in their dealings with America. The chapters on the War of 1812, separately reprinted in 1944 for use in educating United States Army officers, remain the basis for most secondary works on the military history of the period.[18] Adams's tribute to the Negroes of Santo Domingo and his dispassionate account of America's Indian policy may soon be rediscovered; and a mine of rich observation on American national character lies unworked in his volumes, awaiting the return of that topic to fashion. The *History* is still, after a century, a robust child on the playground of clashing interpretations of nineteenth-century American experience. But evidently something else differentiates Adams's work from most histories. His precision of vocabulary, vividness of imagery, extravagance of syntax, fertility in inventing synonyms and in exploiting the resources of iteration; capacity to generalize, courage to trust the reader's powers of comprehension; passionate engagement in past politics, yet discretion in expressing his own judgments; sophistication in proposing contrary points of view for the reader's consideration—these and other qualities conjoin to make Adams's prose something exceptional. The *History* is distinguished by the play of Adams's imagination and the meticulousness of his use of langauge. No other work by an American historian tells so much about the art of historical writing.

Adams's composition might be examined by following the narrative through each of its nine volumes, showing how the author weaves together the strands of his tale. He divides his work according to presidential administrations. Volume 2 ends in 1805 as Jefferson, triumphantly reelected after a conciliatory first term, is caught up in entanglements with England. Volume 4 concludes with Jefferson's departure from the White House in 1809, his embargo policy in ruins. President Madison completes his first term at the end of volume 6, soon after the inauspicious start of the war against England. Most of volumes 7 through 9 tell the military and political history of that war, while the four concluding chapters contrast America's position in 1817 with that of 1800.

Within this structure the work is built upon a complex interweaving of foreign and domestic politics. Adams often isolates a single theme for analysis: He presents in volume 2 a long, clear discussion of British-American relations from 1783 to 1804, and in volume 3 he gives a full account of the Burr conspiracy. But usually he sticks close to chronology. This offers him the chance to show how each of the president's policies was affected by the other, for example, how Jefferson's conduct toward Britain was influenced by his wish to acquire Florida from Spain, by his hope that Napoleon would not frustrate this object, and by his quarrel with John Randolph. But Adams's faithfulness to chronology causes his story to become too complex, and the overall structure of the *History* is not its strong point.

Adams's power lies instead in the details of individual passages, or in the construction of individual chapters. A chronological treatment of the *History* would not define in any systematic way the elements of his art, and perhaps the most satisfactory approach is to take up, one by one, the clues to his method that Adams has dropped in his first volume.

II. Imagination

Imaginative power is the quality most characteristic of the *History*. Adams's text, as much as that of any Victorian novelist, is studded with provocative generalizations. Politics spur him to aphorism: "Governments rarely succeed in forethought, and their favorite rule is to do nothing where nothing need be done" (5:274). "To impose on hostile forces and interests the compulsion of a single will was the task and triumph of the true politician" (3:123). Adams lamented in 1871 that "we have [at this moment] hardly a man in political life who has the knowledge and the ability to make a respectable generalization,"[19] and he feels that this ability marks also the estimable historian. Like literary allusions, generalizations can be but sparingly employed, but so used they challenge the reader's mental inertia and lift history from the particular toward the universal: "Of all supposed facts in history, scandal about women was commonest and least to be trusted" (1:345). "Americans were the professional smugglers of an age when smuggling was tolerated by custom" (1:339). The function of generalizations is that of yeast: Separated unnaturally from the dough, they have little power to delight the appetite, but mixed into their appropriate medium they raise less digestible narrative into a lighter, more palatable prose.

The War of 1812 presents Adams many opportunities to place an event in perspective. In June 1813 the Massachusetts Senate not only condemned the struggle but resolved self-righteously that in such a war "it is not becoming a moral and religious people to express any approbation of military or naval exploits which are not immediately connected with the defence of our seacoast and soil." This outburst impels Adams to distinguish between two types of antiwar activity: "Mere opposition to foreign war rarely injured public men, except while the war-fever lasted. Many distinguished statesmen of Europe and America had been, at one time or another, in opposition to some special war,—as was the case with Talleyrand, Charles James Fox, Lord Grey, Jefferson, and Madison; but opposition became unpardonable when it took a form which could have no apparent object except national ruin" (7:65–66).

Adams also seeks perspective by setting the events of 1801–17 against those of other times. Contemplating the South's devotion to trade regulation as an instrument of diplomacy, evident both in Jefferson's and Madison's administrations, he challenges the reader to survey a fifty-year period. An embargo on America's international commerce, imposed at Jefferson's behest in 1807, was reimposed for a few months during the War of 1812. From the day of its repeal in April 1813, "the restrictive system . . . seemed to vanish from the public mind. . . . Yet so deeply riveted was the idea of its efficacy among the Southern people," Adams remarks, "that at the next great crisis of their history they staked their lives and fortunes on the same belief of their necessity to Europe which had led them into the experiment of coercing Napoleon and Canning by commercial deprivations; and their second experiment had results still more striking than those which attended their first" (7:379).

Another kind of imaginative power is shown in Adams's penchant for psychological analysis. He once alluded to "the unexpected revelations of human nature that suddenly astonish historians," and he delights in constantly proposing psychological interpretations, like a novelist's, which run beyond the narrow limits of scientific proof.[20] One subject of his observation is Timothy Pickering, whose ultra-Federalism had goaded President John Adams to dismiss him from his cabinet in 1800. Pickering gained a certain recompense in 1808, for his success in rallying Massachusetts against the embargo caused John Quincy Adams, who had voted for that measure, to resign from the United States Senate. George Rose, the former British envoy to Washington, congratulated Pickering on his triumph over Adams, and this letter spurs Henry Adams to reflect upon the psychology of American-British relations. His discreet comment upon the tone of Rose's missive is buried several lines after his citation of it, while an unobtrusive generalization about the craving for popularity sharpens his probing of Pickering's psyche. "That he felt, in his austere way, the full delight of repaying to the son the debt which for eight years he had owed to the father was not to be doubted; but a keener pleasure came to him from beyond the ocean. If the American of that day, and especially the New England Federalist, conceived of any applause as deciding the success of his career," Henry Adams surmises,

he thought first of London and the society of England; although the imagination could scarcely invent a means by which an American could win the favor of a British public. This impossibility Pickering accomplished . . . ; and Rose maintained with him a correspondence calculated to make him think his success even greater than it was.

" . . . Let me thank you cordially [wrote Rose from London] for your answer to Governor Sullivan. It was an unintentional kindness on his part thus to compel you to bring to the public eye the narrative of a life so interesting, so virtuous, and honorable. Receive the assurance of how anxiously I hope that though gratitude is not the virtue of republics, the remaining years of that life may receive from yours the tribute of honor and confidence it has so many claims to. . . ."

Flattery like this was rare in Pickering's toilsome career; and man, almost in the full degree of his antipathy to demagogy, yearns for the popular regard he will not seek. Pickering's ambition to be President was . . . evident to George Rose. . . . That Timothy Pickering could become President over a Union which embraced Pennsylvania and Virginia was an idea so extravagant as to be unsuited even to coarsely flavored flattery; but that he should be the chief of a New England Confederation was not an extravagant thought. [4:401–2]

Adams could prove neither that British applause was the special joy of a New England Federalist nor that Pickering felt spite toward the son of John Adams nor that he was ambitious to become president. Yet these were plausible inferences from Henry Adams's close reading of the primary sources and from his acquaintance with New England character. Long experience in the 1850s and 1860s had suggested to him how New Englanders of his century felt about the mother country, and he later wrote of his own father that "almost alone among his Boston contemporaries, he was not English in feeling or in sympathies. . . . Boston admired [Charles Sumner] . . . chiefly for his social success in England and on the Continent; success that gave to every Bostonian who enjoyed it a halo never acquired by domestic sanctity."[21] Knowing Boston from inside the drawing room and England at least from the antechamber, Adams could draw upon a rich experience to guide him in interpreting cryptic documentary evidence.

Psychological observations, like generalizations and literary allusions, punctuate Adams's narrative. Thus "Pickering enjoyed hearing himself called 'honest Tim Pickering,' as though he were willing to imply a tinge of dishonesty in others" (2:169). George Canning, the British foreign minister from 1807 to 1809, "belonged to a class of men denied the faculty of realizing the sensibilities of others. At the moment when he took . . . [a] tone of authority toward America, he gave mortal offence to his own colleague Lord Castlereagh, by assuming a like attitude toward him. He could not understand, and he could never train himself to regard, the rule that such an attitude between States as between gentlemen was not admitted among equals" (5:56).

Adams's interest in human nature appeared as early as 1863 in his bewilderment at certain of his own errors of judgment. The family's butler in London had proved to be a thief and forger, and Henry was beginning to learn how curiously compounded is human character: "Here is a case that has completely puzzled all my preconceived ideas," he confessed to his brother Charles. The butler

lied like a sculpin on every matter where lying was possible, to the last. Yet for months . . . he has been struggling to keep his head above water, and while trusted with large sums of money, has generally devoted it to paying bills. . . . His character is such a mixture of every meanness and weakness that can make human nature contemptible, all covered with a plausible air of candid, gushing honesty and fidelity, that I would like to have had Balzac or Thackeray analyse and dissect this carrion.[22]

As historian Adams had to read human nature from scattered documentary sources—"the liveliest [written] description," he lamented, "was worth less than a moment of personal contact" (1:185)—and eventually he developed the knack of squeezing his sources for every drop they could be made to yield. " 'I have often observed that the smallest things are sometimes better marks [of character] than the greatest,'" he quoted Cardinal de Retz approvingly (1: 186–87). While still a young man he was already trying to decipher the psychology of various gestures and actions. "It is a standing figure, quite in repose," he reported of a statue of Medea meditating the death of her children, sculptured by William Wetmore Story: "The left arm is folded across her, and on the left hand she is resting her right elbow, so that her right hand comes up to her chin. Her head is bent over a little and so rests on the hand. If you understand the attitude, and put anyone into it, you will see in a moment how expressive it is, and how exact it is to suit the instant of determination, or just before the completion of a decisive plan." Although no very precise power of observation was yet evident in this youthful commentary, Adams was at least asking the right questions. Pretending never to read his friends' novels, he nevertheless knew at least two novels of Henry James by 1882; that he learned, however reluctantly, from James's books as from those of Balzac and Thackeray may be inferred from a later comment. As of 1862, he declared with a tinge of irritation, "Henry James had not yet taught the world to read a volume for the pleasure of seeing the lights of his burning-glass turned on alternate sides of the same figure. Psychological study was still simple."[23] Adams further schooled his faculty of observation by writing two novels of his own, and by the 1880s he was prepared to venture exceedingly close psychological readings of his sources.

The British minister to Washington in 1809, Francis Jackson, sent his mother in England a seemingly innocent description of his first reception by Madison. Adams jumps at the clue to Jackson's character but eschews naming the discovered trait: He invites the reader to make his own inference. Equally typically, Adams refrains from insisting upon a moral judgment. Instead he invents an excuse for Jackson, smiling as he does so at a characteristic foible of members of the diplomatic profession:

"While we were talking [Jackson wrote], a negro servant brought in some glasses of punch and a seed-cake. The former, as I had been in conference the whole morning, served very agreeably to wet, or whet, my whistle, and still more strongly to contrast this audience with others I had had with most of the sovereigns of Europe."

Perhaps this passing allusion to previous acquaintance with "most of the sovereigns of Europe" threw a light, somewhat too searching, into the recesses of Jackson's character. The weakness was pardonable, and not specially unsuited to success in his career, but showed itself in private as a form of self-deception which promised ill for his coming struggle. [5:121]

The smile on the reader's face would have vanished had Adams preached, insisted, or spelled everything out.

Adams's most provocative psychological theorizing bore upon British at-

titudes to America, a matter of interest to him since his arrival in London at
the beginning of the Civil War. He agreed with Talleyrand that the English
and the Americans were closely akin to each other, and by the 1880s he had
come to believe that American literary artists normally would do well to
develop their originality within the broad limits of the British tradition.[24]
These views caused him the more irritation at Englishmen's virulent anti-
American feelings, which contributed so much to bringing on the War of
1812. Illustrations of the British sense of superiority were readily multiplied,[25]
but explanation of British rancor was more difficult. Adams quivers with
pleasure as he sets the terms of the problem. "The Somersetshire squire and
the chancery barrister in Westminster Hall—the extremes of national ob-
tuseness and professional keenness—" Adams alleges,

agreed in despising America. The pompous Lord Sidmouth, the tedious Lord Sheffield, the vivacious Canning, the religious Perceval, and the merry-andrew Cobbett
. . . joined hands in spreading libels against a people three thousand miles away, who
according to their own theory were too contemptible to be dangerous. . . . Young
Henry Brougham, not yet thirty years old, whose restless mind persistently asked
questions which parsons and squires thought absurd or impious, speculated much
upon the causes of this prejudice. Was it because the New York dinners were less
elegant than those of London, or because the Yankees talked with an accent, or because their manners were vulgar? No doubt a prejudice might seize on any justification, however small; but a prejudice so general and so deep became respectable, and
needed a correct explanation. [4:73–74]

   Three psychological factors, Adams believed, contributed to British contempt. One factor was related to the theory of American exceptionalism,
and Adams introduces this theme, with ambiguity, near the beginning of the
History: "The experience of mankind proved trade to be dependent on water
communications, and as yet Americans did not dream that the experience of
mankind was useless to them" (1:7–8). This sentence seems to assert that the
experience of mankind would not help the Americans, yet why the term
dream?[26] Was the idea of America's being exceptional an illusion? Doubtless
Adams believed that European experience was useless in regard to inland
transport, but what was to be thought of those American "critics who required, as they commonly did, a national literature founded on some new
conception,—such as the Shawanee or Aztecs could be supposed to suggest"
(9:212–13)? And what judgment would England make upon a nation that
imagined it could live unarmed amidst the broils of Europe? "England required America to prove by acts what virtue existed in her conduct or character which should exempt her from the common lot of humanity." England
"expected her antagonists to fight; and if they would not fight, she took
them to be cowardly or mean. Jefferson and his government had shown over
and over again that no provocation would make them fight; and from the

moment that this attitude was understood, America became fair prey" (4:74).

Speculation about unconscious motives suggested a second factor to account for British prejudice. Adams's paean to the trim sailing vessels that had gone to sea, just off the coast at Beverly Farms, would have been offensively chauvinistic had not every enthusiastic cry for Massachusetts ships been elsewhere balanced by equal castigation of the folly of Massachusetts politicians. Beneath Britain's disdain for America, Adams conjectured,

lurked an uneasy doubt which gave to contempt the virulence of fear. The English nation, and especially the aristocracy, believed that America was biding her time; that she expected to become a giant; and that if she succeeded, she would use her strength as every other giant in the world's history had done before her. . . . Already the American ship was far in advance of the British model. . . . [The British shipowner] already felt, without acknowledging it even to himself, that in war he was likely to enjoy little profit or pleasure on the day when the long, low, black hull of the Yankee privateer, with her tapering, bending spars, her long-range gun, and her sharp-faced captain, should appear on the western horizon, and suddenly, at sight of the heavy lumbering British merchantman, should fling out her white wings of canvas and fly down on her prey. [4:75]

The third factor was the behavior of the Federalist leaders of the state which produced the black Yankee privateer. Adams believed Englishmen were taught to disdain America by Americans who did not respect themselves. One memorable instance of the conduct of such Americans occurred late in 1809 when, upon Madison's dismissing the British minister, Jackson, the Federalists adopted him as one of their own. "Incredible as the folly of a political party was apt to be," Adams rages, "the folly of the Federalists in taking up Jackson's quarrel passed the limits of understanding" (5:158). He writes passionately, with his heart's blood, from the painful experience of the 1860s; and his sympathies here lie entirely with the Democratic-Republicans. "Nothing could be more dangerous to the Americans," he thinks,

than the loss of self-respect. . . . The sense of national and personal inferiority sank astonishingly deep. It passed bounds when it condemned everything American as contemptible, or when the Federalist gentry refused to admit the Democrats of Pennsylvania or the Republicans of Virginia or the Government at Washington into the circle of civilized life. Social self-abasement never went so far as in its efforts to prove to Francis James Jackson, the British minister, that he was right in treating the national government with contempt. [5:211–12]

British attitudes to America have sometimes shown a certain likeness to those of white Americans to blacks; and Adams's sophisticated hypothesis that British contempt was nourished by Jefferson's reluctance to arm in self-defense, that British feeling betrayed the virulence of fear, and that matters were aggravated by the servility toward Britain of Federalist Uncle Toms bears striking similarity to the intelligent theory of a black man, torn by ambivalent feelings toward white people, attempting to account for anti-Negro prejudice.[27]

Although Adams propounded the theory that individual statesmen were mere grasshoppers carried along by the current of uncontrollable historical forces, he seldom in the *History* pursued this idea. His interest was psychological rather than sociological or economic. He understood that good generals won battles, that able diplomats won political victories, that it mattered immensely whether Napoleon or General Moreau was at the head of the French state. He was fascinated by the study of human character, and the most conspicuous evidence of his intellectual vitality lay in his forays into the psychology of men such as Napoleon,[28] Canning, Jefferson, and Madison, and of the British people as they faced America.

A fourth type of imaginative power—beyond Adams's taste for generalizations, for placing events in perspective, and for psychological analysis—appears in his predilection for making comparisons. The word *resemble* was one of his favorites. It is not always easy to distinguish simple comparison from elaborate figures of speech: Harvard College in 1800 "resembled a priesthood which had lost the secret of its mysteries, and patiently stood holding the flickering torch before cold altars, until God should vouchsafe a new dispensation of sunlight" (1:77). "The march [of the British army into Maryland in August 1814] resembled a midsummer picnic" (8:129). Such comparisons alternately stimulate the reader's fancy, lend emotional tone to sober narrative, or suggest Adams's judgment of events: General Ross and Admiral Cockburn "burned the Capitol, the White House, and the Department buildings because they thought it proper, as they would have burned a negro kraal or a den of pirates. Apparently they assumed as a matter of course that the American government stood beyond the pale of civilization" (8:146–47).

The qualities of Adams's mind are evident not only in quick sallies like the ones above but in extended passages throughout the *History*. The author sharpens his analysis of Napoleon's character by likening him to one of the Corsican's eminent antagonists, Toussaint L'Ouverture. Adams relentlessly pursues the parallelism of events, and his comments upon Toussaint—"the most active and indefatigable man that could be imagined,—one who was present everywhere, but especially where his presence was most needed"—deserve to be better known in an era when the great leaders of the black people are being rediscovered. Adams does not romanticize Toussaint, and the presumptions behind his comparison are egalitarian. "In more respects than one," he suggests, Toussaint's

character had a curious resemblance to that of Napoleon,—the same abnormal energy of body and mind; the same morbid lust for power, and indifference to means; the same craft and vehemence of temper; the same fatalism, love of display, reckless personal courage, and, what was more remarkable, the same occasional acts of moral cowardice. One might suppose that Toussaint had inherited from his Dahomey grandfather the qualities of primitive society; but if this was the case, the conditions of life in Corsica must have borne some strong resemblance to barbarism, because the rule of inheritance which applied to Toussaint should hold good for Bonaparte. [1:382–83][29]

Like Toussaint, the Virginian John Randolph, the most talented leader of Jefferson's party in the House of Representatives, possessed so vivid a character as to feed Adams's appetite for comparison. Adams's search for parallelism infuses itself into the structure of his writing; thus in one sentence he attributes six characteristics to James Madison and each finds its exact contrast in Randolph, yet the expression of the details is sufficiently varied that the general form of the sentence is not schematic. "Madison," Adams declares, "was in person small, retiring, modest, with quiet malice in his humor, and with marked taste for closet politics and delicate management; Randolph was tall in stature, abrupt in manner, self-asserting in temper, sarcastic, with a pronounced taste for publicity, and a vehement contempt for those silent influences which more practical politicians called legitimate and necessary, but which Randolph, when he could not control them, called corrupt" (3:120–21).

Every historian unconsciously employs the figures of speech stereotyped into the language. How many statesmen have "plumbed the depths of despair" or "reaped the harvest of disaster"? But Adams's art lay in his listening carefully to the words he used, infusing new life into those old images that crept inadvertently into his text, and inventing new figures that were neither too simple minded nor too farfetched. Often he pursues an image consistently through the whole range of its possibilities, and he discreetly prepares the ground for each image so that it seems to grow naturally from its context. Some of his figures—"the influence of a whale over its captors"—are maritime, as suited an author writing each summer, north of Boston, in a house overlooking the sea. Others—"a mediaeval knight in . . . Arkwright's cotton-mill"—recall his years of teaching about medieval Europe, whose history he did not yet romanticize. One figure may have grown from his experience in the summer of 1871, exploring the wilds of Wyoming: "England and the United States, like two vultures, hovered over the expiring [Spanish] empire, snatching at the morsels they most coveted" (5:305).

To pursue a single image, working out in detail each element of the simile, is Adams's delight.[30] His avocation of chess playing enabled him to convert the lifeless figure of "stalemate" into a vital metaphor for the state of British party politics in 1809.[31] And he relishes representing a prominent member of the British aristocracy—the editor of Gibbon's memoir—as a primitive religionist. Lord Sheffield, Adams observes, felt such devotion to the British navigation laws as could be likened only to the idolatry which a savage felt toward his fetich; one might almost have supposed that to him the State, the Church, and the liberties of England, the privileges of her nobility, and even the person of her sovereign, were sacred chiefly because they guaranteed the safety of her maritime system. . . . The existence of the United States was a protest against Lord Sheffield's political religion; and therefore in his eyes the United States were no better than a nation of criminals, capable of betraying their God for pieces of silver. The independence of America had shattered the navigation system of England into fragments; but Lord Sheffield clung the more desperately to his broken idol. [2:412–13]

Adams's joy in elaborating an image was allied to his hearty laughter at the foibles of human nature. To impale an adversary upon a metaphor was only one of the many possible methods of dispatching him. The American general Alexander Smyth provoked Adams's mirth no less than Lord Sheffield; and the historian, restraining his merriment at Smyth's bombast, dedicates several paragraphs to evoking the genius of that remarkable leader. Adams's language is ambiguous and even more than usually fastidious. On October 24, 1812, Smyth took command of the American forces at Buffalo. Three weeks later, Adams recounts,

the public read in the newspapers an address issued by him to the "Men of New York," written in a style hitherto unusual in American warfare.

" . . . The nation [Smyth announced to the Men of New York] has been unfortunate in the selection of some of those who have directed it. One army has been disgracefully surrendered and lost. Another has been sacrificed by a precipitate attempt to pass it over at the strongest point of the enemy's lines. . . . The commanders were popular men, 'destitute alike of theory and experience' in the art of war."

Unmilitary as such remarks were, the address continued in a tone more and more surprising, until at last it became burlesque.

"In a few days the troops under my command will plant the American standard in Canada. . . . Will you stand with your arms folded and look on this interesting struggle? . . . Has the race degenerated? . . . Shall I imitate the officers of the British king, and suffer our ungathered laurels to be tarnished by ruthless deeds? Shame, where is thy blush! No!"

. . . . .

. . . Everything was prepared, November 27, for the crossing, and once more orders were issued in an inspiring tone:

"Friends of your country! ye who have 'the will to do, the heart to dare!' . . . Think on your country's honors torn! . . . her infants perishing by the hatchet! Be strong! be brave! and let the ruffian power of the British king cease on this continent!"

. . . . .

[Smyth twice embarked his soldiers, and twice abandoned his plan for invasion.] Upon this, General Smyth's army dissolved. "A scene of confusion ensued which it is difficult to describe," wrote Peter B. Porter soon afterward,—"about four thousand men without order or restraint discharging their muskets in every direction." They showed a preference for General Smyth's tent as their target, which caused the General to shift his quarters repeatedly.

The humor of this passage is emasculated by removing the words from their context, a sober narration of American military disasters in 1812, yet the Smyth episode points toward the underlying spirit of the *History*. Adams takes such delight in the act of writing that a sympathetic smile may creep over the reader's face, and lightness of heart may enter his soul as he apprehends Adams's own pleasure. When Adams was in his prime, his intimate friends and his better students at Harvard felt that "his laugh was infectious . . . with a gay twinkle of humor in his eyes and in the wrinkles at their corners," and this facet of his personality infuses the best passages of the *History*.[32] Adams's joy in inventing metaphors, his zest in laughing at the absurdities of the world, his passion for comparison, his love of psychological speculation, his pleasure in generalizing and setting events in perspective— these all create a buoyant, mischievous, sometimes exhilarating prose. A rich imagination disports itself, and the reader smiles to see what trick it will play next. Adams understood that the historian is an artist whose revelation of his own mind is as essential to his art as is that of any novelist or poet.

III. Craft

Compelled like everyone in his profession to be a literary craftsman, a historian may be constrained by the habits of his education or spurred by pride to master the craft. In rare cases a mysterious transformation overtakes his work; by some strange process whose laws can never be adequately defined, soil and climate occasionally nurture the grape whose juice is metamorphosed into a choice wine; what was merely an exceedingly competent piece of craftsmanship suddenly becomes a work of art.

Adams's talent in organizing an extended passage can be seen in his narrative of the Americans' humiliation in August 1814, the rout of their army at Bladensburg, Md., which led to the burning of the Capitol and the White House by British troops.[33] Adams places the reader in the position of the commander of one army, then of the other. The reader experiences first the Americans' uncertainty as to whether the British navy is really going to deposit an invading army upon the Chesapeake coast of Maryland, and during this part of the tale the reader knows as little as did General Winder, the American commander, of British movements. Only then does Adams discuss the British activities of the last two and one-half months. The reader soon experiences the perplexities of the British commander, whose army marched slowly through Maryland for five days without catching view of any American force. Not until the moment the British sight the opposing army does Adams retrogress five days to tell what the Americans had been doing. He follows the Americans until 10:00 A.M. on August 24, the moment when news reached Winder that he had miscalculated British intentions: The enemy was marching to outflank him at Bladensburg, where the Americans would have to face a veteran British army without even the benefit of defensive fortifications.

Once Adams has described the ignominious defeat of the Americans at Bladensburg, he wishes to show Winder's panic as his troops flee down the narrow lanes toward Rock Creek. Again his organization heightens the effect, for he follows the British first. They enter the abandoned capital, set fire to the public buildings, then secretly and swiftly withdraw toward their ships. Once they are miles away from Washington, marching rapidly in the opposite direction from Winder, Adams returns to the hapless American general just as the battle of Bladensburg ends, and shows him driving his troops to further and further flight, quite unaware that the British had no faintest intention of pursuing him. For thirty-three pages Adams has attempted to suppress his feelings about Winder, treating him usually with laborious civility, but now—having made his reader aware that Winder had no further cause for alarm—Adams unleashes his fury at the man responsible for the humiliation of his nation:

Of the commanding general no kind word could be said. Neither William Hull, Alexander Smyth, Dearborn, Wilkinson, nor Winchester showed such incapacity as Winder either to organize, fortify, fight, or escape. When he might have prepared defences, he acted as scout; when he might have fought, he still scouted; when he retreated, he retreated in the wrong direction; when he fought, he thought only of retreat; and whether scouting, retreating, or fighting, he never betrayed an idea. . . . Behind Rock Creek his army would have been safe, and he could certainly have rallied more than a thousand men to stop the panic; but he thought a farther retreat necessary, and went on to the heights. On the heights nothing could reach him without hours of warning, but he rode three miles farther to Tenallytown. At Tenallytown his exhausted men stopped a moment from inability to run farther, yet he seemed angry at their fatigue. Struck by a fresh panic at the glare of the burning city, he pressed his men on at midnight. [8:153–54]

Repeating batteries direct a barrage of invective upon Adams's unfortunate victim, but the overpowering effect depends largely on the quiet way in which, for page after page, the author has organized his materials.

A well-known prose rule requires that sometimes when a transition is to be effected—from one chapter, from one section, or even from one paragraph, to the next—the final sentence should point toward the paragraph to come. No artistic virtue lies in rote application of the rule. Talent appears only in doing the thing so unobtrusively as to serve the function without betraying the method. In his narrative of Bladensburg, Adams hides one transition by introducing an allusion that wholly distracts the reader's attention at the crucial moment. The invading British army has been marching slowly toward Washington without catching sight of the Americans, and at the end of seven pages Adams must summarize the section and turn to the Americans to explain what they have been doing: "Thus for five days, from August 18 to August 23, a British army, which though small was larger than any single body of American regulars then in the field, marched in a leisurely manner through a long-settled country, and met no show of resistance before coming within sight of the Capitol. Such an adventure resembled the stories of Cortez and De Soto; and the conduct of the United States government offered no contradiction to the resemblance" (8:131). The reader hesitates only a moment to infer that the American government was scarcely less disorganized than the Indian tribes for whom Americans manifested such contempt, but at the end of that brief reflection he discovers the transition to be complete. The next section is indeed an account of "the conduct of the United States government" from August 18 until August 24. Similarly unobtrusive transitions are found in the well-known chapter on New England.[34]

Another standard prose rule, important to many historians, requires them to furnish an adequate commentary upon each quotation from a primary source. The writer has to supply essential background information—author, date, context—and to suggest the purpose of his citation. So seldom did Macaulay quote primary sources—his own reaction to William III is more evident than the naked features of the king himself—that he little heeded this rule, but Adams, depending heavily upon quotations, inevitably developed the craft of commentary. Unlike historians who compress a dozen fragmentary citations into a single paragraph, Adams often cites a single source at length, letting it serve not as proof but as illustration. Thus in describing the Federalists' conservatism, he furnishes a quotation so vivid and extravagant that the reader must presume it an invention, and only afterwards does he indicate that a real person, a clergyman, actually spoke the words. Essential information about authorship, date, and context is so skillfully woven into the commentary that the art escapes notice. The graduates of Harvard and Yale

passed from the college to the pulpit, and from the pulpit attempted to hold the college, as well as their own congregations, facing toward the past. "Let us guard against the insidious encroachments of *innovation*," they preached,—"that evil and beguiling spirit which is now stalking to and fro through the earth, seeking whom he may destroy." These words were spoken by Jedediah Morse, a graduate of Yale in 1783, pastor of the church at Charlestown, near Boston, and still known in biographical dictionaries as "the father of American geography." They were contained in the Election Sermon of this worthy and useful man, delivered June 6, 1803; but the sentiment was not peculiar to him, or confined to the audience he was then addressing,—it was the burden of a thousand discourses enforced by a formidable authority. [1: 78–79]

Morse is not an absurd crank but " 'the father of American geography' "; he is alleged to be, not a bigot, but a "worthy and useful man"; and by this indirection Adams the more disarmingly suggests his folly and narrow-mindedness.

Adams's introduction to a quotation goads the reader to ask questions of the primary source, and generally his subsequent comment invites further reflection from an unexpected point of view.[35] Everything depends upon the quickness of the introductory comments and the follow-up. A single tart sentence of Adams's transforms a maundering letter (sent near the beginning of the War of 1812 by the incompetent American general Henry Dearborn to Secretary of War Eustis) into a damning piece of evidence:

"For some time past [Dearborn replied from Boston to Eustis's orders] I have been in a very unpleasant situation, being at a loss to determine whether or not I ought to leave the sea-coast. . . . Having waited for more explicit directions until I begin to fear that I may be censured for not moving, and having taken such measures as circumstances would permit for the defence of the sea-coast, I have concluded to leave this place for Albany before the end of the present week unless I receive orders to remain."

A general-in-chief unable to decide at the beginning of a campaign in what part of his department his services were most needed was sure to be taught the required lesson by the enemy. [6:309]

A bold inference constantly tests the reader's mental alertness, turning him back to the primary source to judge whether the historian has leapt too far. Copious extracts from original sources enable the reader to experience directly the atmosphere of the times and the character of the protagonists; the method can succeed artistically only because Adams avoids laboring a point but instead converts his book, by his sharp running commentary, into a lively debate between himself and his sources.

An essential quality of Adams's prose style, suspect to the modern ear, is its elevated tone: No artistic work, the historian seems to say, can be couched in everyday language. The examples of Racine or Gibbon would seem in their different ways to support this view. Yet Gibbon was too ornate and mannered for modern taste, while the florid rhetoric of Macaulay might quickly satiate a reader's appetite. Adams's problem was to strike a balance between the best classical manner and the everyday prose of an increasingly democratic age. His principal instruments were syntax and diction.

Adams's simplest rule for sentence structure was frequently to separate a verb from the complement or object; and he did this by placing adverbs and adverbial phrases adjacent to their verb. Thus the *Pilot* did not lament the sinking of the British frigate *Java* in set periods; instead it "lamented in set periods the incomprehensible event" (7:16): This deviation from ordinary speech elevates the tone. Indeed Adams's comment upon the style of the *Pilot* gives a clue to his practice. When the object or complement no longer follows directly upon the verb, an artificial tension is created—the "period" is extended. The same effect is achieved in the second sentence by the location of the prepositional phrase: "These epithets would not have disturbed Napoleon. Politics were to him a campaign" (5:259). The everyday arrangement of the words ("Politics were a campaign to him") would have reduced the sentence to the prosaic.

Beyond alteration of normal word order, Adams's most common syntactical device—one certainly employed to excess—was the balancing of coordinate clauses:

When one nation is agreed in the policy of fighting another any pretext will answer, and Government need not even be greatly concerned to give any reason at all; but in the condition of America in 1810, grave dangers might result from setting aside the four or five just issues of war with England in order to insist on an issue that revolted common-sense. . . . [5:343]
The diplomatic outlook had changed since March, 1813, when the President accepted the offer of Russian mediation; but the change was wholly for the worse. England's triumphs girdled the world. [7:356]

Offering rare opportunity for satirical thrusts, this construction at the same time prevented a statement's being too bald or simpleminded: Adams had a horror of spoon-feeding his reader. If he devised a generalization "When one nation is agreed in the policy of fighting another any pretext will answer", he would not smugly halt but must somehow complicate the sentence, measuring it more exactly to the complexity of the world. Fully conscious of the perversity of events, he found in sentences that seemed to point one way but suddenly broke into the opposite direction a syntactical device mirroring his own ironic spirit.

The practice of packing a complicated thought into a single sentence by using semicolons could occasionally support an extravagantly long period, so carefully constructed as to distinguish it completely from the language of ordinary life:

No canvass for the Presidency was ever less creditable than that of De Witt Clinton in 1812. Seeking war votes for the reason that he favored more vigorous prosecution of the war; asking support from peace Republicans because Madison had plunged the country into war without preparation; bargaining for Federalist votes as the price of bringing about a peace; or coquetting with all parties in the atmosphere of bribery in bank charters,—Clinton strove to make up a majority which had no element of union but himself and money. [6:410]

Here, as in the sentence marking Napoleon's entry upon the stage—"Ambition that ground its heel into every obstacle"[36]—Adams contrives, by throwing the verb to the rear, to stretch tension the whole length of an inordinately long sentence; and as so often in his writing, the sting lies in the tail. A beautifully constructed extravaganza of this sort allows the author to express his strongest feelings, whether of admiration, indignation, or disgust:

At St. Domingo, horror followed fast on horror. Rochambeau, shut in Port au Prince,—drunken, reckless, surrounded by worthless men and by women more abandoned still, wallowing in the dregs of the former English occupation and of a half-civilized negro empire,—waged as he best could a guerilla war, hanging, shooting, drowning, burning all the negroes he could catch; hunting them with fifteen hundred bloodhounds bought in Jamaica for something more than one hundred dollars each; wasting money, squandering men; while Dessalines and Christophe massacred every white being within their reach. [2:19–20]

Yet, as shown in his contemptuous discussion of General Winder's activities at Bladensburg, Adams knew the strength of the short sentence.[37] When he describes the famous duel between Vice President Aaron Burr and his victim, Alexander Hamilton, his style moves from complexity to terseness:

Early on the morning of July 11 [1804], in the brilliant sunlight of a hot summer, the two men were rowed to the duelling-ground across the river, under the rocky heights of Weehawken, and were placed by their seconds face to face. Had Hamilton acted with the energy of conviction, he would have met Burr in his own spirit; but throughout this affair Hamilton showed want of will. He allowed himself to be drawn into a duel, but instead of killing Burr he invited Burr to kill him. In the paper Hamilton left for his justification, he declared the intention to throw away his first fire. He did so. Burr's bullet passed through Hamilton's body. The next day he was dead. [2:189]

Another illustration of Adams's skill in varying the length and convolution of sentences appears in his account of the once famous naval battle between the U.S.S. *Constitution* and the British *Guerriere*.[38]

Experiments with syntax were regularly mixed with other stylistic devices. The passage on Napoleon cited earlier (page 138) continues: "Politics were to him a campaign, and if his opponents had not the sense to divine his movements and motives, the disgrace and disaster were none of his. More mysterious than the conduct of Napoleon was that of Armstrong" (5:259). In this last sentence inversion of subject and complement brings to prominence the phrase Adams wishes to emphasize, but the distinction of the passage lies in the choice of words. "None of his" is slightly archaic and more forceful than "not his"; while "divine," rarely used as a verb, exactly suits its context. Its value is increased by the preceding string of hard-hitting monosyllables. Alliteration on *d*'s and *m*'s further distinguishes these sentences from everyday prose.

Indeed, Adams lavishes infinite care upon diction. Evoking the atmosphere of New England at the time of the French Revolution, he selects one series of vivid words—"three-cornered hat," "silver-topped cane," "authority," "best parishioners"—to suggest the established order; a second series—"defiance," "license," "infidelity"—to represent the forces of subversion as they appeared to the Establishment; and a third series to indicate the reaction of Federalist society to the apprehended threat—"repression," "strenuous," "combined effort":

The power of the Congregational clergy, which had lasted unbroken until the Revolution, was originally minute and inquisitory, equivalent to a police authority. During the last quarter of the century the clergy themselves were glad to lay aside the more odious watchfulness over their parishes, and to welcome social freedom within limits conventionally fixed; but their old authority had not wholly disappeared. In country parishes they were still autocratic. Did an individual defy their authority, the minister put his three-cornered hat on his head, took his silver-topped cane in his hand, and walked down the village street, knocking at one door and another of his best parishioners, to warn them that a spirit of license and of French infidelity was abroad, which could be repressed only by a strenuous and combined effort. Any man once placed under this ban fared badly if he afterward came before a bench of magistrates. The temporal arm vigorously supported the ecclesiastical will. Nothing tended so directly to make respectability conservative, and conservatism a fetich of respectability, as this union of bench and pulpit. The democrat had no caste; he was not respectable; he was a Jacobin,—and no such character was admitted into a Federalist house. Every dissolute intriguer, loose-liver, forger, false-coiner, and prison-bird; every hair-brained, loud-talking demagogue; every speculator, scoffer, and atheist,—was a follower of Jefferson; and Jefferson was himself the incarnation of their theories. [1:79–80]

Exact terms are deployed—"minute," "inquisitory," "odious watchfulness"— and frequent reflexives lend emphasis: "the clergy themselves"; "Jefferson was himself." This vigorous language is not weakened by qualification: The power of the clergy was not "like a police authority" but was "equivalent to a police authority." Like Gibbon, Adams is profuse in employing all-or-nothing terms: "wholly . . . only . . . any man once placed . . . nothing . . . directly . . . had no caste . . . no such character . . . Every . . . every . . . every . . . the incarnation." The long-winded "Within limits which had been fixed by convention" is reduced to "limits conventionally fixed," and superfluous verbiage is squeezed from the normal "Once a man had been placed under this ban, he fared badly." Even without reducing the number of words, Adams tightens up another clause and improves both the rhythm and the

alliteration on *d* by discarding a conjunction: "If an individual defied" becomes "Did an individual defy."[39]

Yet for all the pains Adams takes with the diction and syntax of this paragraph, the great stroke of talent lies in substituting a single vivid image—
that of the minister with silver-topped cane walking down the street—for
the abstraction "respectability." Concrete and abstract terms are skillfully
juxtaposed: The personified "spirit of license" confronts the person of the
minister. The literary artist aims, not at proof by means of a hundred footnotes, but at illustration appealing directly to the reader's imagination. The
habit of specifying, of letting a pictorial image stand for a general term or for
a dozen pieces of evidence, is inveterate. Benjamin Franklin did not land in
Philadelphia "poor"; rather, "In 1723 Benjamin Franklin landed at Philadelphia, and with his loaf of bread under his arm walked along Market Street
toward an immortality such as no American had then conceived" (1:60).
New England after the turn of the century was not "lacking in Greek literature"; instead, "as late as 1814 . . . a copy of Euripides in the original could
not be bought at any book-seller's shop" (1:63). King Charles IV of Spain
was "skilful with his tools, and withal a dilettante in his way, capable of
enjoying not only the workmanship of a gunlock, but the beauties of his
glorious picture-gallery,—the 'Feconditá' of Titian, and the 'Hilanderas' of
Velasquez" (1:342).

Another means of making language forceful was to borrow the orator's
device of iteration: the British Orders in Council of November 1807 worked
"to *break the power* and *blot out the memory* of Virginia and Massachusetts
principles" (4:79). "The war of 1812 was chiefly remarkable for the vehemence with which, *from beginning to end*, it was *resisted* and *thwarted* by a very
large number of citizens *who were commonly considered*, and *who considered
themselves*, by no means the least respectable, intelligent, or patriotic part of
the nation" (6:224).[40] This power of saying the same thing in two different
ways—or of saying two different things in the same way—could strengthen
a sentence only if the device did not through overuse, as with Macaulay,
degenerate into mannerism. Not fitted out too often, and arrayed in colorful
language, an idea dressed in more than one costume might gain splendor, as
does the condemnation of Winder cited earlier (page 135). Similarly, elaborate repetition heightens the force of Adams's wonderment at the tactics of
certain Jeffersonian congressmen. When Representative Eppes and his colleagues declared that the United States was solemnly bound by a contract
with Napoleon to stop trading with Britain as soon as the French ruler
should claim to diminish his depredations against American commerce,
Adams understood that the worst possible grounds had been chosen for an
anti-British campaign:

If ingenuity had been provoked to suggest the course which would rouse most repugnance in the minds of the largest possible number of Americans, no device better

suited for its purpose than the theory of Eppes, Cheves, and Rhea could have been proposed; and if they wished to exasperate the conscience of New England in especial to fanatical violence, they came nearest their end by insisting on an involuntary, one-sided compact, intended to force Massachusetts and Connecticut to do the will of the man whom a majority of the people in New England seriously regarded as anti-Christ. [5:343–44]

Respect for his reader's intelligence often leads Adams, avoiding obvious paths, to approach his destinations by indirect routes. When annihilating General Winder he is of course perfectly capable of heavy bombardment, but normally he attacks more subtly. More than once, wishing to convey a sense of Winder's excessively small accomplishment, he uses an excessively short sentence: "The single step taken for defence was taken by the citizens, who held a meeting Saturday evening, and offered at their own expense to erect works at Bladensburg. Winder accepted their offer" (8:132). On August 23, Winder having left his army a few miles east of Washington, the enemy approached: "Winder was summoned back in haste, and arrived on the field at five o'clock as the British appeared. He ordered a retreat. Every military reason required a retreat to Bladensburg. Winder directed a retreat on Washington by the navy-yard bridge" (8:135). But flowery language and more complex sentences appear as soon as Adams shifts to Winder's self-justification; the Latinate vocabulary introduced for a single sentence and the enclosure of four words in quotation marks preserve Adams's distance from the object of his distaste:

The reasons which actuated him to prefer the navy-yard to Bladensburg, as explained by him, consisted in anxiety for the safety of that "direct and important pass," which could not without hazard be left unguarded. In order to guard a bridge a quarter of a mile long over an impassable river covered by the guns of war-vessels and the navy-yard, he left unguarded the open high-road which led through Bladensburg directly to the Capitol and the White House. [8:135–6]

After each outburst into candor, the author reverts to a polite and fastidious language, as if he wished to avoid unnecessary contact with the loathsome creature: "By a quick march at dawn [of August 24] he might still have arrived . . . [at Bladensburg] with six hours to spare for arranging his defence. He preferred to wait till he should know with certainty that the British were on their way there" (8:136–7).

When on the morning of August 24 Winder requested the military counsel of the civilian leaders of the government, Adams's judgment lies disguised behind a solitary ambiguous adjective: "This singular note was carried first to the President" (8:137). The reader is left to make his own inference, and only seventeen pages later does the historian offer an explicit comment upon this transaction. Not once does the word *coward* pass Adams's lips, for the judgment falls harder when the reader supplies it himself. Trained as his father's secretary in the language of diplomacy, long exposed to the circumlocutions of diplomats like Madison, Canning, and Lord Wellesley, and deeply influenced by the usages of English society, Adams was thoroughly impregnated with the principle of indirection.[41]

In praise as in condemnation, Adams senses that indirect expression will heighten his effect. When in 1812 Madison appointed James Winchester of Tennessee to be a brigadier general, the historian comments that "Winchester, another old Revolutionary officer, originally from Maryland, though mild, generous, and rich, was not the best choice that might have been made from Tennessee" (6:292). This remark, not explained for a moment, is his early tribute to Andrew Jackson's military capacity. But the spirit of criticism burns more brightly in Adams's breast than the impulse to laud, and indirection normally masks quiet thrusts at the foibles of his countrymen: General Dearborn "submitted to the Secretary of War what was called a plan of campaign" (6:297). "A people that could feel its vanity flattered by such glories as the war gave in 1813 must have felt the want of flattery to an unusual degree" (7:70).

An essential part of Adams's technique was that he sometimes argues against his own conviction; this is another aspect of his devotion to the indirect approach. When first discussing Madison's appointment of General Winder, a relation of the Federalist governor of Maryland, Adams offers an excuse for the president's blunder: "Political appointments were not necessarily bad" (8:122). Of Jefferson's view in 1801 that the United States did not need a strong navy to protect its commerce, the historian remarks blandly that "this reasoning had much in its favor" (2:330); and the Virginians' faith in gunboats as a substitute for heavier naval vessels prompts the allegation that "their theory was reasonable" (3:352). By withholding his own opinion, Adams forces the reader to think for himself.

This method disguises Adams's judgment upon the War of 1812. Frequently he adopts a belligerent tone toward Britain, yet when he discusses the Americans' position in autumn of 1812 his words are ambiguous. With a barb at the end of more than one clause and a profusion of "———; but ———" constructions, he declares that the experiment of fighting England in order to force her to renounce impressments was

worth trying, and after the timidity of the American government in past years was well suited to create national character, if it did not destroy the nation; but it was not the less hazardous in the face of sectional passions such as existed in New England, or in the hands of a party which held power by virtue of Jefferson's principles. That the British government should expressly renounce its claim to impressment was already an idea hardly worth entertaining; but if the war could not produce that result, it might at least develop a government strong enough to attain the same result at some future time. If a strong government was desired, any foreign war, without regard to its object, might be good policy, if not good morals; and in that sense President Madison's war was the boldest and most successful of all experiments in American statesmanship, though it was also among the most reckless; but only with difficulty could history offer a better example of its processes than when it showed Madison, Gallatin, Macon, Monroe, and Jefferson joining to create a mercenary army and a great national debt, for no other attainable object than that which had guided Alexander Hamilton and the Federalists toward the establishment of a strong government fifteen years before. [6:417–18]

This passionate delight in the irony of events, this sense of the futility of human efforts, is the best-known feature of Adams's mind. He carries matters to irritating lengths in passages of his autobiography, blaming the world and calling attention to himself: "Wherever else he might, in the infinities of space and time, seek for education, it should not be again in Berlin. . . . His attempt at education in treason . . . , like all the rest, disastrously failed."[42] But in the *History* his sense of the world's refractoriness is objective and usually is constrained within reasonable bounds. At the moment in 1812 that Congress declared war upon Britain, "chaos" seemed to him "beyond control. War with England was about to restore commerce with her; alliance with France was a state of war with her. The war party proposed to depend on peace taxes at the cost of France their ally, in the interests of England their enemy; the peace party called for war taxes to discredit the war; both parties wanted trade with England with whom they were at war; while every one was displeased with the necessity of assisting France, the only ally that America possessed in the world" (6:231). This passage, mingling humor with despair, as in the mad scenes of *Lear*, was written after Marian's death; but Adams discovered his most vivid figure of the world's confusion before she died. The insurrection of Madrid against French rule in 1808, he declares,

swept the vast Spanish empire into the vortex of dissolution. . . . Spain, France, Germany, England, were swept into a vast and bloody torrent which dragged America, from Montreal to Valparaiso, slowly into its movement; while the familiar figures of famous men,—Napoleon, Alexander, Canning, Godoy, Jefferson, Madison, Talleyrand; emperors, generals, presidents, conspirators, patriots, tyrants, and martyrs by the thousand,—were borne away by the stream, each blind to everything but a selfish interest, and all helping more or less unconsciously to reach the new level which society was obliged to seek. [4:300–302]

If human action and judgment were thus weak in the presence of powerful subterranean currents, philosophy joined good manners and diplomatic policy in suggesting discretion to the artist. Adams conscientiously believed the author should keep himself in the background. "As a point of literary form," he once hectored his younger brother, "I should first try to appear master of my own temper."[43] Yet the principle of indirection warred with Adams's nature, deep and caustic as it was, whose expression could not always be confined within diplomatic limits. The principal American generals and politicians of 1812 fare ill: By November 1812 "Napoleon, though supposed to be dictating peace at Moscow, was actually in full retreat. Every hope of the war party had already proved mistaken. Canada was not in their hands; no army had been enlisted; the people were less united than ever; taxation and debt could no longer be avoided; and military disgrace had been incurred beyond the predictions of John Randolph and Josiah Quincy" (6:412).

Indignant outbursts like this one, which gain force in contrast with Adams's usually restrained language, are produced by his loyalty to the American republican experiment, disgraced by the Republic's incompetent servants. Yet not the least memorable of Adams's explosions was fired by his loyalty to the ideals of the Civil War. In 1806 the Jeffersonian party enacted a total prohibition of American trade with the blacks of Santo Domingo—a ban sure to please Bonaparte, from whose rule Santo Domingo had revolted. Adams denies that Jefferson and Madison were led by French sympathies, and he attributes their action partly to the conviction that Napoleon "alone could give Florida to the United States without the expense and losses inevitable in a war" (3:140). Once again the craftsman lavishes his varied arts upon a disenchanted recreation of America's history: The act prohibiting trade with Santo Domingo,

taken in all its relations, might claim distinction among the most disgraceful statutes ever enacted by the United States government. Nevertheless, this measure, which bore on its face the birth-mark of Napoleonic features, did in fact owe its existence chiefly to a different parentage. In truth, the Southern States dreaded the rebel negroes of Hayti more than they feared Napoleon. . . . The opportunity to declare the negroes of Hayti enemies of the human race was too tempting to be rejected; and not only did the Southern Republicans eagerly seize it, but they persuaded their Northern allies to support them. John Randolph himself, though then wearying the House day after day with cries that Madison had sold the honor of the United States to France, never alluded to this act of subservience, which would have made any other Administration infamous. [3:142]

A history, no less than *Anna Karenina*—a different distillation of experience—may be a work of art, but no historian to equal the best novelists has yet lived. Adams's *History* lacks the richness of human sympathy necessary to the greatest literature, and it subordinates insufficiently its fine details to a compelling central theme. But no other writer—not Macaulay, nor Gibbon either—has wrestled wholly successfully with the problem of bringing a veracious history into artistic form. Adams cherished the ideal and, preeminently among historians of the United States, he developed such imaginative power and such mastery of the writer's craft as to transform his story into an impressive work of art. His accomplishment is comparable to Henry James's in the most carefully wrought works of that author's middle period, and the method not dissimilar. If one day historians should conceive their calling as something beyond scientific reporting and interpretation—if they should accept again the challenge of combining historical science with literary art—Adams's *History* may suggest something of that "unattainable standard" upon which every great artist has fixed his eye.[44]

CHAPTER 6 · *History as Science*

IF ADAMS aspired to art, he aimed also at accurate reporting and skillful interpretation, and an estimate of his stature requires assessment of his success in
these latter endeavors. He originally intended to write a diplomatic history
of the United States from 1801 to 1815. Although he soon extended his plan,
his account of American-English relations, culminating in the War of 1812,
remained at the center of his *History*. But the internal division of America
during this war (the disaffection of New England from the war which most
of the rest of the country supported) was only one aspect of the wider conflict
between Federalists and Jeffersonians, and this conflict supplied Adams with
his second great theme. The *History* was unrivaled, for two-thirds of a century, as the principal narrative of American affairs during the administrations of Jefferson and Madison. Adams's scholarship and intelligence deterred
more than one able historian, like Edward Channing, from undertaking research in this field. Several biographies and monographs challenged certain
of Adams's assertions, but a cycle of reinterpretations of the War of 1812
returned eventually to points not far distant from those of Adams himself.
At the same time, historians' attitudes toward Jefferson and Madison shifted
dramatically, without producing a major piece of research to undermine
Adams's view of their presidencies. The phenomenon was unique in the
historiography of the United States: No other piece of nineteenth-century
research lived so lustily far into the succeeding century, neither Palfrey's *New
England* nor Bancroft's colonial history nor Rhodes's Civil War nor the forgotten works of Hildreth, Schouler, and McMaster.

But after 1955 the tide seemed to turn. A major diplomatic history of
Adams's period, and several important biographies, appeared. A host of writers flooded the field with specialized monographs, and by 1968 the author of
a reputable survey alleged that the *History* was now outdated as a source of
historical knowledge.

Yet a glance at four recent studies suggests that Adams's work is not superseded. The most authoritative modern diplomatic history of the era is Bradford Perkins's three-volume analysis of British-American relations from 1795 to 1823.[1] This scholar's painstaking research supports almost every one of Adams's theses on the origins of the War of 1812. Like Adams, Perkins declares that in England "encouragement was too little needed, to act almost as though Lord Cornwallis had won the battle of Yorktown."[2] Perkins is equally plain about the nature of British commercial aggression: The Orders in Council of November 1807 took a "nakedly selfish form . . . , with their almost open purpose of gaining for Britain a near monopoly of trade with the Continent."[3] Perkins also shares Adams's low estimate of American strategy: "The policies of Jefferson and . . . [Madison] had convinced England that she need not fear war. . . . [Jefferson and Madison] secured not one important diplomatic objective after 1803. . . . In a state of military and psychological unpreparedness, the United States of America embarked upon a [nearly ruinous] war to recover the self-respect destroyed by Republican leaders."[4] Perkins concurs in Adams's judgment that the embargo was a failure: Although the embargo "was, of course, felt by the belligerents, it proved far more harmful to America, economically and morally, and served chiefly to convince Europe of the cowardice of the United States." Perkins acknowledges that his own harsh verdict on Jefferson's handling of the embargo bill "coincides, except in shading, with the excoriation of Jefferson in Henry Adams, *History*."[5] Finally, the twentieth-century historian is no less severe than his predecessor toward the diplomatic tactics of the Jeffersonians. Perkins confirms Jefferson's mismanagement of the *Chesapeake* affair;[6] he agrees with Adams that in 1810 Madison's "policy, by reinforcing the plausibility of Federalist claims that he was a minion of France, led to disunity of the most dangerous kind";[7] and he is caustic about the change in American war aims in 1812.[8]

The remarkable correspondence between the views of the two historians cannot be attributed to hero worship. While quoting occasionally one of what he calls Henry Adams's "many brilliant passages,"[9] Perkins criticizes unsparingly what he takes to be the shortcomings of the *History*: "Adams is bitterly and sometimes unfairly anti-Jefferson." "He did not and could not examine a number of important sources [on the British repeal of their commercial regulations]. . . . As Irving Brant has shown, [Adams] is not above shading the evidence in a fashion modern historians would consider improper. . . . His attitude toward England is colored with the nationalism of the period in which he wrote. . . . [He fell into] extremely lengthy quotations and paraphrases."[10] Nor can Perkins be accused of lacking originality. His proof that Americans in 1812 regarded Canada primarily as a stick with which to beat Britain, rather than as valuable territory to be conquered for its own sake, and his dissection of the reasons Parliament that year repealed its attack upon America's trade with Europe—these are only two among numerous instances of Perkins's independence of judgment. Historians are not famed for exaggerating the achievements of their forerunners, and the correspondence between Adams's interpretations and those of this twentieth-century scholar is strong confirmation of the reliability of much of the *History*.

The principal disagreement between Adams and Perkins lies in their assessment of British motives. Perkins's kindliness toward certain British leaders helps to illuminate the period before 1805 but is less convincing thereafter. He rightly stresses the psychology of America's efforts to retain national self-respect, yet he undervalues another psychological factor—Britain's overweening sense of superiority during the nineteenth century. Visiting England in the 1950s when Britain's self-confidence and its superciliousness toward America were waning, and writing at a moment when American liberals were impelled to counter the Anglophobia of McCarthyites and the Chicago *Tribune*, Perkins seems to have projected upon British rulers of the early nineteenth century an unhistorical mildness of temper. Adams's London experiences in the 1860s had prepared him to see the Cannings and Percevals in a truer light.

While Perkins may not be an entirely reliable guide to the force of British contempt for America, he corrects and supplements Adams on a host of specific matters.[11] The most important is his demolition of Adams's claim that the American war threat, early in 1812, was the cause for Britain's repealing her Orders in Council.

Adams asks himself above all, What lessons can a student of diplomacy learn from the era? rather than What caused the War of 1812?; consequently his attention to nuances of diplomatic exchanges is sharper than that of Perkins, but his answer to the latter question—while remarkably similar to Perkins's—is not so clearly stated. Adams is the more imaginative writer—his figure of an angry bull conveys at a stroke the idea behind Perkins's chapter entitled "Beleaguered Britain."[12] Adams's diplomatic narrative profits by being set against a rich background of political and military events; his pungent characterization of Perceval and Canning is incomparable; and his devastating judgments upon both Republicans and Federalists challenge national self-complacency. Perkins's excellent volumes by no means supersede Adams's *History*, and they constitute the strongest tribute from a recent historian to the continuing vitality of that work.

A provocative effort at rehabilitating the New England Federalists, whose hesitant steps toward secession stirred Adams's hostility, appears in James Banner's *To the Hartford Convention*. This study of Massachusetts supplements the *History* at many points and, more than Perkins's volumes, forces important changes of interpretation. Yet Banner's central theses remain open to question. The Federalists' most significant characteristic, in his judgment, was their allegiance to republicanism, and he gives credit to George Cabot and Harrison Gray Otis as skillful thwarters of the disunionist passions of New Englanders. A striking feature of Banner's work is the apparent discrepancy between these theses and the evidence he amasses, much of which supports Adams's interpretations. Some of it even suggests that Adams understates his case.

Banner explores the Federalists' allegiance to what they supposed the ideals of the American Revolution, but eventually he acknowledges that, as Adams had argued, the Federalist party system was formed "to confront and turn back the tide of democracy."[13] While Banner denies that most Federalist leaders sought secession, he shows that the pressure for a convention like that of 1814 was already even stronger in 1812 than Adams knew. He admits that the Federalist governor of Massachusetts sent a secret agent to Canada during wartime to inquire about terms for a separate armistice.[14] He concedes that if the national government had refused the disintegrative demand of the Hartford Convention, there would have been a second convention: It "would probably . . . either have declared New England neutral for the duration of the war . . . , or have made a separate peace with England."[15]

If Banner's evidence thus confirms to a considerable extent Adams's interpretation of the New England secession movement, a major disagreement nevertheless separates the two historians in their attitude toward Cabot and Otis. To Adams, Otis was a trimmer whose flirtation with secessionism threatened to lead him to a result he publicly deprecated; to Banner, Otis was a skilled manipulator who channeled popular disunionism into harmless courses. Perhaps this disagreement is more a matter of judgment than of evidence, but not every observer will be persuaded that Adams's verdict is too severe.

Banner's achievement, and it is a substantial one, lies not in destroying Adams's conclusions but in supplementing and slightly amending them. He makes Federalist leaders seem more like normal human beings than does Adams, less like eccentrics. Federalists, Banner shows, deplored the spirit of democracy yet quickly adapted themselves to democratic party practices. The caution of men like Otis was inspired by a greater wish to avoid civil war, a greater reluctance to divide the union, and a greater wish to temper popular extremism than Adams acknowledges.

After accepting each of these points of Banner's, most historians probably will nevertheless conclude that the New England secession movement sprang from conservative alarm at the progress of democracy and that most Federalist leaders, unlike Samuel Dexter, were timid in dealing with the maneuverings of Pickering and his ilk. Adams's *History*, in its vivid portrayal of conservative alarms and in its sophisticated exposure both of the secessionists and their less extreme Federalist colleagues, remains an arresting account of that movement. Undoubtedly the great caution of most Federalist leaders contributed to the fact that the crises ended before the secessionists could achieve their goal. But even Banner grants that the Hartford Convention's "only enduring bequest . . . [was that] it nationalized the doctrine of inter-position and in so doing gave it a legitimacy which it had lacked before."[16]

The most influential attack upon Adams's *History* has come from the biographer of James Madison, Irving Brant, whose defense of this circumspect yet sometimes surprisingly incautious politician occupies six volumes.[17] Time after time Brant assaults Adams's scholarship, and he has persuaded some readers that the *History* is not to be trusted.

Adams's errors, as detailed by Brant, include a number readily pardoned, and a few less easily excused. Sometimes he mistranslated French. For example, he translated literally the French minister's report of a meeting with President Madison, "J'ai cherché ses yeux, et . . . les ai rencontrés. . . . Il était dans un abattement extraordinaire"; and thus he betrayed a serious misunderstanding of what the minister was actually asserting.[18] Adams also failed to discover that the dates which appear on certain primary sources were erroneous. This happened with the letter just mentioned, which the French minister dated incorrectly. Another example of Brant's admirable detective work is his proof that a later French dispatch, headed June 14, 1809, must in fact have been written on June 4.[19]

Adams sometimes left out significant evidence of whose existence he was certainly aware. Thus he omitted to mention Gallatin's suggestion that Jefferson had talked indiscreetly to the French minister of acquiring Florida and Cuba.[20] On other occasions he failed to use evidence that ought to have been known to him. For example, Adams overlooked an article in the *National Intelligencer* that exposed the statistical unsoundness of certain charges made by John Randolph, charges Adams accepted at face value.[21] Finally, he sometimes gave credence to evidence that other sources suggest to be unreliable. Thus Adams believed the report that, twenty-four hours after the burning of the White House, renewed alarm about the British forces "drove Madison from his bed for refuge in the Virginia woods."[22]

Adams was pessimistically conscious of the pitfalls that surround the most conscientious historical investigator, and he implied, with characteristic hyperbole, that probably there were about 20,000 factual errors in his own work:

The historian can hardly expect that four out of five of his statements shall be exact. . . . [He] can only wait in silent hope that no one will read him,—at least with too much attention. He knows the worst. He has taken some patriot at his own estimate, and condemned some traitor at the estimate of the patriot! He has misread some document, adding his own blunder to the deception intended by the author of the document! He has accepted, as authority, an official statement, made, for once, without intent to deceive; and thus, thrown off his guard by the evident absence of dishonest intention, he has fallen into the blunder of taking a government at its own low estimate of itself.[23]

Brant and others have in fact discovered dozens of factual errors in the *History*, and dozens more doubtless remain to be found. Most of these resulted simply from the pressure of collecting, with the help of fallible copyists, interpreting, and bringing into artistic shape a prodigious volume of original material. Adams's research stands up reasonably well to examination, considering how much new material he uncovered and how little he could depend upon the research of other scholars.

Yet Adams's errors do not occur at random—they often work to the disadvantage of the principal Jeffersonians. Brant is rather free in his implications and accusations that Adams deliberately twisted evidence,[24] but there can be no doubt that Adams's impatience with Jefferson and Madison caused him unconsciously to select, omit, mistranslate, or distort a considerable number of pieces of evidence. Although he labored endlessly to attenuate his judgments of what he believed the Virginians' political blunders, his impatience was certain to mar his scholarship. "To do justice to Gallatin," Adams explained in 1883 to a leading Democrat,

was a labor of love. . . . For combination of ability, integrity, knowledge, unselfishness, and social fitness Mr. Gallatin has no equal. He was the most fully and perfectly equipped statesman we can show. . . . [But in regard to Jefferson, Madison, and Monroe] I am incessantly forced to devise excuses and apologies or to admit that no excuse will avail. . . . There is no possibility of reconciling their theories with their acts, or their extraordinary foreign policy with dignity.[25]

Although he usually suppressed his antipathy toward British Tories and New England Federalists, he could not control his distaste for the Virginians.

Part of the explanation was that southerners remained alien to him in a way that New Englanders could never be, nor Britons after his years of residence in England. To be sure, Adams admired George Washington and John Marshall, but these Virginians, he believed, had conferred dignity and strength upon the American Union. He also praised the "severe beauty of George Mason's Virginia Bill of Rights." He felt a sensual attraction to the "thickness of foliage and the heavy smells . . . , the sense of atmosphere . . . , and the brooding indolence" of the South, and he imagined that his feeling caught onto an inheritance from the Maryland family of his grandmother.[26] But Robert E. Lee's son at Harvard was forever incomprehensible to Adams; and in 1862, thinking of the Civil War as a battle against aristocratic principles, Adams had considered his planned first historical article, "Captain John Smith," to be a "rear attack on the Virginia aristocracy. . . . I can imagine to myself the shade of John Randolf turn green."[27] In Washington, a southern town, Adams attempted to overcome his antipathy for southerners: He became familiar with Mississippi's Senator Lamar and with the son of President Zachary Taylor, and he disguised himself as a Virginian in *Democracy*.

But Adams's closest associates in Washington were always either northerners like King, Hay, MacVeagh, Hewitt, and Schurz or members of the foreign legations. The principals of *Democracy* were not the Virginian Carrington but characters modeled after northerners—after Clover and Senator Blaine. Unfamiliarity doubtless contributed to Adams's alienation from the Virginians.

But there was a more profound reason for Adams's distaste: A sense of betrayal entered his feelings. From the British Tories and the New England conservatives he could distance himself, for they plainly were fighting a losing battle against the rise of democracy. Jefferson on the other hand stood "pre-eminent as the representative . . . of what is best in our national . . . aspirations." Tocqueville, whom Adams admired, had declared Jefferson "the most powerful advocate democracy has ever had."[28] Whatever doubts Adams entertained about the future of American democracy, he understood perfectly well—as he continually told his English friends—that America had progressed politically and socially far beyond the class-ridden societies of Europe. He knew that the proper place for liberal-minded Federalists was in the Jeffersonian party, away from conservatives like Pickering, Cabot, and Otis.[29] He proposed the Jeffersonian line against Lodge's Hamiltonianism when teaching at Harvard. The democratic movement obviously represented the side of progress, and Jefferson's leadership promised to ally it with the cause of science.

Jefferson and Madison, furthermore, might have been expected to supply the disinterested leadership that had become the Adams family ideal. Not dependent upon officeholding for their incomes like the machine politicians of the 1880s nor dependent upon the favor of State Street as Daniel Webster had later become, they should have been free to promote the interests of America's promising democratic republican experiment. Gallatin, the closest colleague of Jefferson and Madison in the Democratic Republican administrations, was to Adams almost wholly admirable, and Jefferson might have been equally so. He was not handicapped by "provincial barbarism" like the untraveled American politicians of the succeeding generation,[30] and his mind and character sufficiently resembled Adams's that sympathy might have developed between author and subject, as it had done with Gallatin.

Yet the Virginians, who had so much to offer, seemed to betray their trust. Their diplomatic mismanagement, Adams believed, led to a war that gained little and risked much; their decentralist theories, if practiced, would have reduced the national government to custodianship of foreign affairs; another principle of theirs, had it been put into effect, would have reduced the necessary independence of the judiciary; and they sacrificed American national dignity both by their ill-disguised lust for Florida and by their unrealistic theory of peaceable coercion. In Adams's view, the diplomatic heights were commanded by two bands of armed robbers, English and French, whose contempt for the Republic became the more dangerous as American policy

153

deviated from self-respect and strength: "Few men have dared to legislate as though eternal peace were at hand, in a world torn by wars and convulsions and drowned in blood; but this was what Jefferson aspired to do."[31]

Above all, the Virginians' "States-rights conservatism"[32] threatened the integrity of the Union. Adams believed that by 1800 "the United States had thus far made a single great step in advance of the Old World,—they had agreed to try the experiment of embracing half a continent in one republican system." Pride in his family's association with the American republican experiment increased his loyalty to it. In 1863, smarting under Englishmen's contempt for the American Union, Adams had felt the deepest political emotion of his life when the northern armies finally proved themselves:

With an intensity more painful than that of any Shakespearean drama, men's eyes were fastened on the armies in the field. Little by little . . . one began to feel that, somewhere behind the chaos in Washington power was taking shape; that it was massed and guided as it had not been before. . . .

Life never could know more than a single such climax. . . . As the first great blows began to fall, one curled up in bed in the silence of night, to listen with incredulous hope.

"Henry's feelings about the Civil War," his niece recalled, "were such that I have seen them flame into heat 40 years after." Jefferson's principle of nullification seemed to Adams the deadliest foe to his hope for the success of the American experiment. The Kentucky Resolutions had demonstrated that, to Jefferson, "Union was a question of expediency, not of obligation. . . . Calhoun was the true heir to . . . [Jefferson's] intellectual succession."[33] The democratic society of Pennsylvania and New York could not yet in 1800 have been expected to throw up its own trained statesmen to lead the American republic, but Adams lamented that the leadership had fallen by default to these well-meaning but devious, dangerous, and incompetent Virginia planters.

Some such conception seems to have constituted the "carefully concealed foundation of idea" that lay below the surface of the *History*.[34] Doubtless Adams's work betrays hints of family feeling against Jefferson: "I know nothing in [the expressions of Jefferson and his friends about John Adams]," Henry once wrote resentfully, "that should entitle Mr. Jefferson to more than simple justice,—at least from me."[35] But it would be an error to place the *History* in the filiopietistic tradition of memoir writing. Adams's brother, colleague, and admirer, Charles, launched one of the first onslaughts upon historical ancestor worship, and Henry was no blind admirer of his great-grandfather.[36] Jefferson, Adams confided to John Hay, "is a character of comedy. John Adams is a droll figure, and good for Sheridan's school, but T.J. is a case for Beaumarchàis; he needs the lightest of touches, and my hand is as heavy as his own sprightliness."[37] The historian's complicated feelings about John Quincy Adams should be sufficient warning against treating his work as the expression of an old family quarrel. The source of Adams's mistakes of bias is far less simple.[38]

The notorious Henry-Crillon affair of 1812 provides an excellent test of how far—or how little—Adams's passions and preconceptions distorted his writing. His account of this imbroglio was carefully restudied in 1910 by Samuel Eliot Morison, who sympathized with the New England Federalists;[39] and it has been reexamined by Madison's defender Irving Brant. Adams proves to have steered a cautious course between those later marked out by Morison and Brant—between Morison's vehement assault upon Madison and Brant's undiscriminating defense. Certain errors need to be corrected in Adams's account (one mistake redounding to the Federalists' disadvantage and one to Madison's),[40] but Adams's version is clearer and more succinct than Morison's, and more reliable than Brant's.[41]

To a generation, already passing, that idolized Jefferson, the most serious fault of the *History* has been Adams's lack of sympathy with the Virginia statesman. Obviously Adams sometimes failed to control his irritation with Jefferson, and critics have fixed upon his confession to a friend, as he wrote the *History*, that "Mr. Jefferson is feeling the knife."[42] Yet the New Englander was scrupulous in defending Jefferson from the Federalists' charge that he was under French influence,[43] and he understood full well that Jefferson was a born compromiser, far different from the dangerous fanatic conjured up in the imagination of New England clergymen. Indeed, as uncritical admiration of Jefferson fades, Adams's judgment seems more and more temperate. He rejected out of hand the claim that Jefferson had children by one of his slaves, but the possibility that this story is true has been suggested, with circumstantial supporting evidence, by an intelligent and influential modern historian.[44] The limits of the president's libertarianism are exposed in another recent study.[45] The policy of Jefferson's administration toward the Indians and toward the blacks of Haiti will certainly come under renewed scrutiny, and when this happens Adams will be found to have anticipated serious and well-founded criticisms of what Jefferson did or countenanced.[46] Some historians now stress the ideological similarities between Jeffersonians and Federalists, and Adams undoubtedly emphasized how little Jefferson's domestic policies, when he was president, differed from those of the two preceding presidents. But Adams understood, perhaps more clearly than some recent writers, that Jefferson could not be reduced to the figure of a mere clever pragmatic politician.

Adams's Jefferson is a man of great individuality who represented a peculiar blend of two important ideas: America's democratic aspiration and Southern parochialism. Adams never lets one forget that Jefferson aspired to philanthropy and to raising the status of the average man, nor that he wrote the Kentucky Resolutions, menacing to the future of the Union. Yet when Jefferson was in power his practices often contradicted his theories, as in his government of Louisiana and his Indian policy. According to Adams, Jefferson's administration of domestic affairs reverted in most respects to the principles of his two Federalist predecessors. The most original of his political ideas was his belief in exerting economic rather than military pressure upon the combatants of Europe, and this theory, to which he persistently clung, led in Adams's view to failure, throwing New England again into the hands of archconservatives and robbing Jefferson at the end of his presidency of the popularity he craved.

There are serious defects in Adams's interpretation. He seems to underestimate how important was Jefferson's reversal, at the national level, of the Federalists' narrow-minded policies toward immigrants and political dissenters. He does not acknowledge how far Jefferson's public utterances and his policy of financial retrenchment set an example that strengthened the states'-rights movement later in the century. He is probably too severe on Jefferson's propensity to compromise his principles and does not often enough admit that the president's conciliatory rule was vastly influential in making democratic ideas acceptable to the whole country. Adams's balancing, attenuating habit of mind, and his usually carefully-controlled irony are sometimes overwhelmed by heavy-handed sarcasm at the expense of Jefferson's rhetoric.[47]

Marshall Smelser's *The Democratic Republic, 1801–1815* helps to correct Adams's portrait of Jefferson. Smelser is the author who affirms that, as a source of historical knowledge, Adams's *History* has been "outdated by the prodigious labors of hundreds of scholars" whose findings he reports.[48] Yet doubts gnaw the reader's heart at Smelser's apparent reduction of Jefferson to a clever party manipulator, of colorlessly old-fashioned ideas and honorably pacific intent. Despite Smelser's words of admiration for Jefferson, he may unconsciously do less justice to the Virginian than did Adams. Smelser's Namier-like interest in the details of political management threatens to engulf the reader's awareness of the issues of principle that Adams believed to be at stake between conservative and democrat. The democratic ideas Jefferson expressed in personal letters were perhaps more important than Smelser acknowledges, for, passed on by word of mouth or in letters from his correspondents to other politicians, they exerted a wide influence within the constricted political community of the early nineteenth century. Stressing the similarities between Federalists and Republicans, Smelser treats the strategically placed Massachusetts Senator Timothy Pickering as "merely a figurehead" for younger and less conservative Federalists.[49] His impression is that Jefferson was less of a pacifist than his Federalist predecessors, but he does not underscore the major differences in their attitudes to England, which accounted for the conduct thus debatably interpreted. He seems persistently to underplay Jefferson's decentralist philosophy. The result is to deny Jefferson much of his individuality and to rob him of his stature as the representative both of his country's democratic aspirations and of his section's parochial conservatism. Adams's picture of Jefferson requires substantial retouching, but it appears in these respects a close likeness of the president.

This sketch of four recent studies, while exposing the faults and weaknesses of the *History*, may also suggest its strengths. Adams's principal interest was diplomatic history, and Perkins's exhaustive research has shown that in the field of British-American relations Adams's work was remarkably sound. The evidence produced in Banner's investigation of Massachusetts Federalists supports many of Adams's conclusions. More than any other scholar, Brant has demonstrated mistakes in Adams's reading of the evidence, yet his own errors of judgment create little confidence that the historical structure he builds is as solid as that whose weaknesses he detects. Adams's interpretation of Jefferson's domestic policy is open to substantial criticism, yet even here his work may reveal the truth about Jefferson as clearly as does Smelser's. Far from being outdated, the *History* remains the most impressive critique of Jeffersonian foreign policy ever written, while its narrative of domestic politics during the Jeffersonian era is rich in vivid detail and searching analysis.

In considering the political conflicts of American history, Adams's countrymen have tended to identify with one side or the other: Either they sympathize, like Parrington, with the "liberals," or they identify with the Federalist-Whig-conservative tradition, or they seek the roots of a radical heritage. But the independence of judgment bred into Adams by his family and his long years of looking at America with transatlantic eyes from England encouraged him to assess the weaknesses of both sides—of Federalists and Jeffersonian Republicans, of the British and of Americans—with rare clarity. The greatest strength of his historical work lies in his astringent judgment of all parties to a dispute. To a sympathizer with England like Perkins, Adams is too critical of British arrogance; to a defender of Massachusetts Federalists like Banner, Adams is too sharp with Cabot and Otis; to admirers of Madison and Jefferson, such as Brant and Smelser, Adams's censure of their heroes seems harsh. Measuring all sides with New England severity, Adams seldom errs in his criticism; his unsentimental consideration of America's past sets an example painfully rare in his own, or any other, country.

The construction of the *History* may be likened to that of a Gothic cathedral. The pillars upon which the edifice is erected are America's involvement with England, France, and Spain and the internal conflict of Jeffersonians versus Federalists. Adams's theme of the growth of democratic nationalism resembles the flying buttresses, helping at many points to support the structure yet set to the side and in a subordinate position. The determinist philosophy of the *History* is like the western rose window: prominent, yet only a detail in the whole construction. It is set among rows of statues covering the structure, the vignettes that attest to Adams's fascination with human personality: his vigorous protest against his own fatalist philosophy. The towers rising from the building, visible in the distance above everything else, are expressions of Adams's critical intelligence—the scientific objectivity with which he presents primary sources to his reader's scrutiny, and the severity with which he assesses mankind. The stained glass irradiating the structure with color is Adams's rich imagination, especially his coruscating spirit of satire.

Most of these architectural elements are familiar from preceding pages, and only a word need be said about the remainder. Adams shared the view of many other Americans in the nineteenth century (like Abraham Lincoln) that the cause of American nationalism was that of democracy and republicanism. Sympathizing with this cause, Adams observed how democratic nationalism had waxed during the Jeffersonian era despite obstructions placed in its way. By 1813, after a year of an apparently ruinous war, "the Federalists were greatly and naturally perplexed at discovering the silent under-current which tended to grow in strength precisely as it encountered most resistance from events." While applauding the effect of democracy in raising the average man, Adams feared that social progress might not transform itself into intellectual or moral progress, and he ended the *History* with the moralist's queries to democracy: "What interests were to vivify a society so vast and uniform? What ideals were to ennoble it? What object, besides physical content, must a democratic continent aspire to attain?" But while Adams, following his mentor Tocqueville, alluded frequently to the centralizing tendency of democracy, his principal concern was with high politics. His ideas about the popular movement—the "silent under-current"—of democratic nationalism were less fully developed, and less interesting, than his interpretations of foreign policy and of the conflict between Federalist and Jeffersonian politicians.[50]

Adams's determinist philosophy, or at least the language in which he clothed it, was influenced by Herbert Spencer, Darwin, and Auguste Comte. Spencer's and Darwin's most famous phrase appeared twice in the *History*, but Adams realized that his own practice as historian contradicted his fatalist theory: Governor William Henry Harrison's "account of Indian affairs offered an illustration of the law accepted by all historians in theory, but adopted by none in practice; which former ages called 'fate' . . . , but which modern science has refined into the 'survival of the fittest.' "[51] Spencer's scientific language also reappeared in Adams's image of American history flowing unconsciously, like water, toward equilibrium in a democratic ocean.[52] The young Adams was much affected by Comte,[53] and as early as 1863 he affirmed man's subjection to natural laws. "The laws which govern animated beings," he asserted rather self-consciously, "will be ultimately found to be at bottom the same with those which rule inanimate nature, and . . . I entertain a profound conviction of the littleness of our kind, and of the curious enormity of creation." In regard to the progress of the war "I have come out a full-blown fatalist." By the 1880s Adams had modified this philosophy by exaggerating the weakness of man—"human nature is but a reed shaken by a breeze"—and by substituting "perversity" for "enormity": "Illogical and perverse, society persisted in extending itself in lines which [to the Federalist mind] ran into chaos."[54]

But the younger Adams reveled in "chaos." In 1872, when he had just become engaged to Clover Hooper and when he believed his father had a good chance of becoming president, he exulted to Gaskell that "we are altogether in a chaotic condition." When he wrote the *History* he still found "chaos" a challenge—the function of statesmanship was to impose order upon political chaos, while the historian's role was to celebrate the dominion of disorderly nature over human affairs. If the world's perversity upset well-laid plans and mocked human understanding—"the 'crisis' [of 1813] produced the opposite effect to that which Burke's philosophy predicted"— Adams's tone in the *History* was often that of triumph at the world's incorrigibility.[55]

Adams felt as deeply as any Calvinist predestinarian the utility of human effort; no determinist philosophy clouded his perception that efficient leadership was vital to every enterprise. When his brother Charles invested some of Henry's funds in the Boston, Hartford and Erie Railroad, Henry wanted to know "one fact which to me seems the most important. . . . Who manages the undertaking? If well managed, it will succeed. If badly managed it will fail."[56] He was equally clear about the importance of good management in diplomacy, politics, and war. The determinist philosophy to which Adams occasionally gave eloquent voice was an attractive, but lesser and contradictory, element in the total structure of his *History*.[57]

More significant than Adams's explicit philosophizing was the critical spirit informing every page of his writing. From Germany he had learned the essential principles of scientific history: that the primary source was the foundation of all scholarship; that the reader as well as the historian must experience the primary source; and that the primary source must be torn, scratched, clawed, tapped, listened to, examined from every side—criticized—if it was to reveal its inner meaning.

Primary sources stare from nearly every paragraph of Adams's, and no one can read the *History* without receiving a lasting impression of the subtlety with which original sources can be interpreted and the sophistication with which they can be used to make a point vivid and persuasive. Adams does occasionally refer to a secondary source, but he never engages in a dispute with another historian, and he always offers a primary instead of a

secondary source if he possibly can do so. In a twenty-four page chapter he
may present fifteen long extracts from the primary sources, each about fifteen lines long, and infrequently an extract of forty lines will cover more
than a page of his text. This is the way that university instruction in German-
speaking countries sometimes was (and sometimes still is) conducted; the
original document itself is at the center of discussion, and all of the ingenuity
of the historian is lavished upon gleaning from it whatever it can be made to
yield. Adams's acquaintance with the English life-and-letters manner of
writing biographies—with H. A. Bruce's life of Sir William Napier[58] or perhaps with Mrs. Gaskell's life of Charlotte Brontë—nourished his tendency
to present long extracts, while his seven London years of analyzing diplomatic documents in the legation sharpened his ability to apply Germanic
method.[59]

This method tempts the author to require too much from his reader. The
writer's fascination with his material may blind him to the reader's rightful
impatience—his wish for clarity and conclusions at the expense of thoroughness. Adams was too demanding. Science here warred with art, and Adams
was more faithful to science than was good for his art. Yet if he applied
scientific principles too completely, the principles themselves were not mistaken; the prominence Adams gave to the original source was exemplary.[60]

His critical spirit showed itself also in his caustic analysis of political and
military leadership. It is possible that debacles after 1965, which to some
degree have shaken America's self-confidence, may cause Adams's severity
to become less uncongenial than formerly. Before Vietnam the United States
fought one other war whose disasters had few offsets—the White House and
the Capitol were burned, while the loyalty of New England was at risk—
and Adams's unillusioned analysis of the origins and conduct of the War of
1812 carries a wide significance. If the Jefferson and Madison administrations
were as ill-starred in diplomacy and war as Adams argued, if the leading
Federalists contributed as little as Adams believed to solving the problems
of the time,—if "incapacity in national politics . . . [appeared] as a leading
trait in American character"[61]—then American faith in the generation of the
Founding Fathers and in their less illustrious successors might be diminished. Adams regretted that in 1817 "the public seemed obstinate . . . in believing that all was for the best, as far as the United States were concerned,
in the affairs of mankind";[62] but a century and a half later a reaction against
early optimism began at length to appear. Yet Adams's was not the criticism
of a cynic or a nihilist. He found strength of character or high ability in men
so varied as Albert Gallatin, John Marshall, William Pinkney, Samuel Dexter, General Jacob Brown, and—after the enemy came within sight—General
Andrew Jackson; and he praised both the popular intelligence and the scientific training that often made themselves felt on the American side of the
war. Adams's severity makes a reader more confident in the merit of all that

could pass safely through his gauntlet. Although his tone was sometimes carping, Adams's critical spirit offered at its best a rigorous but just standard for evaluating America's past.

Beyond all these attributes, the *History* is filled with flashes of insight into the character of dozens of its protagonists,[63] lucid analysis of scores of episodes, and the building of thousands of details into a structure of rare excellence. There are nevertheless flaws in the construction of this great work, and after nearly a century it stands in need of substantial restoration. Certain of Adams's major contentions have been convincingly challenged; a vast quantity of supplementary detail has been discovered; and a multitude of factual errors are now evident. One possible remedy would be for a scholar to do for Adams's *History* what J. B. Bury seventy-five years ago did for Gibbon's: to produce an annotated edition of the original work. Such a person might place references at the foot of many pages, correcting, supplementing, or challenging the original text, without overburdening it in detail. Perhaps a historian or group of historians will one day restore in this way the most valuable contribution of any American to the writing of history.

PART III · *Stature*

CHAPTER 7 · *Macaulay and Gibbon*

NINETEENTH-CENTURY American writers are with hazard appraised by American standards. Henry James's merits and demerits become evident by placing him beside Thackeray and George Eliot, but perhaps not by comparing him to Fenimore Cooper or William Dean Howells. Adams's *History*—as he himself always wished—must be set not against those of Prescott and Parkman but against Macaulay's *History of England*, 1685–1702, and Gibbon's *Decline and Fall*. The procedure is excursive, but Adams's achievement can be defined, in its extent and its limits, in no other way.

Similar objects, examined, promptly evince their differences, and their individuality. The three histories prove no exception. At first glance Macaulay's *History* might appear to be the elder brother, or at least the first cousin, of Adams's. It covers a similar time span in much the same detail, and the literary method of its author has at points affected Adams's. Yet the spirit of the two works is sharply different. Gibbon's *Decline and Fall of the Roman Empire* was a more important influence upon Adams. But here, too, differences run deeper than might be suggested by simply contrasting Gibbon's twelve-century span with Adams's mere sixteen years.

When Adams thought of historical writing, he thought instinctively of Gibbon and Macaulay. Discussing with his publisher whether to distinguish the first chapters of his *History* as a separate introduction, Adams argued naturally from the example of his predecessors: "Gibbon ran his introductory chapters into his narrative, and Macaulay actually broke off his narrative to insert his introductory chapter." Macaulay was, to Adams, the outstanding British historian of the nineteenth century, and he sometimes read the Englishman afresh to whet his own style. He unconsciously associated the idea of a book's being interesting with Macaulay. Of Adams's own first four volumes he wrote to Gaskell, "I mean them to be readable. By the by, can you find out for me who is a man named Morison, who has written a very clever sketch of Macaulay?"[1]

But Adams's praise of the Morison biography suggested his own doubts about Macaulay. In criticizing the illustrious historian, Morison followed a circuitous route: "There are writers . . . whose merit consists neither in profound originality nor special flavour, but in a general wide eloquence and power, coupled with a certain commonplaceness of thought, of whom Cicero may be taken as the supreme type. . . . Macaulay . . . has a certain distant resemblance to Cicero."[2] Morison commended Macaulay for making history as interesting as a novel, but demurred at his prolixity, present-mindedness, and lack of general ideas. Adams, at the age of nineteen, had already implied that Macaulay was much less substantial than Gibbon;[3] and when in old age he alluded to Macaulay, his circumlocution rivaled Morison's. Like Morison, Adams objected to the lack of general ideas in Macaulay, and he also queried Macaulay's style. The whole of British historical writing in the nineteenth century, Adams claimed, was "antiquarianism or anecdotage, for no one except Buckle had tried to link it with ideas, and commonly Buckle was regarded as having failed. . . . Adams had the greatest admiration for Macaulay, but he felt that any one who should even distantly imitate Macaulay would perish in self-contempt. . . . Macaulay's method was more doubtful than the style."[4]

It was Gibbon, not Macaulay, for whom Adams felt genuine respect, and Gibbon was the historian who came to his mind as he completed his own *History*. When the last word of the narrative was written, Adams walked in his garden "in imitation of Gibbon."[5] Adams's too frequent references in the *Education* to his having sat in Rome, like Gibbon, "on the steps of the Church of Santa Maria di Ara Coeli"—and his protestation that "the thought of posing for a Gibbon never entered his mind"—smack of conceit; yet the experience at Rome in 1860 was bona fide and had proved decisive in Adams's life. When first in Rome the twenty-two-year-old American had been prompted to read the famous passage from Gibbon's *Autobiography* describing the moment when the idea of writing the *Decline and Fall* started to his mind: "I feel," Henry then wrote to his brother, "much as if perhaps some day I too might come to anchor like that."[6]

Adams sometimes read Gibbon for pleasure, as in the summer of 1869; he later goaded his wife into reading the *Decline and Fall*; and in the first chapter of the *History* he invited his reader—much more discreetly than in the *Education*—to measure his work against Gibbon's. Gibbon's prose style deeply affected Adams, but Adams also valued this "great man" for his humor, for "his vast study," for his "active mind," and for his raising large questions. Adams believed that America would one day become a great empire, as had Rome, and that the American experiment might fail as had the Roman and the Christian experiments. He was fascinated by the spectacle presented in Gibbon's pages. When Adams declared himself a child of the eighteenth century, he referred partly to his education to his father's eighteenth-century tastes and to his early reading of eighteenth-century historians in his father's library. Although Henry acquired a liking for some nineteenth-century writers, he avowed near the end of his life that it was Gibbon who had been his "idol."[7]

The ends to which Macaulay directed his mental powers lie open to dispute, but the magnitude of his talent, in certain directions, is not to be doubted. He was a rare storyteller. Lucidly and plausibly he interpreted the Revolution of 1688 and its aftermath, while his pages furnish a memorable record of the pieties of early Victorian England. The story of the escape of James II's infant child when William of Orange's Protestant army was approaching London from the west in December 1688 is told in abbreviated clauses as full of suspense as any adventure tale:

The night was bleak: the rain fell: the wind roared: the water was rough: at length the boat reached Lambeth; and the fugitives landed near an inn, where a coach and horses were in waiting. . . . Three Irish officers were also on board [the yacht at Gravesend]. These men had been sent thither in order that they might assist Lauzun in any desperate emergency; for it was thought not impossible that the captain of the ship might prove false; and it was fully determined that, on the first suspicion of treachery, he should be stabbed to the heart.[8]

Terse topic sentences urge the reader across the thicket of paragraphs, as pricks of the spur goad a hunter. "The Commissioners read and stood aghast" (p. 1063). "The gentry were not less refractory than the clergy" (p. 1064). The author organizes his materials with crystalline clarity. Having discussed the barriers to William of Orange's descent upon England, Macaulay wishes to show how the folly of James II and Louis XIV removed those barriers. He introduces the sections on James and Louis with painstaking care: "Not only was the King of England, as he had ever been, stupid and perverse: but even the counsel of the politic King of France was turned into foolishness. Whatever wisdom and energy could do William did. Those obstacles which no wisdom or energy could have overcome his enemies themselves studiously removed" (p. 1060). A dozen pages later, his discussion of James II completed, Macaulay recapitulates and turns to Louis XIV with a paragraph only one sentence long: "While James was thus raising against himself all those national feelings which, but for his own folly, might have saved his throne, Lewis was in another way exerting himself not less effectually to facilitate the enterprise which William meditated" (p. 1072).

Lucidity and simplicity of presentation are Macaulay's hallmark. He is capable of a nicely turned phrase: "Sidney, whose notions of a conscientious scruple were extremely vague" (p. 1053). And he sometimes fills out vivaciously the periods of an elegantly constructed sentence: "Such was his [John Wildman's] cunning that, though always plotting, though always known to

be plotting, and though long malignantly watched by a vindictive government, he eluded every danger, and died in his bed, after having seen two
generations of his accomplices die on the gallows" (p. 518). Seeking everywhere the picturesque, the author populates his pages with vivid scenes and
descriptions that make some of Henry Adams's passages seem pallid. Macaulay dwells on the pageantry when William's army enters Exeter:

The Dutch army, composed of men who had been born in various climates, . . .
presented an aspect at once grotesque, gorgeous, and terrible to islanders who had, in
general, a very indistinct notion of foreign countries. First rode Macclesfield at the
head of two hundred gentlemen, mostly of English blood, glittering in helmets and
cuirasses, and mounted on Flemish war horses. Each was attended by a negro,
brought from the sugar plantations of the coast of Guiana. The citizens of Exeter,
who had never seen so many specimens of the African race, gazed with wonder on
those black faces set off by embroidered turbans and white feathers. Then, with
drawn broadswords, came a squadron of Swedish horsemen in black armour and fur
cloaks. . . . Newsletters conveyed to every part of the kingdom fabulous accounts of
the size and strength of the invaders. It was affirmed that they were, with scarcely an
exception, above six feet high, and that they wielded such huge pikes, swords, and
muskets, as had never before been seen in England. . . . Much curiosity was excited
by a strange structure mounted on wheels. . . . But nothing caused so much astonishment as the bridge of boats. [Pp. 1132–36]

Small wonder that many Englishmen and Americans devoured this appetiz-
ing fare.

Macaulay praises the overthrow of James II as a "preserving" revolution,
just as many Americans have applauded the American Revolution as a conservative defense of established, customary rights against the encroachments
of another tyrannical British monarch. Macaulay holds that the Anglican
Church erred in preaching nonresistance in every case and in teaching "that
hereditary monarchy, alone among our institutions, was divine and invio-
lable" (p. 1308). He is persuasive in condemning James II and in lauding the
scope of William's policy, and his judgmen. is sometimes acute and independent, as in his discussion of Lord Grey's problems with his cavalry during
Monmouth's rebellion. He sometimes shows psychological penetration. Thus,
in accounting for George Savile Halifax's changing sides in 1688, he remarks
that Halifax was not the man to invite William to descend upon England:

His intellect was inexhaustibly fertile of distinctions and objections, his temper calm
and unadventurous.

. . . . .

The tendency of Halifax's mind was always to see the faults of his allies more
strongly than the faults of his opponents.

. . . . .

[But in December Halifax saw that an amicable arrangement between James and William was no longer possible.] He also felt, it may be suspected, the vexation natural to a man widely renowned for wisdom, who finds that he has been duped by an understanding [James II's] immeasurably inferior to his own, and the vexation natural to a great master of ridicule, who finds himself placed in a ridiculous situation. His judgment and his resentment alike induced him to relinquish the schemes of reconciliation on which he had hitherto been intent, and to place himself at the head of those who were bent on raising William to the throne. [Pp. 1050, 1188, 1220–21]

Macaulay's understanding of the world is considerable, his learning great, and his comparisons often illuminating.

Yet Macaulay's work is defective. His prose is riddled with conventional imagery and stereotyped phraseology; he often fails to use his sources to furnish reliable, individualized characters of his protagonists; and his pages are filled with obeisance to the established values of early Victorian England. While declaiming against the crude demagogue who inflames the passions of the mob, Macaulay verges on being the well-bred demagogue who woos the middle classes with complacent adulation of the status quo. His success with his reading public was in substantial measure a tribute to the conventionality of his mind and to the earnest, self-righteous tone with which he flattered the prejudices of his readers.

If Macaulay finds a word which, sparingly used, might lend variety to his text, he satiates the reader's appetite. The archaism "thither," used once in the story of the infant Prince of Wales's flight to Gravesend—"Three Irish officers . . . had been sent thither"—does no harm; but in the account of Monmouth's rebellion it becomes a cliché, contributing to Macaulay's maudlin account of the Duke's last moments. At the Tower of London the historian sighs for womankind:

Many of the chief inhabitants of . . . [Bristol] were Whigs. One of the ramifications of the Whig plot had extended thither.

. . . . .

[The rebels] hastened to Philip's Norton, where they halted on the evening of the twenty-sixth of June. Feversham followed them thither.

. . . . .

. . . In truth there is no sadder spot on the earth than that little cemetery [at St. Peter's Chapel in the Tower of London]. . . . Thither have been carried, through successive ages, by the rude hands of gaolers, without one mourner following, the bleeding relics of men who had been the captains of armies, the leaders of parties, the oracles of senates, and the ornaments of courts. Thither was borne, before the window where Jane Grey was praying, the mangled corpse of Guilford Dudley. . . . Here and there, among the thick graves of unquiet and aspiring statesmen, lie more delicate sufferers; Margaret of Salisbury, the last of the proud name of Plantagenet, and those two fair Queens who perished by the jealous rage of Henry. Such was the dust with which the dust of Monmouth mingled. [Pp. 586, 588, 620]

Conventional sentiment is one of Macaulay's stocks in trade: One of Feversham's officers "seized the unhappy maiden, refused to listen to her errand, and brutally outraged her. She fled in agonies of rage and shame" (p. 596). Besides women, there is another stimulus to devout expression: "The Saviour of mankind himself, in whose blameless life malice could find no act to impeach, had been called in question for words spoken. False witnesses had suppressed a syllable which would have made it clear that those words were figurative, and had thus furnished the Sanhedrim with a pretext under which the foulest of all judicial murders had been perpetrated" (pp. 573–74). When the time arrives for Macaulay to render judgment, religious principle proves consonant with manly virtue. The Duke of Monmouth, captured and facing execution, fails the test of a hero; centuries of English history contribute to the historian's expansive peroration:

And all was lost; and nothing remained but that he should prepare to meet death as became one who had thought himself not unworthy to wear the crown of William the Conqueror and of Richard the Lion-hearted, of the hero of Cressy and of the hero of Agincourt. . . . Within a hundred years, two sovereigns whose blood ran in his veins, one of them a delicate woman, had been placed in the same situation in which he now stood. They had shown, in the prison and on the scaffold, virtue of which, in the season of prosperity, they had seemed incapable, and had half redeemed great crimes and errors by enduring with Christian meekness and princely dignity all that victorious enemies could inflict. . . . [To Lady Wentworth] who had sacrificed everything for his sake he owed it so to bear himself that, though she might weep for him, she should not blush for him. [Pp. 608–9]

To Macaulay's sensibility, a device suited to oratory is likely to be equally appropriate to the written page. His characterization of James II's adviser the Earl of Sunderland—"The artful minister found that . . . , from the moment at which he began to counsel well, he began to counsel in vain" (p. 1019)—would doubtless sound well from the rostrum; but in print the turn of phrase appears facile. Macaulay's generalizations sometimes flatter the reader's sense of rectitude instead of challenging his intellect: "In every age the vilest specimens of human nature are to be found among the demagogues" (p. 576). Even when the historian grasps an interesting idea, he is likely to embellish it so elaborately—as though the reader were slow to comprehend—that it can become dull: "The prosecution of the Bishops . . . was the first and the last occasion on which two feelings of tremendous potency, two feelings which have generally been opposed to each other, and either of which, when strongly excited, has sufficed to convulse the state, were united in perfect harmony. Those feelings were love of the Church and love of freedom" (p. 1035).

Macaulay's analysis of the problems facing William of Orange as he meditates his descent upon England is lucid, yet even here things are stated twice for fear the auditor may have missed them the first time. The author is as immodest as a monograph writer in advertising the novelty of his own interpretations, but he is more certain of the epic qualities of his hero, who must surmount three different sets of obstacles:

> . . . Of all the difficulties with which he had to struggle, the greatest, *though little noticed by English historians*, arose from the constitution of the Batavian republic.
>
> . . . . .
>
> There was yet another difficulty *which has been too little noticed by English writers*. . . .
>
> Such were the complicated *difficulties* of this great undertaking. Continental *statesmen saw a part* of those *difficulties*, British *statesmen another part*. One *capacious and powerful* mind alone took them all in at one view, and determined to surmount them all. *It was no easy thing* to subvert the English government by means of a foreign army without galling the national pride of Englishmen. *It was no easy thing* to obtain from that Batavian faction which regarded France with partiality, and the House of Orange with aversion, a decision in favour of an expedition which would confound all the schemes of France, and raise the House of Orange to the height of greatness. *It was no easy thing* to lead enthusiastic Protestants on a crusade against Popery with the good wishes of almost all Popish governments and of the Pope himself. Yet *all these things William* effected. *All his objects*, even those which appeared most incompatible with each other, *he attained completely and at once*. The whole history *of ancient and of modern* times records no other such triumph of statesmanship. [Pp. 1057, 1060][9]

Each phrase—"completely and at once"—is amplified for maximum resonance, and parallel construction perhaps runs out of hand. William of Orange, when but a child, already spurs Macaulay's propensity toward an orotund rhetoric: "With *strong natural sense, and rare force of will*, he found himself, when first his mind began to open, a *fatherless and motherless* child, the chief of a *great but depressed and disheartened* party, and the heir to *vast and indefinite* pretensions, which excited the *dread and aversion* of the oligarchy then supreme in the United Provinces" (pp. 811–12).[10] This sentence might perhaps stand on its own, but the mannerism soon becomes familiar: "And yet this revolution, of all revolutions the least violent, has been of all revolutions the most beneficent" (p. 1310). Anthony Hamilton "became the chronicler of that brilliant and dissolute society of which he had been not the least brilliant nor the least dissolute member" (p. 1450). Macaulay's imagery and phraseology do not always vibrate with fresh life: "Already that dawn which had lately been so bright was overcast; and many signs portended a dark and stormy day" (p. 1314). The statuesque figures of the bishops who resisted

James II risk losing their individuality as they play out their prescribed roles in Macaulay's epic: "Meanwhile several of the Bishops were *anxiously deliberating* as to the course which they should take. . . . A *grave and learned* company was assembled. . . . a *zealous and uncompromising* friend of the Church. . . . inferior to none of his brethren *in courage and in zeal* for the common cause of his order. . . . On the following day came *the excellent Ken*, Bishop of Bath and Wells . . . and Sir John Trelawney, Bishop of Bristol, a baronet of *an old and honourable* Cornish family" (pp. 994–96).[11]

The danger of individuals being reduced to puppets upon Macaulay's stage is increased by his method of employing primary sources. When Lord John Churchill and others deserted James II and the royal army retreated from Salisbury, the king consulted his principal advisers in London. They recommended that he offer the rebels amnesty. "You talk wholly about other people's safety, and say nothing of my own," replied James, according to the Dutch ambassador's dispatch, which Macaulay cites.[12] But this language is not colorful enough, so the author translates the Dutch report of James's words to suit his sense of what such a monarch ought to have said: "My Lords, you are strangely anxious for the safety of traitors. None of you troubles himself about my safety" (p. 1169). Rarely do Macaulay's sources furnish even a direct quotation like this one; in their absence he invents one conversation after another, transposing the indirect discourse of his sources into factitious direct quotations, freely embellished by his own imagination.

This procedure creates a specious sense of immediacy, but when Macaulay could supply the reader with an authentic quotation from a primary source, he normally prefers to paraphrase it. "The difference between . . . [Monmouth's] expedition of 1685 and the expedition of 1688," the author justly observes, "was sufficiently marked by the difference between the manifestoes which the leaders of those expeditions published" (p. 1103); yet he offers no quotation from either manifesto to heighten the sense of this difference. Monmouth's declaration, we are told, was "set forth in the prolix and inflated style of a bad pamphlet" (p. 564), but we do not see for ourselves. Monmouth's craven letter to James II, begging for his life; James II's second Declaration of Indulgence; the petition of the seven bishops; the invitation to William of Orange to come to England, signed in cipher by seven temporal and spiritual leaders—parts of these famous documents might be quoted to give the reader a genuine experience of events and characters, but in none of these cases does Macaulay do so. Instead of trusting the reader to read primary sources for himself, he fobs him off with counterfeit conversations.

Certain views with which Macaulay disagrees—such as Filmer's justification of the course of Archbishop Sancroft—the historian states fairly, but his treatment of seventeenth-century Irish Catholics is unbalanced. Hearsay evidence is treated as though fact, and hyperbole races unchecked:

The Celtic population . . . , finding themselves suddenly transformed from slaves into masters, were impatient to pay back, with accumulated usury, the heavy debts of injuries and insults. The new soldiers, it was said, never passed an Englishman without cursing him and calling him by some foul name. They were the terror of every Protestant innkeeper; for, from the moment when they came under his roof, they ate and drank everything: they paid for nothing; and by their rude swaggering they scared more respectable guests from his door.*

*. . . I cannot find that Charles Leslie, who was zealous on the other side, has, in his Answer to King, contradicted any of these facts. [Pp. 1430–31]

Macaulay declares at the beginning of this passage that the Catholics "had long suffered oppression"; and sometimes he acknowledges the sufferings of Irishmen under English rule—or at least the sufferings of the dispossessed Irish landowners: A beneficent government, he thinks, would have alleviated "by a judicious liberality the misfortunes of the ancient gentry" (p. 1431). But behind a powder of fair-mindedness his narrative is covered with the pock marks of racial, religious, and class contempt. Macaulay's words might be those of an anti-Negro historian depicting the disorder of America's post– Civil War South, when the proper relations of society were inverted and the passions of supposed savages stimulated against their betters. Cobblers and tailors displaced gentlemen; an inferior race rose in insurrection against the superior Anglo-Saxons; men with outlandish accents threatened civilization:

> . . . A Roman Catholic who had never distinguished himself at the bar except by his brogue and his blunders, was Chief Justice of the King's Bench. . . . [Some of the new Aldermen and Sheriffs] had been servants to Protestants; and the Protestants added, with bitter scorn, that it was fortunate for the country when this was the case; for that a menial who had cleaned the plate and rubbed down the horse of an English gentleman might pass for a civilised being, when compared with many of the native aristocracy whose lives had been spent in coshering or marauding.
>
> . . . . .
>
> . . . [Tyrconnel] had with little difficulty stimulated the ignorant and susceptible Irish to fury. . . . Many companies [in the Irish army] were commanded by cobblers, tailors, and footmen.
>
> . . . . .
>
> . . . Whatever was bravest and most truehearted in Leinster took the road to Londonderry.
>
> . . . . .
>
> . . . The English inhabitants of Ireland . . . spoke English with remarkable purity and correctness. [Pp. 1429–30, 1450, 1452, 1457, 1484]

This travesty of objectivity may be contrasted, both in tone and content, with Henry Adams's evenhanded account of the relations between two other hostile groups, the American whites and the Indians. Adams treats the whites severely, but does not sentimentalize the Indians:

> . . . The practice [by whites] of hunting on Indian lands, in violation of law and existing treaties, had grown into a monstrous abuse. . . .
> . . . Harrison reported that contact with white settlements never failed to ruin [the Indians]. . . . Their drunkenness so often ended in murder that among three of the tribes scarcely a chief survived.
>
> . . . . .
>
> By treaty, if an Indian killed a white man the tribe was bound to surrender the murderer for trial by American law; while if a white man killed an Indian, the murderer was also to be tried by a white jury. The Indians surrendered their murderers, and white juries at Vincennes hung them without scruple; but no jury in the territory ever convicted a white man of murdering an Indian.[13]

Macaulay's chapters on Ireland are his least trustworthy, but the pungent class attitudes and the seasoning of rectitude there served up garnish the whole work. His strategy is to intone, with sobriety, that the whole English "nation" supports—and that it did in the glorious past support—that particular combination of aristocratic and middle-class values to which he himself pays homage. The Revolution of 1688 is tamed and domesticated: Based as it was on the principles inherent in "our ancient and noble statutes," it was "strictly defensive, and had prescription and legitimacy on its side" (p. 1306). When the nation turned against James II, it effected England's final revolution. People of property can slumber undisturbed by fears of anarchy, Macaulay protests, for no revolution will ever be needed again. The settlement of 1689 laid the foundation for all necessary future reforms. Every right-minded person believes this: "In all honest and reflecting minds there is [now] a conviction that the means of effecting every improvement which the constitution requires may be found within the constitution itself" (p. 1311). To establish this state of affairs, the nation rose in its majesty in 1688, each class of society acknowledging its due order within the social hierarchy.

The values, to defend which the nation then united, included no breath of egalitarianism, no hint of universal suffrage: At the convention of 1689, Macaulay exults, "the assertors of liberty said not a word about the natural equality of men and the inalienable sovereignty of the people." Almost every word and act of the Revolution exhibited, instead, "a profound reverence for the past" (p. 1310). The nation thoroughly understood the value of good blood: "The people of Cornwall, a fierce, bold, and athletic race . . . were greatly moved by the danger of Trelawney [Bishop of Bristol], whom they reverenced less as a ruler of the Church than as the head of an honourable house, and the heir through twenty descents of ancestors who had been of great note before the Normans had set foot on English ground" (p. 1018). Macaulay himself acknowledges the claims of aristocracy,[14] and his tone is grave when he touches religion. Sunderland resolved "to recover the royal confidence, by an act which, to a mind impressed with the importance of religious truth, must have appeared to be one of the most flagitious of crimes" (p. 1019). A church is not a "church," it is a "house of God"; an aristocratic woman is "a daughter of the noble house of Berkeley"; elderly bishops are "divines of venerable age and dignity" (pp. 1184, 522, 1018); and in this pageant there is no flicker of humor. Macaulay never laughs, scarcely ever smiles, and had he been American, he might have been taken by Englishmen to illustrate the earnestness of his compatriots.

Alarmed by the revolutions of 1848—especially in highly civilized countries like France and Germany—Macaulay was frank that property rights were ultimately more valuable than liberty, for upon them "civilization" was grounded. Historical research and horror of socialism fused into a homogeneous alloy. He was creating for nineteenth-century England a myth of its past, to be celebrated in a burst of national unity as his countrymen rejoiced in a heritage unlike that of any other nation on earth. "Here, and here only, a limited monarchy of the thirteenth century had come down unimpaired to the seventeenth century" (p. 1306); and during that century giants had walked upon the earth: "There was no place for a lowminded agitator . . . among the grave statesmen and generals who partook the cares of the resolute and sagacious William" (p. 1103). The seventeenth century's great achievements had guaranteed that in 1848 England—"a loyal nation, rallied in firm array round a parental throne" (p. 1312)—would enjoy order amidst European anarchy. Macaulay penned his most famous peroration in November 1848, inveighing against democratic and socialist doctrines promulgated by "bad men who longed for license and plunder." These doctrines "which, if carried into effect, would, in thirty years, undo all that thirty centuries have done for mankind, and would make the fairest provinces of France and Germany as savage as Congo or Patagonia, have been avowed from the tribune and defended by the sword. . . . The truest friends of the people have with deep sorrow owned that interests more precious than any political privileges were in jeopardy, and that it might be necessary to sacrifice even liberty in order to save civilisation" (p. 1312).

Macaulay's is a strange and wonderful evocation of the fears of middle-class England as it entered the Victorian era, and his appropriation of seventeenth-century heroes to the defense of the nineteenth-century status quo will ever remain richly suggestive to students of the Victorian ethos. The historian's sympathies comprehend the Long Parliament as well as the larger-than-life figures of 1688–89, and occasionally his emotional rhetoric stirs the reader, against his better judgment. He is a racy storyteller, an influential interpreter of the late seventeenth century, a powerful mythmaker; yet it is doubtful whether he can be regarded as a literary artist of the first rank. His pages are calculated to move the feelings without challenging the mind; his prose is clichéd, facile, inflated, filled with stereotyped oratorical devices; his method of using sources is fallacious, while his characters sometimes verge upon the statuesque, better suited to epic poetry than to a realistic art. His account of events in Ireland is outrageously partisan, while his blending of history with mythmaking risks prostituting the former to the latter. His humorless tone and his sententious presumption of high-minded rectitude are monuments to the least attractive features of his age. He has ill served his cause. "If Macaulay represents literary history," the twentieth century might exclaim—not sorry to witness its predisposition confirmed—"it is a derisible object." This logic is immaculate, and only the premise faulty.

Gibbon is an artist of different stature. The scope of his work is grand, his erudition comprehensive, his objectivity often admirable, his critical spirit as he approaches his sources generally exemplary. Certain of his passages are terribly funny. He reflects some of the best of eighteenth-century values, especially in his devotion to intellectual freedom and in his rationalist approach to human affairs. Yet the most distinctive feature of the *Decline and Fall* is the magnificent brocade of its prose.

Opening Gibbon's pages, one immediately recognizes an unusual intellect. This historian's diction is more vigorous and original than Macaulay's; his sentences and paragraphs more complex yet equally lucid; his expression profuse but nevertheless economical; his generalizations often deft, his adjectives frequently provocative, his assertions masterfully indirect and not insistent. His objects were to write in a "style bold and elegant," to show through keen observation that he "had studied mankind," to quicken his narrative by sparks "of philosophy . . . [and] taste."[15]

His generalizations illuminate the long twilight of the Roman empire: "The slaves of domestic tyranny may vainly exult in their national independence" (5:320). Quick provocations to thought, often suggesting a cynical view of human nature or a perception of the vicissitude of human affairs, are generally introduced into longer sentences so as not to stand naked: "Persuasion is the resource of the feeble; and the feeble can seldom persuade: the ambassadors of the emperor [Constantine Palaeologus] attempted, without success, to divert Mahomet [II] from the execution of his design" (7:164). Observations stated not quite in the form of explicit generalization reflect again Gibbon's study of mankind: "The Koran inculcates, in the most absolute sense, the tenets of fate and predestination, which would extinguish both industry and virtue, if the actions of man were governed by his speculative belief" (5:361).

Gibbon's command of the arts of indirection equals his skill at generalization. The Turkish ruler Mahomet II combined the fearsome authority of a despot with the determined purpose of a man possessed by a great design; his troops besieging Constantinople in 1453 employed a recent invention, and Gibbon, proceeding circuitously, discusses the use Mahomet made of this instrument, deliberately obliging the reader to exert effort to see the drift of his remarks: "Among the implements of destruction, he studied with peculiar care the recent and tremendous discovery of the Latins; and his artillery surpassed whatever had yet appeared in the world. . . . Fourteen batteries thundered at once on the most accessible places. . . . Yet, in the power and activity of the sultan, we may discern the infancy of the new science. Under a master who counted the moments, the great cannon could be loaded and fired no more than seven times in one day" (7:169, 178–79). Time after time Gibbon points first and only later names what he has called attention to: "When the tyrant Caligula was suspected of an intention to invest a very extraordinary candidate with the consular robes, the sacrilegious profanation would have scarcely excited less astonishment, if, instead of a horse, the noblest chieftain of Germany or Britain had been the object of his choice" (2:181). When the author wishes to characterize the ancient Arabian language, and at the same time to suggest the living conditions on the Arabian peninsula, his method is oblique: "In Arabia as well as in Greece, the perfection of language outstripped the refinement of manners; and her speech could diversify the fourscore names of honey, the two hundred of a serpent, the five hundred of a lion, the thousand of a sword, at a time when this copious dictionary was entrusted to the memory of an illiterate people" (5:324–25).

The uses of indirection are various. While allowing the historian to transform textbook description into a work of art, it is also his happiest tool for avoiding the appearance of complacency at the moment he is passing judgment: Mahomet II "was doubtless a soldier, and possibly a general" (7:161). Nothing could be more unlike Macaulay's self-righteousness than Gibbon's thrust at the eighteenth-century rationalization for certain contemporary political practices. Gibbon declares that at the Council of Milan (355 A.D.), the integrity of the bishops "was gradually undermined by the arguments of the Arians, the dexterity of the eunuchs, and the pressing solicitations of a prince [Constantius], who gratified his revenge at the expense of his dignity, and exposed his own passions, whilst he influenced those of the clergy. Corruption, the most infallible symptom of constitutional liberty, was successfully practised: honours, gifts, and immunities were offered and accepted as the price of an episcopal vote" (2:372). Indirection serves also as the sharpest pin with which to puncture bombast. Behind the mask of a "decent reverence" for the boasts of Christians about the superiority of their soldiers to Turks,[16] Gibbon smiles at how the outnumbered defenders of Constantinople abandoned aggressive sallies in front of their walls, retreating into purely defensive tactics. The Greeks "soon discovered that, in the proportion of their numbers, one Christian was of more value than twenty Turks" (7:177).

Gibbon weaves a profuse diction and a convoluted syntax into a rich pattern. His verbs are diverse, polysyllabic, exact, often used in the original, root, sense: "The Propontis was *overspread* with three hundred and twenty sail. . . . The far greater part must be *degraded* to the condition of storeships. . . . This line of fortification . . . [the writer] Phranza . . . *prolongs* to the measure of six miles. . . . They were prudently content to *maintain* the rampart with their missile weapons. . . . Several breastplates and bodies were *transpierced* by the same shot. . . . Nor had the art been yet invented of *replenishing* those subterraneous passages with gunpowder" (7:173, 177–79).[17] When his fecund imagination supplies the words to describe the resistance of Constantinople's Greeks to the spread of Roman Catholic ritual, Gibbon's manner resembles Macaulay's, but his practice is more lively: "No sooner had the church of St. Sophia been polluted by the Latin sacrifice than it was deserted as a Jewish synagogue, or an heathen temple, by the clergy and people; and a vast and gloomy silence prevailed in that venerable dome, which had so often smoked with a cloud of incense, blazed with innumerable lights, and resounded with the voice of prayer and thanksgiving" (7:177). His use of parallel construction again resembles Macaulay's but is more vital: "To fill the ditch was the toil of the besiegers; to clear away the rubbish was the safety of the besieged; and, after a long and bloody conflict, the web that had been woven in the day was still unravelled in the night" (7:179). The sentences of the eighteenth-century historian are much more complex than Macaulay's, the straight line of a simple period being constantly interrupted by interjected phrases. In the later volumes most sentences comprise two, three, or even four periods. Such constructions challenge the reader's intellect—provoking him, for example, to reflect upon the validity of *raison d'état* as justification for deceit—while simultaneously they furnish him the pleasure, as though he were listening to a line of early eighteenth-century music, of following the inflections of performer's voice from beginning to end of a complex musical phrase:

Falsehood and insincerity, unsuitable as they seem to the dignity of public transactions, offend us with a less degrading idea of meanness than when they are found in the intercourse of private life. In the latter, they discover a want of courage; in the other, only a defect of power; and, as it is impossible for the most able statesmen to subdue millions of followers and enemies by their own personal strength, the world, under the name of policy, seems to have granted them a very liberal indulgence of craft and dissimulation. Yet the arts of Severus cannot be justified by the most ample privileges of state-reason. He promised only to betray, he flattered only to ruin; and however he might occasionally bind himself by oaths and treaties, his conscience, obsequious to his interest, always released him from the inconvenient obligation. [1:116][18]

The brilliance of individual sentences is not yet so surprising as the steady elevation of tone that Gibbon sustains over 3,300 pages, wave following wave of elegantly shaped words.[19]

Respect one feels: astonishment, admiration; but not quite affection. The character of Gibbon's humor suggests the problem. There is often the well-bred, salacious cynicism of gentlemen sipping port at their club: By the Koran

the boundless licence of polygamy was reduced to four legitimate wives or concubines. . . . A special revelation dispensed . . . [Mohammed] from the laws which he had imposed on his nation; the female sex, without reserve, was abandoned to his desires; and this singular prerogative excited the envy, rather than the scandal, the veneration, rather than the envy, of the devout Musulmans. If we remember the seven hundred wives and three hundred concubines of the wise Solomon, we shall applaud the modesty of the Arabian, who espoused no more than seventeen or fifteen wives; eleven are enumerated who occupied at Medina their separate apartments round the house of the apostle, and enjoyed in their turns the favour of his conjugal society. . . . Gabriel again descended with a chapter of the Koran, to absolve him from his oath, and to exhort him freely to enjoy his captives and concubines without listening to the clamours of his wives. In a solitary retreat of thirty days, he laboured, alone with Mary, to fulfil the commands of the angel. [5:378–79]

Voyeurism sometimes is accompanied by deadpan satire upon scholarly pedantry; three footnotes support the authority of a single sentence:

Perhaps the incontinence of . . . [Mohammed] may be palliated by the tradition of his natural or preternatural gifts:* he united the manly virtue of thirty of the children of Adam; and the apostle might rival the thirteenth labour** of the Grecian Hercules.***

 *Sibi robur ad generationem . . . ; and Abulfeda mentions the exclamation of Ali, who washed his body after his death, "O propheta, certe penis tuus caelum versus erectus est". . . .
 **I borrow the style of a father of the church. . . .
 ***The common and most glorious legend includes, in a single night, the fifty victories of Hercules over the virgin daughters of Thestius (Diodor. Sicul. tom i. l. iv. p. 274 . . .). But Athenaeus allows seven nights . . . and Apollodorus fifty for this arduous achievement of Hercules, who was then no more than eighteen years of age. [5:380]

When not devising rude jokes, Gibbon lavishes irony upon religious ideas, Mohammedan, pagan, but especially Christian: "In the field of Ceramio, fifty thousand [Saracen] horse and foot were overthrown by one hundred and thirty-six Christian soldiers, without reckoning St. George, who fought on horseback in the foremost ranks" (6:192). The two styles of satire are not mutually exclusive. The sexual experiences of Christian nuns stimulate the bachelor-historian's curiosity:

It was the amusement of the Saracens to profane, as well as to pillage, the monasteries and churches. At the siege of Salerno, a Musulman chief spread his couch on the communion-table, and on that altar sacrificed each night the virginity of a Christian nun. As he wrestled with a reluctant maid, a beam in the roof was accidentally or dexterously thrown down on his head; and the death of the lustful emir was imputed to the wrath of Christ, which was at length awakened to the defence of his faithful spouse. [6:171]

Gibbon's sense of humor, like that of an adolescent, is squandered too largely upon sex and upon flogging the horses of Christianity.[20] He is capable of writing a paean to intellectual freedom, against the tyranny of religious intolerance; but too much of his energy is devoted to negation, to heavy-handed sarcasms against "superstition." His laughter is piercing, but frequently cynical. His bawdry, unlike Shakespeare's, does not grow from sympathy for mankind.[21] The *Decline and Fall* appeals most strongly to cynics, for Gibbon delights in nourishing the disposition to think ill of the world: the Arians "prudently assumed those modest virtues which, in the fury of civil and religious dissensions, are seldom practised, or even praised, except by the weaker party" (2:347).

The limits of Gibbon's humor and of his view of human nature point toward a certain poverty of thought and feeling, toward the aridity of a bibliophile. They suggest a lack of intellectual daring except in his anti-Christian iconoclasm. Even here he may have felt that the rationalist cynicism of well-bred gentlemen was ready, by 1776, to support him[22]—indeed, to make his views somewhat fashionable. His reflections upon the revolutions of human affairs are not always illuminating; nor are his generalizations of uniform interest: "The counsels of princes are more frequently influenced by views of temporal advantage than by considerations of abstract and speculative truth" (2:293). Parts of Gibbon's narrative—covering as it does 1,200 years in only 3,300 pages—must betray the character of an elegant chronicle, for his narrative is sometimes deficient in interpretative comment; this might even be said of his celebrated account of the Normans in southern Italy. When Gibbon has something interesting to say, the artifice of his style heightens the effect. But when his thought is commonplace, the stylistic mannerism may ring hollow: "The indigent and solitary prince prepared, however, to sustain his formidable adversary; but, if his courage were equal to the peril, his strength was inadequate to the contest" (7:171).

Gibbon's greatest weakness is the uniformity of his tone. Only occasionally are his pages exhilarating. Too often they seem, despite the skill expended upon their inscription, cold, lifeless, and unmoving. It is a highly stylized writing but ultimately less successful than Racine's; for the French dramatist was confined within the limits of an evening's performance, while Gibbon's stage was nearly unbounded; and the formality of Racine's verse constrains the tempestuous development of human passions, while Gibbon infuses no such agitation into the souls of his protagonists.

Gibbon's diction is stereotyped. His characters "sigh" or "tremble" wearisomely; the populace "accuses" the obstinacy of their rulers; ambitious men constantly hope to strip "the purple" from usurpers; and even the most delicious of ambiguous modifiers is worn through overuse: Mohammed "enjoyed the satisfaction of beholding the increase of his faint congregation . . . , to whom he seasonably dispensed the spiritual nourishment of the Koran. . . . Both Caled and Anrou, the future conquerors of Syria and Egypt, most seasonably deserted the sinking cause of idolatry. . . . [The impiety of some of the Persian doctors] has afforded a seasonable warning against the worship of saints and martyrs" (5:353, 367, 395). Nouns sometimes replace each other like the dancers of a tired quadrille: The fathers of the Nicene Council "beheld, with surprise and respect"; Phranza "informed his master, with grief and surprise"; the impatient sultan "perceived, with astonishment and grief" (2:362; 7:173, 180).

Syntactical tricks also become clichéd. Gibbon's manner of amplifying a thought by interjecting a parallel phrase into the smooth flow of a period is at first delightful, but the capacity of an artistic genius—of a Beethoven—to surprise his audience by freshly varying important details whenever something predictable seems about to happen, is not his: "I will not transcribe, nor do I firmly believe, the stories. . . . He studied the lessons, and soon surpassed the example, of his father. . . . After humbling the pride, Mahomet accepted the submission, of the Caramanian. . . . The second order announced, and in some degree commenced, the siege. . . . I must repeat, though I cannot credit, the evidence of Phranza" (6:161–64, 182).

Gibbon is a cold fish. When a fleet of five Venetian vessels attempts to break the naval blockade imposed by a numerous but inferior Turkish fleet, Gibbon's language is as stylized as ever, but genuine feeling is absent: "The reader who has present to his mind the geographical picture of Constantinople, will conceive and admire the greatness of the spectacle. . . . The rampart, the camp, the coasts of Europe and Asia, were lined with innumerable spectators, who anxiously awaited the event of this momentous succour" (7:181). "Anxiously awaited . . . momentous succour": Although the words are there, emotion is filtered off. Gibbon's rhetorical machine devours the raw materials of experience, churning out an elegant but standardized product. Phrasemaking becomes an end in itself. The historian runs the risk, selecting words for effect, of appearing insincere: "The fields of Cannae were *bedewed* a second time with the blood of Africans" (6:168).[23]

Gibbon lacks the humanity of the finest artists. He has nothing of the insight of a rationalist like Santayana into the historical significance of the Christian myth. His adolescent jeers and his fixation upon the weakness, hypocrisy, and superstition of religious men betray a limited spirit. Gibbon's narrative of the revolutions of twelve centuries will continue to fire the imaginations of hundreds of English-speaking readers; the elevation of his tone is imposing; yet the sometimes mechanical quality of his prose, together with the narrowness of his soul, must disappoint the hopes of those who value historical art.

The examples of Macaulay and Gibbon help to define Adams's strengths and weaknesses. Not unnaturally, Adams's is the most reliable of the three histories. Profiting from the development of scientific method in Germany, its author does not invent speeches for his characters, as do Gibbon and Macaulay; and unlike those two historians, Adams quotes copiously from primary sources, making his narrative a more veracious record of the past. He goes farther below the surface than Macaulay, who dwells lovingly upon the sound and fury of events. Adams's concentration upon sixteen well-documented years of modern history allows him, by contrast to Gibbon, the benefits of detail: His character studies of Napoleon, Canning, Jefferson, and Madison and his analysis of the nuances of British feeling toward America are more subtle than anything that Gibbon's sources permit him to achieve, while his account of the origins of the War of 1812 tells more about the complexities of how nations fall into war than Gibbon could suggest. The *Decline and Fall* is amazingly accurate, considering the number of years and continents it touches, but Bury's footnotes nevertheless show how many major mistakes Gibbon made. Firth's *Commentary on Macaulay's History* exposes similar weaknesses in that work; and although Adams's *History* is riddled with minor errors, his work remains more trustworthy than either Gibbon's or Macaulay's.

Lack of scope is the Achilles' heel of Adams's volumes. Gibbon has important things to say about momentous events—the Fall of Rome, the rise of Christianity, the spread of Mohammedanism, the vicissitudes of human affairs in the Mediterranean basin over a millenium. Macaulay's subject is narrower, but he has the intellectual grasp to work out a clear and plausible interpretation of the Revolution of 1688 which affects one's whole view of British history. By comparison Adams is confused. Although he has intelligent things to say about the War of 1812, he stands on all sides of the fence: British policy amply justified the Americans in going to war, but the Americans' declaration of war was for them a risky blunder, yet the war's consequences were beneficial. Perhaps this view of events corresponds most exactly to the facts, but as an interpretation it lacks coherence. Adams's picture of Jeffersonian democracy is no less disappointing: He sympathizes with the democratic movement while deprecating its excesses, such as the impulse to curb judicial independence; he abhors the threat to Union implicit in those states' rights views cherished by leading Jeffersonians; and he shows that Jefferson temporized in his domestic policy, that his practice varied substantially from his theory. But this last theme is not rich enough to bear the stress Adams lays upon it. He attends too much to the detail of Jeffersonian practice, too little to the broad consequences of the president's enunciation of democratic but decentralist principles. Adams mentions the development of democratic nationalism but offers no fully developed interpretation of the phenomenon.

The obverse side of this coin is that the American writer often gets bogged down in detail, as in certain of his accounts of diplomatic negotiation. Having discovered hundreds of new documents in a field never previously treated by an important writer, Adams is infected with the modern historian's disease of "making historical dictionaries,—trying to be true in every possible direction at once."[24] He composes many of his pages simply so that there will be a clear public record of events, the truth about which previously was hidden in the archives. But his wish to write a sound monograph wars with the artist's need to subordinate insignificant detail. In this respect his attempt to combine both scientific method and artistic presentation was a preventable failure.

Sympathy, Macaulay's strong point, is evident in the souls of neither Gibbon nor Adams. Macaulay makes the reader feel the emotions of his protagonists. He wrings every possible drop of sentiment and drama from situations like those of the captured Duke of Monmouth or the besieged defenders of Londonderry. Adams, on the contrary, lacks the power of pathos: His analysis of character is shrewd, and he makes his reader think, but the reader does not at the same moment feel. The carping tone that sometimes enters Adams's voice is related to his deficiency in sympathy.

Mental liveliness was what Macaulay most glaringly did not show. Gibbon was much more sophisticated than Macaulay, but Adams's was nevertheless perhaps the most interesting of the three minds, as a glance at his and Gibbon's autobiographical writings or their humor suggests. Gibbon's brilliant jokes often focus on sex and superstition, but Adams's most memorable sallies—like his thrusts at Lord Sheffield or General Alexander Smyth—deflate all manner of pomposity and pretension. His psychological analysis is more penetrating than Gibbon's, his reading of character more subtle. The quick play of his imagination buoys one's spirit, while Gibbon's cynicism is somewhat sterile.

Macaulay's other principal failing is the bombast and cliché of his prose style. By contrast Gibbon, as everyone knows, is a master of diction and syntax. Yet Adams's literary craftsmanship may be regarded as superior to that of the great eighteenth-century historian: It is more varied, easy, natural, and sincere—far less uniform in tone—than Gibbon's. Adams's imagery is richer, and he maintains much of Gibbon's mastery of the elements of sentence and paragraph construction. Adams strikes a happy medium between the ornateness of eighteenth-century style and the formlessness and ineptness of some twentieth-century writing.

Thus Adams's *History* is more authentic than the *Decline and Fall*, his literary craftsmanship possibly superior to Gibbon's, and his mind perhaps livelier; but his sympathy is as defective as Gibbon's, and his lack of scope severely narrows his achievement. Macaulay's intellectual and stylistic failings diminish the force of his dramatic, conventional declamation. Gibbon, despite his lack of sympathy, is justly considered the outstanding literary historian in the language. But history lingers in an early stage of its development. The three historians practiced an art that has not yet produced its Bach, Mozart, or Beethoven.

PART IV · *Fame*

CHAPTER 8 · Mont-Saint-Michel and Chartres *and* The Education of Henry Adams

ADAMS'S TALENTS found new forms of expression between his completion of the *History* in 1890 and his death in 1918. Pursued by restlessness, he would take his nieces for a summer in Scotland, accompany Clarence King to Cuba, visit the Camerons in South Carolina, and return ever and again to France, while passing most winters in Washington. His strongest attachment was to Elizabeth Sherman Cameron, wife of one of Pennsylvania's powerful Republican senators. The offspring of Adams's old age were a paean to Chartres cathedral and an autobiography that will be read (though occasionally with bemusement) as long as the American nineteenth century survives. These works cannot fully be understood without probing Adams's peculiar psyche, whose complexities unfolded themselves there. Adams's relation to Mrs. Cameron also needs a word of comment.

I

Except for his wife, who died in 1885, the most significant woman in Adams's life was Marian Adams's friend Elizabeth Cameron, with whom he certainly had fallen in love by 1891. Of the few letters Adams ever wrote to Marian, only those from the spring of 1885 have survived, and they are brief, constrained, and tense, as suited the emotional crisis she and he experienced when her father was dying. Adams's letters to Elizabeth Cameron, on the other hand, are expansive, imaginative, full of romantic love. The temptation might exist to attribute to Mrs. Cameron a rich and beneficial effect upon Adams's writing and to contrast her influence with that of Marian. A respected British authority upon America once went so far as to suggest in the

187

anonymous pages of the *Times Literary Supplement* (Oct. 28, 1965) that Elizabeth Cameron's only child, who must have been conceived two months or
so before Marian Adams's suicide, was perhaps an illegitimate child of the
otherwise childless Henry Adams.

Were this speculation well-founded, it would challenge the view of Adams's
marriage and of Marian's relation to the writing of his *History* that underlies
the foregoing interpretation of Adams's career. It would also challenge the
view, to be developed later, that the emotional force of *Mont-Saint-Michel and
Chartres* derives principally from Adams's grief at Marian's death, even two
decades after the event. Although the suggestion—based on a shred of London gossip—that Adams slept with Elizabeth Cameron in 1885 has been
effectively queried by Ernest Samuels, the matter is so vital to one's understanding of Adams's creative life that additional evidence may be worth ex-
amining.[1]

Elizabeth Sherman's was an unusual family. Her uncle William is considered by some the outstanding general of the Civil War, while her uncle John,
a Republican senator from Ohio, was associated with important national
legislation: from the Reconstruction Act of 1867 to the Sherman Anti-Trust
Law of 1890. The third brother, Charles, an Ohio judge, was Elizabeth's
father, and her marriage in 1878 at the age of twenty-one to the widower
Don Cameron—more than double her age—appears to have been regarded
by him as an important dynastic alliance. For her it was a disastrous error
that went far toward ruining her life.

Though fourteen years younger than Marian Adams, Elizabeth became a
close friend of hers in Washington in 1881, and Henry liked her fresh ingenu-
ousness. He had scant respect for Don Cameron (he was unwilling to give
the senator introductions to his friends in England)[2] but he took pains to
smooth Elizabeth's path when she and her husband traveled there in 1883.
Adams jested to Hay in the tone they both affected toward other young
women like Miss Anne Palmer and Miss Kitty McLane that at the Camerons' house "Don and I stroll round with our arms round each other's necks.
I should prefer to accompany Mrs. Don in that attitude"; and he addressed
letters of gallantry to her: "I shall have you carved over the arch of my stone
door-way."[3] The strongest indication of what may have been a mild infatuation was his making Elizabeth the model for the second heroine of *Esther*:
the bright, young, artless westerner Catherine Brook.

Adams's love letters to Elizabeth Cameron in 1891 and 1892—six years
after Marian's death—show the strength of his feeling by that time, and she
is believed to have been at the center of his emotional life for the rest of his
years. But the evidence against his having fathered an illegitimate child in
1885 is overwhelming. Elizabeth invited the Adamses to accompany her that
summer to California, where she planned to visit her husband, who was
going to be there several months for his health. Henry inclined to accept the

invitation, and Marian wished to stay away from the gloomy associations of Beverly Farms after her father's death in mid-April. But Marian's depression quickly set in, and Henry concluded she was not up to a Western trip. He and Marian spent a few weeks at resorts in West Virginia; then her illness obliged them after all to seek the obscurity of Beverly Farms.

Probably Elizabeth went to California, and probably she and her husband later came back to Harrisburg, Pa. She returned to Washington, "terribly used up," late in November.[4] Her child—born about June 25, 1886—would have been conceived sometime in the neighborhood of October 1 and perhaps she suffered morning sickness. During these months Henry was constantly with Marian, as he had been every day of their married life since 1872 except for her brief New York trip in 1883. From September 6 to 12 Henry was away from Beverly Farms, going to and returning from the American Historical Association's convention in Saratoga Springs, N.Y., but he undoubtedly took Marian with him. His companion at Saratoga was not his brother Charles, for Charles's diary shows that he remained in Massachusetts during those days, and the C. Adams at the convention about whose "prevalence" Henry complained was the prominent historian Charles Kendall Adams.[5] Henry's venture to Saratoga with Marian was not a success: "I came away before Schuyler spoke; and deserted him somewhat basely. We froze there"; and another disappointing result of the trip was that Henry and Marian missed John Hay when he unexpectedly visited Boston on September 12: "Our little trip to Saratoga in search of history had a tragic ending since it cost us your visit."[6] Continuing to be with Marian each day, Henry started with his ill wife on October 14, by train, from Boston to Washington. His geographical separation from Elizabeth and his constant attendance upon Marian as well as other considerations made it certain that he could not have been the father of Elizabeth's child.

Of these other considerations, one is that at Christmas 1885, a few weeks after Marian's suicide, Henry gave a piece of her jewelry to Elizabeth as a remembrance: "The little trinket which I send you with this, was a favorite of my wife's. Will you keep it, and sometimes wear it, to remind you of her?"[7] Six months later, when Elizabeth's baby girl was born in Washington, she wanted to name it after her dead friend, but Henry's permission could not be asked, for he was on his way to Japan. Elizabeth's child ended with a name that happened to be the closest possible to "Marian": Martha.[8] Henry soon learned what Elizabeth's wish had been, and there is no wonder that he cherished this child for the rest of his life. Later that summer, while Henry was still abroad, Elizabeth, Martha, and sometimes Don Cameron lived, at Henry's invitation, in the Beverly Farms house he had built with Marian: "A great many of the neighbors" called on Elizabeth. These were not the actions and the language of a guilty couple, seeking to hide something. However Henry felt he had failed Clover, it was not his relation to Elizabeth that troubled him. Even five years later, when Adams undoubtedly was in love with Elizabeth, he had never slept with her: "French novels are not the only possible dramas. One may be innocent as the angels, yet as unhappy as the wicked."[9] Widowers have from time immemorial fallen in love with the good friends of their dead wives, and the gossip about Henry's relations with Elizabeth illustrates primarily the peril of being born eminent.

Although the letters Henry addressed to Elizabeth in the early 1890s had the glow of unfulfilled love, it may be doubted whether her influence upon him was so fruitful as has sometimes been suggested. On the contrary, one's impression is that, although Adams was in some respects unpleasant as a young man, he had very good luck in marrying a woman who brought out the best in him; but that when he was older—and when Elizabeth Cameron was his closest female friend—many of the submerged tendencies of his bachelor days reappeared and became exaggerated. J. Lawrence Laughlin, a graduate student of Adams's who later became a professor of political economy at Harvard, was a well-informed and objective observer who understood how Clover's death had affected her husband: At Beverly Farms before 1885 "the air of happiness, congeniality, and comradeship was infectious. . . . [Adams was] deep and sensitive in his affections. . . . After the loss of his wife he was seemingly a different man within. His latent tendencies became more pronounced."[10] These tendencies had already marred the tone of certain passages of the *History*, but they wrought havoc in parts of *Mont-Saint-Michel* and the *Education*. If the curiously uneven quality of these last two books is to be interpreted, something must be said of the unattractive traits that lay beside the agreeable ones in Adams's complex psyche.

As a young man Adams was awkward in society, easily embarrassed, prone to low spirits. His defense against such afflictions was to take the offensive against the world: He stood upon his own dignity and assumed a lofty tone toward others. The spiky exterior he presented in public belied his sensitivity toward members of his family and his aptitude for intimate friendship. But, as Henry James understood, Adams suffered the deadly sin of pride. Although he tried with a good deal of success to hide his passion, he lusted for "consideration" and craved the acclaim that would confirm his sense of superiority. His ambition was for literary fame. He was anxious about exposing himself to humiliation, and the public's indifference to his *History* seemed to him a crushing blow. He attempted to prevent the world's ever learning how much he had staked on winning its applause with the *History*. *Mont-Saint-Michel* and the *Education* were written in reaction against what he supposed to have been one of the two great failures of his life.

Adams's "sensitive and timid nature"—as he characterized it somewhat indulgently in the last sentence of the *Education*—sprang from both physical and psychological origins. Certain disabilities may have resulted from his near-fatal bout of scarlet fever at the age of three. His development seemed cause for chagrin: Weighing as a young man only about 125 pounds, and just five feet three inches tall, he claimed that in his youth he "never was strong enough to fight, along with other boys." By the age of twenty-five he was conscious of growing bald. Possibly he suffered from mumps the next year: He had had some "little trouble, and have to be cautious and quiet. But my organs appear to have very nearly regained the natural size." He often exhausted himself in London, studying until two in the morning, and by 1865 called himself "a miserable and worn-out ruin." At the age of thirty-one he was "very-very bald." Extremely self-conscious, he often experienced feelings of inferiority due in good part to his small stature. "You have a physique, brass and a disposition for society," he once complained to Charles. "I suffer under a want of all these qualities, and perpetual and incessant mortification on that account."[11]

He was easily embarrassed. In 1859, living at Dresden with a German academic family, Adams was driven to self-mockery by his social awkwardness. He and the whole family had been to an afternoon concert, grouped around tables in a kind of tea room: "I sat next the amiable Fräulein (who looked deuced pretty and all the Lieutenants envied me)," he reported to his mother, "and I think, take the four hours through, I may have spoken about ten words an hour; in the interval sitting still and looking at my kid gloves." The first years in England did not improve matters. "I wish you or John were here to be funny and amuse people," Henry despaired to Charles. "You know I never could do it. . . . I wish I were fifty years old at once, and then I should feel at home." "I am slowly but certainly becoming a dead-head." To be an American was often a handicap in England, yet to hold high social position in America—Adams imagined—barred sympathy with the common lot. Beyond these embarrassments, the mere fact of being an Adams exposed one to popular abuse. My position "subjects me to . . . being pilloried in print on the slightest excuse," he warned the editor of the *North American Review* in 1867; "in other words my name is a trifle too heavy for me. . . . Perhaps it would be as well not to *print* my name to the article now in your hands. I have suffered so much from publicity that I prefer over-caution."[12]

Adams was afflicted by recurrent low spirits. He once pretended to lay his troubles to gloomy weather. "The [autumn] season of the year grinds the very soul out of me," he informed Gaskell morosely: "My nerves lose their tone; my teeth ache, and my courage falls to the bottomless bottom of infinitude. Death stalks about me, and the whole of Gray's grisly train. . . . If ever I take too much laudanum, the coroner's jury may bring in a verdict of wilful murder against the month of November." The jury might have done better to indict dyspepsia. Although Adams was a gobbler of food, his recurrent severe indigestion had other roots; it was probably the outlet for an irritability of which he attempted to check outward expression. During the Civil

War the hostile environment of London constantly galled him, testing his power to subdue wrath: "My effort has always been here to suppress all expression of feeling." But the young man's greatest source of exasperation was his mother. Each time he had to escort her and his sister Mary upon a trip he was a model of self-control toward his parent, but his feeling demanded relief. "I like of all things to be independent," he groaned to Charles, "and of all things detest women's fuss and tongues." He exploded again from Italy in 1865, "You know . . . how I abominate this family work. . . . The battle is perpetual between . . . [the children—that is, Mary and Brooks] and their mother. And if there is one thing that I flinch under, it is the sound of perpetual dispute." In the face of his mother's constant petty worrying, Henry had "learned to be silent, but in return, I must have my laugh."[13]

Facetiousness was one resource. Henry's satirical account of his mother's sitting before a crackling wood fire, fussing about the draughts and her homesickness, shows how her personality spurred his wit. Four-hour rambles provided another outlet—indigestion goaded Adams into those excursions that developed his delight in the countryside around Washington. He often succeeded in suppressing outward signs of wrath: "I never remember seeing Uncle Henry in a temper," one of his nieces testified, "—indeed, he said that a temper fit gave him a bilious attack." Once he was more candid about the relation between dyspepsia and self-command. His attending the historical convention at Saratoga filled him with a wish "to murder the average college professor. . . . Luckily for my nervous system, Eugene Schuyler has so much less self-control than I, that he relieved my feelings by making no concealment of his."[14]

Irritable and lacking self-confidence yet cursed by self-esteem, Adams took the offensive against a world that threatened to overwhelm him. He stood upon his own dignity, assumed a tone of authority toward others, and tried to drown self-criticism in criticism of the world about him. According to a Harvard classmate, as an undergraduate he already "rather prided himself upon his aloofness, and assumed a disdainful tone towards his associates and towards everything connected with the College." He acknowledged the failing in ironic mockery of "that grace and suavity of manner for which I am famous," but his shyness was too great for him to do without protective armor. After the news of the Union victory at Vicksburg in 1863, he went to the Cosmopolitan Club in London, "where the people all looked at me as though I were objectionable. . . . I saw very clearly how unpleasant the news was which I brought. . . . I feel such a dislike for the whole nation, and so keen a sensitiveness to the least suspicion of being thought to pay court to any of them, and so abject a dread of ever giving anyone the chance to put a slight upon me, that I avoid them and neither wish them to be my friends nor wish to be theirs." Adams was pleased to find when he brought Marian to England on their wedding trip that she too was capable of reserve: We "have been prancing about town all the afternoon leaving cards," he wrote Gaskell upon their arrival in London, "—mostly on Americans, however, as Madame is proud and will call on no British female who doesn't intimate a wish to that effect." Six years later Henry and Marian still consciously moved with hauteur when in England and France, but on the Iberian peninsula they could relax: "As no one [here in Spain] pretends to being anything, our American amour-propre has a vacation."[15]

Adams assumed an air of authority toward those who might threaten to overawe him. When in 1870 at the age of thirty-two he was producing his first issue of the *North American Review*, he addressed slightly imperious missives to its distinguished contributors. Soliciting an article from Jacob Cox, a former Union general and former governor of Ohio ten years Adams's senior (Cox had just resigned from Grant's cabinet because the president would not actively support civil service reform), Adams adopted the tone of an experienced man of affairs: "I have directed that all manuscript should be in by Dec. 1st. . . . I shall probably issue a circular in advance. You can see therefore how essential it is to me to have your active support." "To appear with [a statement on your part of the true principles of national reform] . . . in my hand at the outset of my editorial career is of decisive consequence to me. . . . Let me know when I can count upon it and I will make my arrangements accordingly."[16]

Toward those not of his own class, Adams occasionally behaved insufferably. He used to say that he had overcome his resentment of his short stature by bad manners picked up in England on purpose, and by 1867 he was ready to boast about his aggressiveness toward a group of French workingmen. One August day he returned by rail from Versailles to Paris, in company with his mother, Mary, and Brooks: "Our train was overfilled," he explained to Gaskell,

and at a station about half way a great crowd of *ouvriers* in blouses could not get seats. . . . A big devil tried to force his way in, so I put my shoulder against him and pitched him out into his friends' arms. Upon this the crowd flared up into a regular French passion. . . . My big friend I saw howling in the middle of the mob, shaking his fist at me and shrieking at cet homme-là. . . . It must have been nearly a minute before the guard came and just then the train started. One blouse did then come in, but the rest, my *vengeur* among them, were left on the platform howling.[17]

If the world seemed likely to overwhelm him, Adams would reply by assault and by expressing contempt for it. In the letter reporting the Versailles scrape, he urged Gaskell to "run over to Paris by all means. Otherwise you will be deprived of the precious privilege of abusing it; a privilege which I value so highly that I have done little else but exercise it since I arrived there." Criticized once for conceit, Adams admitted the charge but protested weakly that it was "not due to admiration of myself but to contempt for everyone else." He claimed to object to "all that is because it is," and an access of tension would cause him to redouble his attacks upon the world. Thus to Lodge he explained in 1876 that "you will find no little of the nervousness and wretchedness of the last week, worked off into criticisms of your essay."[18]

Yet despite his lofty tone and his critical nature, Adams had considerable capacity to inspire affection. In 1868, fresh in Washington from his seven years in England and opening his short career as political journalist, he presented his two faces to a not unsympathetic Massachusetts lawyer. "I found a strange young man there [at Attorney General Evarts's house]," Moorfield Storey recalled, "who was monopolizing the conversation, as it seemed to me, and laying down the law with a certain assumption. I took quite a prejudice against him during this brief acquaintance, but the next day I met him in the street and he was so charming and his voice was so pleasant that my prejudice vanished, and we formed a friendship that was lasting."[19] Strangers, Adams seemed to feel, must be overawed by one means or another, but in his family or with intimate friends he was a different person.

He was his father's favorite child—"Henry is of the gentle and easy sort" in contrast to his brusque brother Brooks, Charles Francis confided to his diary—and was also, despite his suppressed impatience, the closest of all the children to his mother. To his brother Charles he was such a faithful correspondent that, soon after the battle of Gettysburg, the soldier hinted at his feelings about Henry's letters: "You cannot imagine how welcome they have been. . . . You [in London] are all models of thoughtfulness in this respect and, while you will never know how much pleasure your letters have given me, I can never express to you how much their regularity has touched and gratified me." Brooks Adams, ten years Henry's junior, wrote that up until Henry's serious illness in 1912 he "had, all through my life, been nearer to me than any other man." Henry was also the favorite brother of his elder sister Louisa and the only blood relative at her bedside in Italy when she died from tetanus after a riding accident. "Oh Henry," his mother wrote from Quincy just after receiving the cryptic telegraphic report of Louisa's death in 1870, "that we could be sure you was there, and that those dear eager eyes, may have looked her last on the home face she especially loved." Louisa's death bound Henry closer to his father; Henry had "passed through a trial such as is not the fate of many, of your age," Charles Francis wrote a fortnight later: "It will endear you the more to us all, that you have gone through it so devotedly."[20]

When Henry and Marian lived in Washington their two closest friends were John Hay, later secretary of state, and the peripatetic geologist Clarence King. Hay, dexterous as a writer yet rather less sprightly than Adams, was the junior partner in their close friendship. Residing in Cleveland in 1883, he joined the Adamses in commissioning Henry Hobson Richardson to build adjacent houses on Lafayette Square in Washington, and three days after Marian's death he explained what the Adamses had meant to him. "The darkness in which you walk has its shadow for me also," he wrote:

You and your wife were more to me than any other two. I came to Washington because you were there. . . . In the presence of a sorrow like yours, it is little for your friends to say they love you and sympathize with you—but it is all any body can say. Everything else is mere words.

Is it any consolation to remember her as she was? that bright intrepid spirit, that keen fine intellect, that lofty scorn of all that was mean, that social charm which made your house such a one as Washington never knew before, and made hundreds of people love her as much as they admired. No, that makes it all so much the harder to bear.

With Clarence King, admiration went in the other direction: Adams, impressed by this swashbuckling figure, seemed only gradually to recognize that King, although undoubtedly touched by genius, was also in his regal progresses through Europe something of a charlatan. More seriously infected than even Charles Adams by the poisonous hope of winning a fortune, in western mines, King gave the impression of occasionally using his friendships for his own ends. But he suffered a nervous breakdown in 1893, induced by his involvement in the financial panic that year, and when he left the Bloomingdale Asylum to travel to Cuba with his most devoted friend, his gratitude to Adams was heartfelt. His words resembled those of Marian Adams in 1873 and 1885. "That pessimistic Angel Henry," he reported to John Hay, "has been more kind and gentle and healing in his way with me than, as Ruskin expresses it, 'an eternity of clear grammatical speech would explain.' He was simply delightful, genial and tropical in his warmth, physically active as a chamois."[21]

Devotion to Marian's nieces was a great consolation to Adams in his last years, and they, like his own family earlier, returned his affection. Louisa Hooper Thoron reminisced years later, "You couldn't possibly live with him and not find him tender-hearted, human, kind to his entourage, considerate, warmly loyal, staunch." When another Hooper niece married in 1898, she remembered to write to Henry. "I send you once again my heart's love, darling Uncle," she exclaimed: " . . . I never knew such infinite tenderness as yours that you show to children—it surpasses everything I have known. . . . This is the morning of my wedding-day, and I feel you near to me as I have always." Adams's best students at Harvard were acquainted with the hearty smile and the gay, infectious laugh with which, during the years before Marian died, he welcomed his friends.[22]

Nevertheless Adams's personality was host to a virus even more dangerous than his defensive contempt for the world at large—his craving for public acclaim: "Man, almost in the full degree of his antipathy to demogogy, yearns for the popular regard he will not seek." At first he imagined he would win applause in politics: To him as a child, "that there should be a doubt of his being President was a new idea."[23] The sense that he was born something rather special never left him. Was it entirely accidental that in 1885 Clover rode a horse named "Daisy" while Henry's beast was "Prince"? Brooks Adams supposed his brother's ambition took a nonpolitical form— that above all he wished acknowledgment of his position in society. But during the most productive years of Adams's life his true passion was neither political nor social: What he primarily lusted for was recognition of his literary powers.

The subject of literary fame had fascinated him as early as 1863, when he chanced to hear Robert Browning and Sir Edward Lytton protesting the unimportance to them of being known to future generations. "It was curious," the young American mused, "to see two men who, of all others, write for fame, or have done so, ridicule the idea of its real value to them." Henry admitted to Gaskell that "you and I both have always had a foolish weakness for combining social and literary success," and occasionally he hinted at his feelings to other correspondents. Thus, when advising his student Henry Cabot Lodge, he could admit his perfectionism without self-consciousness: "The question for you is not by any means whether you can do a great deal, but whether that which you choose to do, be it much or little, shall be done perfectly, so as to give you credit worth your having." And to Oliver Wendell Holmes, Jr., just founding his reputation as a jurist, Henry acknowledged that "nothing is pleasanter than to receive proof that we are not without respect in our generation." How well Adams loved to make a splash was shown in his long-continued jousting with John Hay about the authorship of *Democracy* and his glee over the house Richardson was building for him: It "is a new form of domestic architecture. . . . I forsee it will rouse a riot."[24]

But generally Adams tried to keep his passion a secret. "I rather grudge the public my immortal writings," he once wrote, straying from complete candor: "I neither want notoriety nor neglect, and one of the two must be imagined by every author to be his reward. My ideal of authorship would be to have a famous *double* with another name to wear what honors I could win. How I should enjoy upsetting him at last by publishing a low and shameless essay with smutty woodcuts in his name!"[25] This anticipatory joy at exposing the double's lust for fame surely derived from Adams's own effort to hold that craving in check. Here was another clue to his treatment of Jefferson: The president was in some respects Adams's double, and the author's impulse to expose a double was partly the historian's motive toward his protagonist. Jefferson "shrank from whatever was rough or coarse," Adams wrote, drawing a character not unlike his own, "and his yearning for sympathy was almost feminine. . . . [He] longed like a sensitive child for sympathy and love."[26] The popularity that President Jefferson had achieved by the time of his overwhelming reelection in 1804 was soon lost through his disastrous embargo policy, and Adams seemed not dissatisfied to see his double upset: "By repealing the embargo [in February 1809], Congress avowedly and even maliciously rejected and trampled upon the only part of Jefferson's statesmanship which claimed originality. . . . [To Jefferson] the supreme bitterness of the moment lay . . . in the sudden loss of respect and consideration."[27]

Not popularity but "consideration" was Adams's desideratum. He congratulated Cabot Lodge on an oration in 1879: "You have got through this ordeal very happily, and I am sure with an increase of consideration." Brooks Adams employed the same term when trying to understand Henry's impulses, and Henry used the word in suggesting how he felt about literary achievement and its reward. "If he worked at all," he declared of himself as journalist, "it was for social consideration. . . . [Artists] find their return in the pride of their social superiority as they feel it. Society commonly . . . encourages their attitude of contempt." This resembled the language of Gilbert Osmond when in addressing Isabel Archer he hinted at his own great passion. "I took my measure early in life," Osmond said: "I was simply the most fastidious young gentleman living. There were two or three people in the world I envied—the Emperor of Russia, for instance, and the Sultan of Turkey! There were even moments when I envied the Pope of Rome—for the consideration he enjoys."[28]

Henry James did not model Gilbert Osmond on Henry Adams, and the differences between the fictional character and Adams were extreme. It may be suspected, nevertheless, that the novelist's analysis of Osmond's worldliness derived partly from his observation of Adams, whom he had known at close quarters for several years. If so, James placed his finger upon Adams's greatest weakness. James concentrated Osmond's craving for consideration into his name: *monde*. Scorning almost everyone and denying that he cared for the judgment of the world, Osmond thirsted in fact for its applause: "This base, ignoble world, it appeared, was after all what one was to live for; one was to keep it for ever in one's eye . . . to extract from it some recognition of one's own superiority. . . . Indifference was really the last of his qualities; . . . [Isabel] had never seen any one who thought so much of others." Adams, like Osmond, so wished to gain the applause of the world that he tried vigorously to disguise the craving. He speculated in 1883 whether it might not be better to delay publication of the *History*—as later he withheld the *Education*—until he was in his grave. "I would rather let the stuff lie till I'm dead," he claimed to Gaskell: "There is a sort of pleasure and triumph in proving to oneself that one does not care a nickel cent for the opinion of one's fellow men. At all events I am not yet in a hurry to say: Plaudite! " Like Gilbert Osmond flaunting his possessions in the face of Caspar Goodwood, Adams enjoyed the sensation of pretending indifference when the world knocked upon his door for admission. "Reeve is hunting for another article," he once wrote of the *Edinburgh Review*'s editor, "and I would like to teach him to beg." In later years Adams and James pursued the subject of consideration: Adams denying to the last that he lusted for it, James smiling at his disavowals just as Adams himself had once queried Robert Browning's denial. After James received in 1892 renewed signs of the world's acclaim, he wrote to Adams that something nice had happened which "makes me feel famous—and doesn't discourage that psychological lust—au contraire—on which you freely animadvert."[29]

For a few years after 1868 Adams had been deeply involved in reform politics, and his rejection of a political career was certain to increase his desire for literary laurels. Soon after he began work upon the *History*, he exposed some of his feelings about politics by praising his esteemed Gallatin "because he could and did refuse power when he found what vanity it was, and yet became neither a cynic nor a transcendental philosopher." Adams too succeeded in fighting off cynicism as long as he could retain faith in literary gods. But if his turning from politics sharpened his appetite for literary success, he felt the greater need to disguise this craving. When *John Randolph*—which of all Adams's historical writings proved the greatest popular success—was being printed in 1882, he declared that "a book to me always seems a part of myself, a kind of intellectual brat or segment, and I never bring one into the world without a sense of shame."[30] Why shame? Was this not because the time of publication was the moment most likely to betray a writer into exposing his secret hunger?

Equally upsetting, publication opened the author to possible humiliation. When Adams alleged that he dreaded "notoriety more than dyspepsia," he told a half-truth, for notoriety could take the shape of either acclaim or ridicule. He certainly loved the former, but his horror of the latter was profound. "I am a sensitive cuss and a coward," he admitted to John Hay. "When I get a real whipping I feel kind of low about it."[31] He could never forget the public roasting he had received in 1862: "To my immense astonishment and dismay," he had then written, "I found myself this morning sarsed through a whole column of the Times, and am laughed at by all England. . . . For the present I shall cease my other writings as I am in agonies for fear they should be exposed."[32] This emotion lay dormant like a mountain bear, ready to be roused by any pinprick of public criticism. Even the carvings on the new Richardson house had the power, if the journalists should play their easy game of Adams-baiting, to revive the monster: "I turn red, blue and green of nights thinking about it, and hiding my head under my pillow. . . . [I would rather be eaten on toast] than spitted on newspapers."[33]

Against public humiliations Adams erected a variety of defenses. "I rather pride myself on the capacity to hold my tongue," he observed in 1881. This was Jefferson's defense too, early in 1809, when Congress repealed his embargo and refused even to approve his appointment of an old personal friend to be minister to Russia. Adams believed there was a conflict between preserving one's dignity and gaining the respect of the crowd. "These mortifications, which rapidly followed each other in the last days of February [1809]," he wrote in the *History*, "were endured by Jefferson with dignity and in silence. Perhaps senators would have better understood and might have more respected a vigorous burst of anger, even at some cost of dignity, than they did the self-restraint of the sensitive gentleman who had no longer a wish but to escape from Washington and seek peace in the calm of Monticello." Silence, the only means of maintaining one's dignity, was the object of Adams's relentless effort when the great disaster of his life struck him with his wife's death in 1885. But silence was no sufficient defense against the humiliations of authorship for publication exposed one to the public. One of Adams's strategies was a laudable modesty. Thus when he issued in 1877 his invaluable collection of primary sources, *New England Federalism*, there was a contretemps with the publisher: "I have even had the binding altered," he informed Lodge, "so as to take my name off the back where it was put, contrary to my express order. . . . As there is nothing of mine in it but the preface and the index, it is ridiculous to put my name on the back like an author's."[34] Similarly Adams scorned to parade before his readers a footnote reference to his own authorship of a learned article. If Adams's proof that Napoleon was responsible through one of his ministers for restoring slavery to Santo Domingo required reference to his own research, published in a French journal, at least the author's name could be deleted.[35] Later in life, after the *History* failed to capture the popular imagination, Adams erected a more formidable barrier against exposure to public indifference. He printed *Mont-Saint-Michel and Chartres* and *The Education of Henry Adams* privately. "I prefer the humiliation of paying for the whole," he said, "rather than betray my solitude."[36]

The festering sore was the relative failure of his main work. Macaulay's *History* sold 140,000 copies, Adams's in ten years scarcely more than one-fiftieth of that number.[37] The humiliation was far greater than Adams could publicly admit, though he nibbled like a mouse at the edge of the wound. "The utmost that any writer could hope of his readers now is that they should consent to regard themselves as nephews," he claimed in the preface to *Mont-Saint-Michel*, "and even then he would expect only a more or less civil refusal from most of them. Indeed, . . . there is only one familiar instance recorded of a nephew who read his uncle. The exception tends rather to support the rule, since it needed a Macaulay to produce." Privately, to Samuel Eliot Morison, Adams alleged that he had given up writing American history for lack of appreciation. The poor sales of the *History* "seemed to him proof that the American public did not care for his contributions to their history, so he decided to write only for his own amusement, and for a close circle of appreciative friends."[38]

How much the public's lack of interest in the *History* rankled was shown in one of the most unpleasant episodes of Adams's life. His elder brother John and his brother-in-law Edward Hooper were both, in 1892, members of Harvard's seven-man governing committee. Charles Adams, recognizing the merit of the *History* but also conscious that three previous generations of Adamses had received the honorary LL.D. from Harvard, "induced Hooper to bring [Henry's] . . . name up, and the degree was voted to him." But Henry—to the intense puzzlement and indignation of his brothers—rudely refused the honor. When President Eliot notified him of his selection, Adams in Washington pretended he had a disabling sprained ankle and could not attend the ceremony, then contemptuously put in an appearance at Hooper's house in Cambridge only a few hours after the award-giving. Charles was enraged about "the honor he so ostentatiously didn't inconvenience himself by a single train to accept. . . . A more brutal, unnecessary and ingeniously offensive and aggressive discourtesy never was perpetrated on the college."[39]

The pool of passions that lay below the scum of Adams's conduct was, to his brother, unfathomable. Henry had acted "all out of pure Miss Nancy affectation," Charles sputtered. But the incident deserved a different explanation. Fifteen years earlier Henry had removed himself from Harvard to Washington because, rather than perform as a large frog in the familiar small ponds of Cambridge and of provincial Bostonian society, he wished to test his powers of jumping in the Washingtonian lake. He was writing for America, not for his native province: "I am writing for a continent of a hundred million people fifty years hence." He could accept an honorary degree from Western Reserve University in Cleveland because Cleveland was part of America, but Harvard was the old family precinct upon which he had turned his back. Yet, although there were some complimentary reviews of the *History* when it was published, no one could fail to observe that the world was not breathless to read the work. When the *History* was completed, Adams fled the country for an eighteen-month circumnavigation of the globe, thinking thus to disguise his nervous interest in the response to its publication. But no matter how far he betook himself from Scribner's office in New York, he could not obscure the fact that no deafening roar of acclaim was there to be heard if only he were a little nearer American shores. The disaster of 1885 had gravely weakened Adams's resistance, and now the depths of his humiliation were in proportion to the heights of his ambition; when he thought of the *History* he turned red, blue, and green, hiding his head under his pillow. His second disastrous seeming-failure had struck him across the face, and in his stinging bitterness and humiliation of spirit, where better could he strike than against the family, the college, and the provincial society he hoped he had outgrown? His reaction to Clover's suicide was in any case causing him to retreat from the world; and in the depths of his unhappiness after her death, in the bitterness of the apparent failure of his thirteen-year literary labor, he turned against the *History* itself. He mocked even the perfectionist care he had taken with cartography and index, symbolic of the devoted attention he had lavished upon the research and artistry of his great work, and he turned in despair to his closest reminder of his dead wife. "There are not nine pages in the nine volumes that now express anything of my interests or feelings; unless perhaps some of my disillusionments," he exclaimed to Elizabeth Cameron: "I care more for one chapter, or any dozen pages of *Esther* than for the whole history, including maps and indexes; so much more, indeed, that I would not let anyone read the story [of *Esther*] for fear the reader should profane it."[40]

II

This excursus into the less agreeable side of Adams's personality and into his disappointments may explain some features of the two well-known books he wrote during his embittered old age. Not the masterpiece it has sometimes been called, *Mont-Saint-Michel and Chartres* is a volume whose merits ought nevertheless to retain for it a certain rank in American letters. Its mixture of genres is attractive, for it is partly an intelligent guide to Chartres cathedral, partly a fragmentary cultural history of France during three medieval centuries, and partly the public confession of a soul conscious of "the cry of human suffering." While concentrating upon French architecture from about 1140 to 1250, Adams ranges as early as the *Song of Roland* in the eleventh century and as far afield as the life of Francis of Assisi. The focus of the book is Chartres, yet half of it discusses the medieval poetry and philosophy that help to explain the cathedral.

But the book's failings obtrude sharply. A cultlike atmosphere permeates some passages, leaving the reader overcome at the feet of Adams's deities yet elevated above the mass of what the author regards as vulgar, materialistic Americans. Toward his countrymen Adams is scathing. He declares that "the measure of this devotion"—the devotion of medieval France to the Virgin Mary—"which proves to any religious American mind, beyond possible cavil, its serious and practical reality, is the money it cost."[41] Adams values essences not subject to physical law: "The grand air of the twelfth century," he thinks, "is something like that of a Greek temple; you can, if you like, hammer every separate stone to pieces, but you cannot hammer out the Greek style" (pp. 73–74). Those who tamper with sacred tablets court retribution, and Adams takes pride in his non-Chaucerian feathers. "Chaucer translated Dante's prayer in the 'Second Nonnes Tale,'" Adams observes: "He who will may undertake to translate either [Dante's or Petrarch's];— not I! The Virgin, in whom is united whatever goodness is in created being, might possibly, in her infinite grace, forgive the sacrilege; but her power has limits, if not her grace; and the whole Trinity, with the Virgin to aid, had not the power to pardon him who should translate Dante and Petrarch" (p. 249). Adams insists upon the range of his connoisseurship of artistic and commercial forms: "One would think this simple enough; easily tested on any illuminated manuscript, Arab, Persian, or Byzantine; verified by any Oriental rug, old or new; freely illustrated by a Chinese pattern on a Ming jar, or cloisonné vase; and offering a kind of alphabet for the shop-window of a Paris modiste" (p. 131). This is poor training for the superior but untutored American tourist to whom Adams directs his lecture.

The literary devices that animated the *History* degenerate in *Mont-Saint-Michel*, through overuse and the author's languor, into mannerisms. Commonplace thought attempts to disguise itself behind alliteration: "Our age has lost much of its ear for poetry, as it has its eye for colour and line, and its taste for war and worship, wine and women" (p. 29). Parallel construction no longer functions properly, for the tone has become sentimental. "It was in the year 1131 or thereabouts," Adams says, "that Roger began the Cathedral at Cefalu and the Chapel Royal at Palermo; it was about the year 1174 that his grandson William began the Cathedral of Monreale. No art—either Greek or Byzantine, Italian or Arab—has ever created two religious types so beautiful, so serious, so impressive, and yet so different, as Mont-Saint-Michel watching over its northern ocean, and Monreale, looking down over its forests of orange and lemon, on Palermo and the Sicilian seas" (p. 4). Nor does strained parallelism hide the sluggishness of certain metaphors: "While the crusaders set out to scale heaven by force at Jerusalem, the monks, who remained at home, undertook to scale heaven by prayer" (p. 284). Schematic sentence structure reduces promising comparisons to pat images: The bourgeois capitalist of the Middle Ages "watched the Virgin with anxious interest. The bourgeois had put an enormous share of his capital into what was in fact an economical speculation, not unlike the South Sea Scheme, or the railway system of our own time; except that in one case the energy was devoted to shortening the road to Heaven; in the other, to shortening the road to Paris" (p. 96). Adams now tolerates hackneyed phrases that nullify the old devices for building tension: "The nineteenth century moved fast and furious, so that one who moved in it felt sometimes giddy, watching it spin; but the eleventh moved faster and more furiously still" (p. 32). The elderly author's generalizations have become tawdry and querulous: "The world grew cheap, as worlds must" (p. 9).

The most painful evidence of Adams's intellectual weariness lies in his reduction of complex issues to simple antitheses—male versus female, unity versus multiplicity—and in his repetitiveness. While he finds the spirit of twelfth-century Chartres to have been "feminine," that of eleventh-century Mont-Saint-Michel was "masculine"; and masculine means "serious":

We [Normans] were a serious race.

. . . . .

. . . Wherever we find [eleventh-century Norman work] . . . we shall find something a little more serious, more military, and more practical than you will meet in other Romanesque work, farther south. . . . [In the sixteenth century] the simple, serious, silent dignity and energy of the eleventh century have gone.

. . . . .

The promenoir . . . is an exceedingly beautiful hall, uniting the splendid calm and seriousness of the Romanesque with the exquisite lines of the Gothic.

. . . . .

. . . [At Coutances] the mere seat of the central tower astride of the church, so firm, so fixed, so serious, so defiant, is Norman. [Pp. 4, 9–10, 36, 47]

Not commanding the primary sources on French medieval history, Adams fits his materials to sterile formulas instead of letting them speak directly in all their richness and diversity.

This pigeonholing—this reducing of cultural history to the study of simple essences inherent in national groups—goes hand-in-hand with the well-known racism that found public expression during Adams's declining years. "Between Norman blood and Breton blood," he alleges, "was a singular gap"; and Thomas Aquinas profited from uniting "the two most energetic strains in Europe," the Norman and the imperial Swabian (pp. 349, 343). Adams mildly chastises the Virgin Mary for her anti-Semitism,[42] but—despite his intellectual debt to Frank Palgrave and despite his family association with Charles Kuhn, Louisa Adams's husband, whom Adams mistakenly supposed to be of Jewish descent—he himself breaks into open contempt of "Jew theatre-managers" (p. 278) and traders. "The windows of Chartres," he declares, have "the charm that the world has made no attempt to popularize them for its modern uses, so that, except for the useful little guide-book of the Abbé Clerval, one can see no clue to the legendary chaos; one has it to one's self, without much fear of being trampled upon by critics or Jew dealers in works of art" (p. 179).[43]

Stereotyping also colors Adams's discussion of the qualities of women, and his reputation as a feminist can be sustained only in part. Although he often rises above conventional lore, he sometimes theorizes about "feminine" attributes, adding a dash of Latin for good measure:

. . . The great ladies who dictated taste at the Courts of France and England, . . . like all women, liked moderate shadow for their toilettes.

. . . . .

. . . The Virgin was by essence illogical, unreasonable and feminine. . . .

. . . . .

. . . To her, every suppliant was . . . to be judged apart, on his own merits, by his love for her. . . .

. . . . .

... She cared for her baby, a simple matter, which any woman could do and understand. That, and the grace of God, had made her Queen of Heaven. The Trinity had its source in her—totius Trinitatis nobile Triclinium—and she was maternity. She was also poetry and art. In the bankruptcy of reason, she alone was real. [Pp. 98, 259, 274, 322]

Mont-Saint-Michel and Chartres seems in many ways to reveal only the ruins of its author's power, yet its strengths remain. It guides beginners modestly through Chartres cathedral and amidst medieval French poetry and philosophy. Adams goads the voyager to observe and reflect upon things that might otherwise pass unnoticed. At Chartres he calls attention to the contrast between one statue on the western portal and another on the northern porch, both perhaps representing the Queen of Sheba; he points to an irregularity in construction designed to accommodate the extraordinarily large western rose; he shows how the rich border of one of the western lancet windows compensates for the window's narrowness; and he pauses at the seven great windows which rise high above the curve of the choir. His commentary is no mere copy of Viollet-le-Duc's: Adams frequently differs from his mentor, and constantly he spurs his reader to speculate on what the architecture meant to the people of the Middle Ages. When he turns to medieval poetry and philosophy, his observations are sometimes equally suggestive. He evokes with imaginative power a gathering of laymen and monks at Mont-Saint-Michel, where a jongleur sings the *Song of Roland*; and his comments upon the rhyme and rhythm of that song make it accessible to laymen. Adams narrates with a connoisseur's appreciation the tale of *Nicolette and Aucassin*. In rendering the spirit of French mysticism, he betrays his own sympathy for this approach to religion.

Yet *Mont-Saint-Michel and Chartres* is more than a superior guidebook: It is an ambitious study of one side of the cultural history of medieval France. Adams is provocative about the position of women and of the Virgin Mary in French society: In the Oriental game of chess, brought home from Syria by the pilgrims or crusaders, "the King was followed step by step by a *Minister* whose functions were personal. The crusaders freed the piece from control; gave it liberty to move up or down or diagonally, forwards and backwards; made it the most arbitrary and formidable champion on the board, while the King and the Knight were the most restricted in movement; and this piece they named Queen, and called the Virgin" (p. 203). Adams insists that he is trying "to catch not a fact but a feeling" (p. 14). Seeking parallels between art forms, especially between poetry and architecture, he attempts to deduce the social attitudes that underlie this artistic expression. Although his formulas are schematic and oversimplified, his expression hyperbolic, Adams's search for parallels can be stimulating. The quality of Chrétien de Troyes's verse, he suggests, "is something like the quality of the glass windows—conventional decoration; colours in conventional harmonies; refinement, restraint, and feminine delicacy of taste. . . . Christian's world is sky-blue and rose, with only enough red to give it warmth, and so flooded with light that even its mysteries count only by the clearness with which they are shown" (p. 212). His interpretation of religion resembles what Santayana was reaching at the same time. Religion, the principal occasion for art, was to Santayana a symbolic representation of experience: Man "has to imagine what the angels would say, so that his own good impulses (which create those angels) may gain in authority."[44] Adams puts the matter less well, for he patronizes the Middle Ages. The Virgin Mary, he claims, was an ideal raised by man whose "worship elevated the whole sex"; the cathedral at Chartres was "a toyhouse to please the Queen of Heaven. . . . This church was built for her . . . exactly as a little girl sets up a doll-house for her favourite blonde doll" (pp. 336, 250, 88–89).

The Mariolatry of twelfth- and thirteenth-century France provides *Mont-Saint-Michel* with its central theme, but Adams's picture of France's devotion to Mary is not fully reliable; for the book is in substantial measure not medieval history but a convoluted autobiographical confession—not so much a lament to the decline of some fabled "Age of Faith" as the secret, unuttered cry of a man who had flung his aspirations up to the sky but was crushed into silence, and beyond pain, by his wife's death. Although the Virgin Mary of Adams's pages is sometimes an archetypal woman with child, she—along with the great French ladies of the twelfth and thirteenth centuries who so fascinated Adams—often bears striking resemblance to the woman who had most filled his imagination. "The French woman of the Middle Ages," he believes, "was a masculine character. . . . The superiority of the woman was not a fancy, but a fact. . . . Both physically and mentally the woman was robust, as the men often complained, and she did not greatly resent being treated as a man. . . . [At Chartres] the Virgin permitted no one to approach her, even to adore" (pp. 197–98, 136).[45] Adams's tone becomes almost lyrical as he narrates Adam de la Halle's tale of *Robin and Marion*: The satire is "directed wholly against the men. . . . [Robin] is tamed by his love of Marion, but he has just enough intelligence to think well of himself, and to get himself into trouble without knowing how to get out of it. Marion loves him much as she would her child; she makes only a little fun of him; defends him from the others; laughs at his jealousy; scolds him on occasion; flatters his dancing; sends him on errands" (pp. 241, 244).

The signs of Adams's feeling for Marian are scattered through the book. The language he later used when referring to his communion with his dead wife was that of *Mont-Saint-Michel and Chartres*: "I have gone on talking, all that time, but it has been to myself—and to her. . . . I can sit now for hours, quite still, with my hands before me, thinking of [her and Anna Lodge]."[46] And his listening to artists talking in the cathedral was his wife's story in

Esther. Sitting in Chartres Cathedral "in the subdued afternoon light of the apse, one goes on for hours reading the open volumes of colour, and listening to the steady discussion by the architects, artists, priests, princes, and princesses of the thirteenth century about the arrangements of this apse" (p. 175). As he turns finally from Chartres, Adams identifies himself with a mother who has lost her child, and his voice breaks as in no other of his works: Mary's

quiet, masculine strength enchants us most. . . . People who suffer beyond the formulas of expression—who are crushed into silence, and beyond pain—want no display of emotion—no bleeding heart—no weeping at the foot of the Cross—no hysterics—no phrases! . . . We shall see . . . [Chartres] no more, and can safely leave the Virgin in her majesty, with her three great prophets on either hand, as calm and confident in their own strength and in God's providence as they were when Saint Louis was born, but looking down from a deserted heaven, into an empty church, on a dead faith. [Pp. 194–95]

On the last page of the book Adams's praise of Chartres again gives vent to feelings that his nature forced him to suppress in his own life: The "haunting nightmares of the Church are expressed as strongly by the Gothic cathedral as though it had been the cry of human suffering. . . . The delight of its aspirations is flung up to the sky. The pathos of its self-distrust and anguish of doubt is buried in the earth as its last secret."

Adams's elaborately indirect way of writing about himself finds a different outlet in his third-person narrative of *The Education of Henry Adams*. Dilettantism spoils much of *Mont-Saint-Michel*, but Adams was a more expert observer of the nineteenth century than of the Middle Ages. This most famous of modern American autobiographies is far more compelling than many portions of its companion piece. The best thing about the *Education* is Adams's captivating account, in the first two-thirds of the book, of his experiences before 1872. His preface—and the Editor's Preface which Adams himself wrote but had Henry Cabot Lodge sign—were parts of a pretense that Adams's sole object was didactic rather than autobiographical.[47] But he took obvious pleasure in telling of his own life, and the first section of the book rings with intelligence and shrewd observation.

One passage after another has become famous for the picture Adams drew of New England, England in the 1860s, and the Washington where Grantism, he claimed, had wrecked his life. Adams evokes a Boston led by men of the professional classes: Self-respecting Unitarian scholar-clergymen gave tone to society; John Quincy Adams's independence grew from the best New England tradition; upright gentlemen conducted a Free-Soil newspaper from Charles Francis Adams's library. In England, Henry Adams's loyalty to the American democratic republican experiment was hardened by the flames of British anti-Americanism during the Civil War, yet his happy association with the Gaskell family directed him toward a literary-scholarly career. Grant symbolized the political and social changes destroying the old order. But the world's confusion was not caused by Grant alone nor by the Industrial Revolution: The most memorable chapter in the *Education*, "Chaos," centers on Adams's first painful coming to terms with death, in Italy and afterwards at Mont Blanc.

When Adams recreates honestly the emotions and experiences of his life, his writing is at its strongest:

Many a boy might be ruined by much less than the emotions of the funeral service [of John Quincy Adams] in the Quincy church, with its surroundings of national respect and family pride. By . . . [a] dramatic chance it happened that the clergyman of the parish, Dr. Lunt, was an unusual pulpit orator, the ideal of a somewhat austere intellectual type, such as the school of Buckminster and Channing inherited from the old Congregational clergy. His extraordinarily refined appearance, his dignity of manner, his deeply cadenced voice, his remarkable English and his fine appreciation, gave to the funeral service a character that left an overwhelming impression on the boy's mind. He was to see many great functions—funerals and festivals—in afterlife, till his only thought was to see no more, but he never again witnessed anything nearly so impressive to him as the last services at Quincy over the body of one President and the ashes of another.[48]

Similarly, Adams's account of his first meeting Charles Milnes Gaskell, on the steps of old Sir Henry Holland's house in London, breathes something of the atmosphere of a declaration of love;[49] and when he left England in 1868 at the age of thirty, he felt an emotion which, thirty-five years later, he could not disguise: "London had become his vice. He loved his haunts, his houses, his habits, and even his hansom cabs. He loved growling like an Englishman, and going into society where he knew not a face, and cared not a straw. He lived deep into the lives and loves and disappointments of his friends. When at last he found himself back at Liverpool, his heart wrenched by the act of parting, he moved mechanically, unstrung" (p. 236).

In this first section of the *Education*, where Adams describes his life before 1872, he writes in the manner of a discursive essayist, passing easily from topic to topic, throwing off provocative comments at random. A character sketch of Henry's father leads to a definition of the divisions within Boston society; portraits of Sumner, Dana, and Palfrey issue into a discussion of the upper-class bourgeoisie that governed France, England, and New England; the fact of Unitarian supremacy in Boston causes Adams to reflect on the disappearance of religion. Miscellaneous observations and generalizations punctuate the narrative: "The faculty of turning away one's eyes as one approaches a chasm is not unusual, and Boston showed, under the lead of Mr. Webster, how successfully it could be done in politics" (pp. 34–35). Vivid images prevent Adams's discussion from becoming abstract: Richard Henry Dana "affected to be still before the mast . . . , and only as one got to know him better one found the man of rather excessive refinement trying with success to work like a day-laborer, deliberately hardening his skin to the burden, as though he were still carrying hides at Monterey" (p. 29). The scope of Adams's reference lends his narrative richness and density, although few topics are analyzed in depth: "The literary world had revolted against the yoke of coming capitalism—its money-lenders, its bank directors, and its railway magnates. Thackeray and Dickens followed Balzac in scratching and biting the unfortunate middle class with savage ill-temper" (p. 61). This discursive method allows Adams to hide many a literary judgment in the briefest of phrases: "The Boston mind . . . , in its uttermost flights, was never *moyenâgeux*. One felt the horror of Longfellow and Emerson, the doubts of Lowell and the humor of Holmes, at the wild Walpurgis-night of Swinburne's talk" (p. 141).

Although the *Education* is known in America for its description of Boston and Washington, Adams's picture of England is scarcely less interesting. He pursues at too great length and with too rancorous a tone his search for the motives of Palmerston's and Russell's American policy, but his sketches of Englishmen like John Bright are as vigorous as that of, for example, Charles Sumner, and his portrayal of English society as suggestive as that of New England. Adams's range of allusion is wide, and hyperbole increases the force of his language. John Bright "was a liberal hater, and what he hated he reviled after the manner of Milton, but he was afraid of no one. He was almost the only man in England, or, for that matter, in Europe, who hated Palmerston and was not afraid of him, or of the press or the pulpit, the clubs or the bench, that stood behind him" (p. 190). British manners fascinated Adams. Satire and affection are strangely blended in his picture of the English gentleman as he entered

a drawing-room where he was a total stranger. . . . [He places] himself on the hearthrug, his back to the fire, with an air of expectant benevolence, without curiosity, much as though he had dropped in at a charity concert, kindly disposed to applaud the performers and to overlook mistakes. This ideal rarely succeeded in youth, and towards thirty it took a form of modified insolence and offensive patronage; but about sixty it mellowed into courtesy, kindliness, and even deference to the young which had extraordinary charm both in women and in men. [P. 202]

The superior quality of many passages of the *Education* appears when Adams's portrait of Clarence King is set against John Stuart Mill's sketch, in his own *Autobiography*, of John Sterling. Mill was more attached to Sterling, he says, than to any other man; yet in writing of his friend he patronizes him. Mill's prose is stilted, and his character study a list of abstract virtues.

His talk of liberty and duty measures the distance from the mid-Victorian to the late Victorian and post-Victorian era. Sterling

was indeed one of the most lovable of men. His frank, cordial, affectionate, and expansive character; a love of truth alike conspicuous in the highest things and the humblest; a generous and ardent nature which threw itself with impetuosity into the opinions it adopted, but was as eager to do justice to the doctrines and the men it was opposed to, as to make war on what it thought their errors; and an equal devotion to the two cardinal points of Liberty and Duty, formed a combination of qualities as attractive to me, as to all others who knew him as well as I did. . . . The advance he always seemed to have made when I saw him after an interval, made me apply to him what Goethe said of Schiller: "Er hatte eine fürchterliche Fortschreitung."[50]

By contrast Adams radiates admiration in describing Clarence King. Adams's talk about "the New York woman" checks momentarily the force of his prose, but it remains markedly more vigorous and imaginative than the political philosopher's. Adams feels more strongly than Mill, yet he is not blind to King's propensity to gamble on mining speculations nor to his slightly untrustworthy, imperial manner. King

had everything to interest and delight Adams. He knew more than Adams did of art and poetry; he knew America, especially west of the hundredth meridian, better than any one; he knew the professor by heart, and he knew the Congressman better than he did the professor. He knew even women; even the American woman; even the New York woman, which is saying much. Incidentally he knew more practical geology than was good for him, and saw ahead at least one generation further than the text-books. That he saw right was a different matter. Since the beginning of time no man has lived who is known to have seen right; the charm of King was that he saw what others did and a great deal more. His wit and humor; his bubbling energy which swept every one into the current of his interest; his personal charm of youth and manners; his faculty of giving and taking, profusely, lavishly, whether in thought or in money as though he were Nature herself, marked him almost alone among Americans. He had in him something of the Greek—a touch of Alcibiades or Alexander. [P. 311]

Every reader of the *Education* has his favorite passages to witness Adams's insight into character and society or to illustrate the more attractive side of the cynicism into which he had fallen. Frequently his style is brilliant, as when he symbolizes his turn from American political history to medievalism by a retrospective glance at his youth: "The happiest hours of the boy's education were passed in summer lying on a musty heap of Congressional Documents in the old farmhouse at Quincy, reading 'Quentin Durward,' 'Ivanhoe,' and 'The Talisman,' and raiding the garden at intervals for peaches and pears" (p. 39). Age had not killed the restless play of his imagination:

"The Legal Tender decision . . . fell on one's head like a plaster ceiling, and could not be escaped" (p. 277).

If the *Education* is the most interesting and artistic of American autobiographies, it is also a major document in American intellectual history. Adams challenges the simple ideologies of his generation with a skepticism whose edge cuts deep. The Free-Soil faith of his youth does not explain how George Washington, whom Adams never ceased to admire, could be the product of a slaveholding regime. The Unitarian faith of Boston cannot account for the callous cruelty with which nature destroys the most finely developed human organisms. The evolutionary faith of the later nineteenth century does not elucidate the sequence leading from Wenlock Abbey to the architectural horrors of the Industrial Revolution.

In rebelling against the heritage of his youth and against certain nineteenth-century dogmas, Adams appealed to a curious mixture of traditional American attitudes and new ideas that were to become twentieth-century dogma. His assault upon the academy—his claim that his book learning was useless, that experience alone proved educational, that reason is weak, that the senses need to be allowed free play, that instinct must not be blighted in babyhood—harmonized with the pragmatic, antirationalist, "Redskin" tendency of American thought, and it was the more welcome as coming from an archdeacon of the "Paleface" New England tradition. Similarly, Adams's portrayal of himself as a feeble failure appealed to an old American belief that the aristocratic elements of the social amalgam could only be sources of weakness. Yet Adams's critical stance toward American provinciality, his tentative discussion of the power of sex, and his recognition of the other powerful subterranean forces that lie below the surface of social convention insured for the *Education* an enthusiastic greeting from the avant garde of 1918. Since then the *Education* has become for many readers a sort of twentieth-century Bible, presenting a powerful "image of modern man in a multiverse."[51] The Industrial and democratic revolutions had confused many members of Adams's generation, and the unsettling events of the twentieth century made him a spokesman for an uncertain age. Much of Adams's pain was genuine, his sense of man's weakness deeply felt; and the coincidence of his loss of spiritual confidence with that of countless contemporaries made the *Education* seem to be much more than a self-portrait.

Yet when acknowledgment has been made of the *Education*'s fine qualities as an autobiography and of its significance in American intellectual history, something remains to be said, and part of this must be negative. Not every important document in intellectual history is a work of philosophical power. It may be suspected that commentators, rightly discriminating certain strengths of the *Education*, have exaggerated others. Adams communicated forcibly a mood of disillusion but was less successful in the philosophical formulation—and even the artistic expression—of this mood. Oliver Wendell Holmes, Jr., was not wholly wrong in his belief that Adams's "philosophizing didn't amount to much. But he did first class work—wrote the best piece of American history there is."[52]

The *Education* falls into two clearly defined sections, the first ending before Adams married at the age of thirty-four in 1872, the second recommencing twenty years later in 1892. While the first part includes most of the best autobiographical passages, the second mirrors the disintegration of Adams's life after the *History* was complete. Feeling himself defeated in love and in art, Adams retreated into scientific speculation that sometimes appeared to verge on madness. "As one's sixtieth year approached," he observes,

the artist began to die; only a certain intense cerebral restlessness survived . . .

. . . . .

[In 1901] he knew not in what new direction to turn, and sat at his desk, idly pulling threads out of the tangled skein of science. . . . He covered his desk with magnets, and mapped out their lines of force by compass. Then he read all the books he could find, and tried in vain to make his lines of force agree with theirs. . . . [The magnet] staggered his new education by its evidence of growing complexity, and multiplicity, and even contradiction, in life. . . . [He was] maundering among the magnets. [Pp. 350–51, 396–98]

Except for two or three chapters and scattered passages elsewhere, this second part of the *Education* seems less well written than the first. Silence, Adams's ostensible ideal at this stage of his life, would have been better than some of these pages. Yet the perversity of fate—her arm jogged by the clever but disillusioned author as she cast the die—is such that the *Education* has become known for just those ideas and images that find culminating expression in this second part: For the discussion of sex in "The Dynamo and the Virgin"; for the quasi-scientific speculations of the concluding chapters; and for the image of himself that Adams projects over his Washington career as a passive, submissive elderly gentleman, sadly displaced from active life by politicians like Grant and Cameron and relegated after 1877 to the derisory role of offstage companion to statesmen.

Adams's voice was part of the twentieth-century protest against those Victorian attitudes toward sex misleadingly termed Puritanic. "Any one brought up among Puritans," he regrets,

knew that sex was sin. In any previous age sex was strength. . . . The true American knew something of the facts, but nothing of the feelings [associated with this force]. . . . [Adams asked himself] whether he knew of any American artist who had ever insisted on the power of sex, as every classic had always done; but he could think only of Walt Whitman; Bret Harte, as far as the magazines would let him venture; and one or two painters, for the flesh-tones. All the rest had used sex for sentiment, never for force. . . . Adams was a quintessence of Boston . . . and Adams's instinct was blighted from babyhood. [Pp. 384–87]

Beyond these few comments Adams's discussion hardly progresses, and in the *Education* his theories (as contrasted to his sketch of his lively elder sister Louisa) are even less feminist than the remarks in *Mont-Saint-Michel*. Just as Adams repudiated after 1890 the principles of his career as historian, so he turned against those implicit in the life of his dead wife. Behind the screen of his "trick of affirming that the woman was the superior" (p. 442), Adams falls back upon the conservative's usual allegation that the world must choose from only two possibilities: It must opt for either the old social relations or a revolutionary overturning of accepted values. He professes to believe that "the woman's . . . axis of rotation had been the cradle and the family. . . . If her force was to be diverted from its axis, it must find a new field, and the family must pay for it. So far as she succeeded, she must become sexless like the bees" (p. 446).

If Adams's feminism leaps gracefully away like a startled deer under inspection, his scientism proves a scarcely less elusive creature. The ever repeated message of the *Education* is that the world is chaos. The most memorable passage is Adams's account of his sister Louisa's death of tetanus, in Italy. Her ten days of torture sharpened his sense of anarchy: Before 1870

he had never seen Nature—only her surface—the sugar-coating that she shows to youth. . . . For the first time, the stage-scenery of the senses collapsed; the human mind felt itself stripped naked, vibrating in a void of shapeless energies, with resistless mass, colliding, crushing, wasting, and destroying what these same energies had created and labored from eternity to perfect. . . . [Afterwards] for the first time in his life, Mont Blanc for a moment looked to him what it was—a chaos of anarchic and purposeless forces. [Pp. 287–89]

Emotion here wells up from Adams's reaction to Clover's suicide, nowhere even hinted at in the *Education* except in a rarely candid sentence of this same passage about Louisa's death: "Flung suddenly in his face, with the harsh brutality of chance, the terror of the blow stayed by him thenceforth for life, until repetition made it more than the will could struggle with; more than he could call on himself to bear" (p. 287).[53] With Clover's breakdown fresh in his recollection, Adams might well declare that in psychology "the only absolute truth was the sub-conscious chaos below [the conscious mind]" (p. 433).

If Adams sees the world as chaos, what is to be made of his presidential message in 1894 to the American Historical Association, suggesting that some new Galileo might soon proclaim momentous laws of history; of his claim that mathematics was above all the tool he had needed for his career but was never properly taught; and of the concluding chapters of the *Education*, enunciating a "Dynamic Theory of History" and a "Law of Acceleration"? How does this apparent flight into scientism relate to Adams's concurrent turn toward aestheticism in *Mont-Saint-Michel*?

Part of the answer is that Adams was mentally exhausted and confused, that he came to make a virtue of being self-contradictory, that he projected upon the world the "Babel of . . . vague and ill-defined and unrelated thoughts and half-thoughts and experimental outcries" that he sensed within.[54] He knew that "his theory and practice were . . . at variance" (p. 420). His practice had been overwhelmingly empiricist—in his skepticism about Lyell's uniformitarian creed in geology, in the painstaking analysis of men and parties that comprises the *History*, and throughout his career—but his theory would be abstract and scientific. He felt that, while each episode in the *History* could stand on its own feet, he had failed to give coherence to the nine-volume work. Now he would compensate by stating coherent theories and laws.[55] The oversimplified generalizations of *Mont-Saint-Michel* and the laws of the *Education*—Adams's turn to the fine arts and his ventures in "arithmetic"—were two different forms of a single reaction against the demanding, detailed analysis of the *History*. Exhausted by his long labor, disappointed in his hopes, finding his life in ruins and his grasp of affairs relaxing, Adams as an old man pursued the snare of achieving at least intellectual mastery over a rebellious world. The geopolitical speculations of the second part of the *Education* and its scientific ruminations are cut from the same cloth.

Yet Adams's empiricist, antitheoretical nature could not be downed. "His theory," he acknowledged, "never affected his practice. He knew . . . that English disorder approached nearer to truth, if truth existed, than French measure or Italian line, or German logic" (p. 420). His chapter "A Dynamic Theory of History" presents no theory but simply a materialist, empiricist sketch of past history, sensible as far as it goes though too sketchy to have much value; while his "Law of Acceleration," which he conceives as the heart of his "Dynamic Theory," is not a scientific statement of order in historical development. Rather it disguises behind scientific allusions Adams's sense that the disorder of the world was running steadily out of hand, that his effort to comprehend history was becoming futile. A mood of impending catastrophe communicates itself, but Adams's expression is repetitive, his science inexpert; and the sometimes artificial tone of Adams's pessimism raises suspicion about his candor.

Adams had inherited his melancholic disposition from his mother, and as early as 1863 he was bewailing man's "impotence and ignorance." His active career as historian and his happy marriage put these ideas into abeyance, but his apparent failures of the 1880s resuscitated his despondent streak. There had always been a factitious element in his melancholy. Like his mother, Adams reveled in gloom: In 1863 he found "amusement" in viewing the world "through rather brown media."[56] His relish in flaunting pessimism and failure before the world shines from most chapters of the *Education*. There was genuine pain, but there was also insincerity, and the disingenuous note weakens the force of Adams's complaint against the world. His satisfaction in exaggerating the world's confusion—diminishing the claims of reason— is so great as to lessen the persuasiveness of this version of irrationalism.

Whether Adams's creed can indeed be termed irrationalist has been questioned by two of his best-known interpreters. J. C. Levenson finds in the *Education* a philosophy that successfully fuses sense and intellect, and he believes Adams offers the optimistic message that "we must know how to discard the past . . . and see the startling novelty of the present, but we can do these things intelligently only if we know the past." Robert Sayre thinks Adams's search for order is in itself constructive, even if it is doomed to be frustrated: "The image of disorder is so clearly presented and the search for education so enfolding that the book builds and informs even as it despairs."[57] The strongest evidence to support these interpretations appears in the last ten pages of the book, where Adams suggests that human powers of comprehension may possibly keep pace with the world's increasing complexity.

But a work of art is not like a detective story, whose final pages should confound the expectations aroused earlier in the book. On the contrary, the denouement of such a work will be effective only when it grows organically from what precedes. For hundreds of pages the *Education* is futilitarian, the assertion on page 496 being typical: Adams "had never been able to acquire knowledge, still less to impart it." Adams implies, furthermore, that no one else understands more than he, for the world's complexity has run out of hand.[58] But suddenly there is a volte-face: Adams promises to be docile toward "the new American," born since 1900, who "must be a sort of God compared with any former creation of nature" (p. 496). So addicted to irony and paradox had the elderly Adams become that he did not always know what he believed, but this flattery of "the new American" smacks of dissimulation.

One may doubt whether the gentle benediction Adams pronounces at the end of his sermon represents his real feelings. "I have urged you to step quickly if you are to keep pace with the world," Adams seems to tell the reader. "My law of acceleration tends at least to encourage foresight and to economize waste of mind. I have done all I can to prepare you for the world, and now I send you forth with my blessing."[59] This mild message is in itself attractive, but it is belied by the anathemas that, on so many other occasions, the tired prelate has pronounced upon a refractory world. One such outburst, taken at random, expresses better than Adams's benediction the essential mood of the *Education*. "The law of the new multiverse explained," according to Adams, "the persistently fiendish treatment of man by man. . . . All that a historian won was a vehement wish to escape. He saw his education complete, and was sorry he ever began it. . . . He repudiated all share in the world as it was to be" (P. 458). Even at the end of his benediction Adams's pessimism cannot be stifled, for the last words of the book express once again his horror of the world, here entirely heartfelt: Clarence King and John Hay were dead and Adams would soon die, but "perhaps some day—say 1938, their centenary—they might be allowed to return together for a holiday . . . ; and perhaps then, for the first time since man began his education among the carnivores, they would find a world that sensitive and timid natures could regard without a shudder" (p. 505).[60]

If Adams's discussion of sex is cursory, and his scientism abortive, the most striking feature of the *Education* is Adams's lack of frankness about his career. Occasionally one may feel him to verge on the heroic in his denial of the ambition that for years had given meaning to his life. Even when he comes closest to avowing the truth, he alludes with utmost indirection to his aims, pretending that his work was social rather than artistic. "He had no notion," he claims, whether his books "served a useful purpose. . . . [Among contemporary American artists and men of letters] Clarence King, John Hay, and Henry Adams had led modest existences, trying to fill in the social gaps of a class which, as yet, showed but thin ranks and little cohesion. The combination offered no very glittering prizes, but they pursued it for twenty years with as much patience and effort as though it led to fame or power, until, at last, Henry Adams thought his own duties sufficiently performed and his account with society settled" (pp. 315–16). But ordinarily Adams denies in toto what he had been up to for twenty years, and one may become alienated by this unnatural exercise in self-mutilation. When interpreting Napoleon's motives for selling Louisiana, Adams defined his own impulse: "The depths of his nature concealed a wish to hide forever the monument of a defeat." Adams sought to protect himself from biographers by inoculating the public with a dose of self-criticism. He might then avoid the humiliation of having people deride his supposed failure to fulfill soaring ambition. "I mean to do [my autobiography]," he had written twenty years earlier; "after seeing how coolly and neatly a man like Trollope can destroy the last vestige of heroism in his own life, I object to allowing mine to be murdered by anyone except myself."[61]

Adams's exercise in literary suicide took the form of self-depreciation. Alleging that in New England one often amused oneself with "the pleasure of hating—one's self if no better victim offered" (p. 7), Adams carried self-mortification beyond bounds. He was a worm, a French poodle, above all an arthropod: He "wandered about in . . . [British society] like a maggot in cheese. . . . He was a spider and had to spin a new web in some new place with a new attachment. . . . Mr. Boutwell turned him out of the Treasury with the indifference or contempt that made even a beetle helpless. . . . No mosquito could be so unlucky as to be caught a second time between a

Secretary and a Senator who were both his friends. . . . One was almost glad to act the part of horseshoe crab in Quincy Bay" (pp. 197, 209, 274, 448). He was passive, docile, submissive, "an elderly and timid single gentleman in Paris, who never drove down the Champs Élysées without expecting an accident, and commonly witnessing one" (p. 494). This ostentation of self-belittlement masked self-esteem, and the judgment upon Tolstoy's *Confession* applies as well to Adams's *Education*: "The general impression created by the book," writes Henry Troyat, "is an unhealthy one of public exposure and flagellation. . . . [At the end of the book one wonders whether this display is not] an orgy of masochistic pride, for self-criticism, when performed in broad daylight, can produce a kind of intoxication, and the setting oneself up as an example not to follow may be another way of attracting attention."[62] Adams understood that his own protest that he never succeeded in gaining education was really a boast. "Since the time of Socrates, wise men have been mostly shy of claiming to understand anything" (p. 407).

But joined with self-advertisement was genuine self-repulsion. Adams distorts the facts and ideals of his career beyond recognition. At the outset his principles had been individualistic; he had declared in 1869 that his path "was never chosen in order to suit other people's tastes, but my own. . . . [In America] the tendency is incessant to draw everyone into the main current. I have told you before that I mean to be unpopular, and do it because I must do it, or do as other people do and give up the path I chose for myself years ago."[63] But now in the *Education* he affects to guide young men toward conformity. Their minds should "react . . . on the lines of force that attract their world. . . . Susceptibility to the highest forces is the highest genius" (pp. 314, 475). Adams had labored tirelessly to achieve his ambition—"Work and read ten hours a day, till my mind is scoured like a kitchen copper. . . . The only thing I want is that . . . [the world] should read my books"[64]—but now he pictures himself as an insignificant "private secretary"; a person who "never got to the point of playing the game at all; he lost himself in the study of it"; a mere "stable-companion to statesmen" (pp. 155, 4, 317). Each of these phrases alludes covertly to his career as writer of history, but few readers of the *Education* could be expected to take up these clues—or the hints in his fascinating but perverse chapter "Twenty Years After"—when Adams carefully creates the image of a feeble, lifelong trifler: In Paris in 1860 "he tried to acquire a few French idioms, without even aspiring to master a subjunctive, but he succeeded better in acquiring a modest taste for Bordeaux and Burgundy and one or two sauces. . . . [As teacher at Harvard] he had accomplished nothing that he tried to do. . . . The secret of education still hid itself somewhere behind ignorance, and one fumbled over it as feebly as ever" (pp. 96, 304, 389). Craving "consideration," Adams finally achieved it posthumously—pretending he had never meant his self-portrait for mass viewing—by creating the image of himself as a ridiculous figure no longer seriously challenging American susceptibilities. Even after 1890 he was by no means merely an ineffectual dilettante. But for him to project such an image across his earlier life was an act of audacity. Perhaps a person has as much right to create fiction out of the materials of his life and pass it off as autobiography as he does to commit suicide, but the act in this case was that of a defeated man. Readers of the *Education* may have been flattered, if mystified, by Adams's profession of obeisance to the twentieth-century American, to whom "the nineteenth century would stand on the same plane with the fourth—equally childlike" (p. 497). Insincerity abounds, yet Adams's denial of the value of his own endeavors is naturally taken as a principal message of the *Education*. This betrayal of the ideals that had shaped his work as historian testifies to his pathetic sense of defeat. Adams's work as literary artist was part of a great nineteenth-century European movement, and to encourage the twentieth century to look upon the nineteenth as childlike was a bad joke.

The decline of Adams's mental vigor after 1890 vitiated certain passages of the *Education*. Adams contents himself too often with phrases of meretricious cleverness—"Here, on the Wenlock Edge of time" (p. 229). Alliterative sport devalues the seriousness of Charles Adams's military duties: Charles was thrown "into the furnace of the Army of the Potomac to get educated in a fury of fire" (p. 112). Henry Adams's thoughts and phrases can sound stereotyped. While in 1861 Adams knew little, "the President and Secretary of State knew least of all. . . . Adams knew no more about it [the Chinese situation in 1900] than though he were the best-informed statesman in Europe. . . . [When the Russo-Japanese War impended,] as usual, Adams felt as ignorant as the best-informed statesman" (pp. 111, 392, 462). Sometimes he is not candid about his own thoughts, yet he insists upon calling attention to himself, and the combination of disingenuousness with self-importance spoils the passage. The most decisive proof of Charles Francis Adams's unfitness to be minister to England, Henry declares, was that, in Henry's opinion, "Mr. Adams had chosen a private secretary far more unfit than his chief. . . . In the mission attached to Mr. Adams in 1861, the only rag of legitimacy or order was the private secretary, whose stature was not sufficient to impose awe on the Court and Parliament of Great Britain" (pp. 110, 113).

But the powers Adams had exercised in the *History* were merely relaxed, not destroyed, and no enumeration of the defects of the *Education* can diminish the intelligence and artistry of many of its pages. It is a triumphant evocation of Adams's early life in Massachusetts, London, and Washington, and the first two-thirds of the book will survive for their brilliant, if selective, recreation of an unusual life. The *Education* is also a work of significance in American intellectual history. It will always remain more popular than the *History*—more accessible, less demanding, less professional. Yet Adams's account of his sister Louisa's death in Italy shows that he might have written an even more remarkable—and a truer—*Education* had he chosen to be candid about his relations with his brother Charles, his friend Gaskell, and his wife Clover; and if he had attempted to think through the forces and experiences that formed him as a historian. The pity is that instead of telling this story, as he might incomparably have done, he chose to bury his passions privately, and with a vengeance.

CHAPTER 9 · *The Sense of Failure*

HENRY ADAMS, in his active middle years, was not a frustrated politician, nor a trifling dilettante, nor a hungry onlooker at other men's banquets. He lived life to the full in his chosen artistic career. His field was historical writing, and he worked at a propitious moment: He profited both from the tradition of literary history as cultivated in England and practiced by his Boston predecessors and from the development of scientific history in Germany. For thirteen years he endeavored, with a concentration of effort scarcely possible except to a person of independent means, to shape the materials of political history into a work of art. As a literary craftsman he was madly perfectionist. He considered and reconsidered every sentence, chiseling, planing, filing, honing, until it seemed capable of no further refinement.

Scholarship and literary pursuits came naturally to the son of Charles Francis Adams, who himself had found more satisfaction in editing the diary of John Quincy Adams than in his own political career. Henry Adams's personal contact with the eminent Boston historians Palfrey, Motley, Parkman, and Bancroft convinced him that a historian's career might be an honorable one. Years of cooperation, competition, and conflict with his elder brother Charles whetted Henry's literary ambitions. His long residence in Great Britain was crucial in determining his career, for he gained courage there to follow his own bent and to set for himself an unattainably high literary standard. "I hope," he once wrote from England, "to reach the point when I shall be able by working hours over a sentence, to make it perfect."[1]

Adams's marriage to Clover Hooper was the best possible spur to his career. A woman of formidable mental and conversational power, she had grown to maturity in the literary society of Boston and Cambridge, where her close association with Henry James long preceded her husband's. She was ambitious for Adams; she goaded him into work; she filled his imagination. Her spirit of mockery delighted him, and the intellectual ebullience of their comradeship infused itself into the *History*, composed, as it was, largely under her influence.

219

Henry Adams was at the peak of his artistic strength in the 1880s, when he was writing his *History*, and it is here that any attempt to evaluate his successes and failures must begin. Describing to a successor at Harvard his aims as a teacher, Adams also defined his purposes in the *History*. "I tried and failed [to discover]," Adams claimed in 1886, "some system of teaching history which should be equally suited to a fixed science and a course of belles lettres."[2] Notwithstanding this claim of failure, the real reason Adams left teaching was his wish to aim higher—he sought "original results." Yet his effort to marry science and art in his *History* was not, despite all praise which that work deserves, in every respect successful.

Adams suffered both emotional and intellectual shortcomings. He had not enough sympathy to explore the full tragedy of Thomas Jefferson, who experimented freely with the vision of a liberal political system but lacked courage or even a deep wish to upset his own slaveholding society. Nor had Adams quite the intellect, like a powerful magnet, to draw the particles of his diplomatic and political narrative into a sufficiently clear pattern.

Adams probably sensed these limitations. His revulsion against the *History*, though greatly magnified by his unappeased lust for "consideration," cannot be attributed exclusively to this source, for the beginnings of his reaction antedated the public's refusal to acclaim his work. The only portion of Adams's diary to escape consumption in his pitiless fireplace covers the year when he completed the draft of his *History*, and bitterness had already eaten like acid to the core of his being. "The narrative was finished last Monday," he wrote at Quincy in September 1888: "In imitation of Gibbon I walked in the garden . . . and meditated. My meditations were too painful to last. The contrast between my beginning and end is something Gibbon never conceived. Spurred by it into long meditated action, I have brought from Boston the old volumes of this Diary, and have begun their systematic destruction. I mean to leave no record that can be obliterated." These meditations were intimately bound up with Adams's feelings about his wife. He dated his troubles, not from the time of Clover's death, but from her breakdown in the spring of 1885. By May 1888 he had already made substantial progress on the last volumes of the *History* and could "see the day near when I shall at last cut this only tie that still connects me with my time. . . . I have been sad, sad, sad. Three years!" A few days later: "I have had a gloomy week, not quite so desperate and wild as in my worst days, but, so far as I can remember, equally hopeless and weary."[3]

Perhaps desperation stemmed from Adams's sensing in himself insufficiencies as a husband allied to his limitations as a writer. Although Marian's depression had roots in her life before she met him, her widower must have wondered how far he had been to blame for failure to reach and bring to life the bright intrepid spirit overwhelmed by the long illness of 1885. Was there something about his own personality, gentle and tender toward her though

Adams certainly had been, that—as Henry James supposed—had dimmed Marian's earlier brilliancy? If Henry Adams before 1885 was too exclusively a cerebral being, if his instinct was blighted from babyhood, he—Casaubon-like as he distantly feared himself to be—might bear a share of responsibility for that *froideur* of Marian's which in *Esther* he seemed to hint at. Lack of a larger human warmth—the influence upon Henry of his father's personality is unmistakable—may have contributed to disaster in Henry Adams's personal life, as it detracted from his literary power.

Convicted to the marrow by the failures, real and imagined, of his earlier years, Adams attempted after 1890 to reconstruct his life on new principles, as he believed John Quincy Adams to have done after his own early failures. Henry Adams's new principles might lead him to a freer emotional life; they would embolden him in his theorizing; they would justify him in relaxing from his long labor of close historical analysis. He could stop working for his country and would be free to work for himself alone.

The products of Adams's volte-face were books attractive to a wider audience than the *History*. *Mont-Saint-Michel* and the *Education* avoided the specialist character of a nine-volume work written according to the prescriptions of scientific history. Yet Adams's intellectual and emotional limitations affected his later books as much as his earlier. Although he essayed bold generalizations—eleventh-century Norman "seriousness," the accelerating "multiplicity" of the twentieth century—his mind was not strong enough to project a series of illuminating theories, supported with valuable subsidiary detail. He veered from being too particular, in the *History*, to being over-general in his later books. And the failures of tone in *Mont-Saint-Michel* and the *Education*—showy contempt for vulgarity, self-important ostentation of self-belittlement—grew from his earlier weakness in sympathy.

Adams did not after 1890 elude his earlier shortcomings, but he lost certain strengths that distinguished the *History*. From 1877 to 1890 Adams's conscientious and serious research had made him absolutely expert in his field, and his artistic powers were at full force. Twentieth-century scholarship is gradually overtaking Adams's, but whether its art will rival his remains an open question. Adams's mastery of the English language and his imaginative vitality may make our century, rather than his, seem the lesser developed.

Henry Adams's life is not to be seen in the distorting mirror he himself constructed. His literary art is as vital as the first day born, and our century would blunder were it to take the old man at his own low estimate of himself. Henry Adams's failure was, in great measure, myth.

Genealogical Chart
Notes
Bibliographical Note
Index

Adams Family

John Adams   m.   Abigail Smith Adams
(1735–1826)   Letter writer
President, 1797–1801

John Quincy Adams   m. Louisa Johnson Adams
(1767–1848)
President, 1825–29

Charles Francis Adams   m.   Abigail Brooks Adams
(1807–1886)   (1808–1889)
Minister to England,
1861–68

| Louisa Adams Kuhn (1831–1870) | John Q. Adams (1833–1894) Democratic candidate for governor of Massachusetts | Charles Adams, Jr. (1835–1915) Railroad reformer and author | Henry Brooks Adams (1838–1918) | Mary Adams Quincy (1845–1928) | Brooks Adams (1848–1927) Author |

Notes

Abbreviations

AP	Adams Papers, Massachusetts Historical Society, Boston
CA	Charles Francis Adams, Jr.
Cater	*Henry Adams and His Friends: A Collection of His Unpublished Letters*, ed. Harold Dean Cater (Boston, 1947)
CFA	Charles Francis Adams
CMG	Charles Milnes Gaskell
Cycle	*A Cycle of Adams Letters, 1861–1865*, ed. Worthington Chauncey Ford, 2 vols. (Boston, 1920)
Education	*The Education of Henry Adams*, ed. Ernest Samuels (1918; rpt. Boston, 1974)
Ford	*Letters of Henry Adams: 1858–1891 . . . 1892–1918*, ed. Worthington Chauncey Ford, 2 vols. (Boston, 1930, 1938)
HA	Henry Adams
HCL	Henry Cabot Lodge
History	Henry Adams, *History of the United States . . . during the . . . [Administrations] of Thomas Jefferson [and] James Madison*, 9 vols. (New York, 1889–91)
MA	Marian Adams
MHS	Massachusetts Historical Society, Boston
RH	Robert Hooper
Thoron	*Letters of Mrs. Henry Adams*, ed. Ward Thoron (Boston, 1936)

Introduction

1. Carl Becker, *Everyman His Own Historian* (New York, 1935), pp. 166, 160; Yvor Winters, *In Defense of Reason* (London, 1960), p. 414.

2. William H. Jordy, *Henry Adams: Scientific Historian* (New Haven, 1952); J. C. Levenson, *The Mind and Art of Henry Adams* (Boston, 1957), pp. 116, 351, 350; Ernest Samuels, *Henry Adams: The Major Phase* (Cambridge, Mass., 1964).

3. See, e.g., Ernest Samuels, *The Young Henry Adams* (Cambridge, Mass., 1948); Earl N. Harbert, *The Force So Much Closer Home: Henry Adams and the Adams Family* (New York, 1977).

4. Winters, *In Defense of Reason*, p. 415.

CHAPTER 1 · *Family*

1. HA to CA, Sept. 7, 1861, Apr. 23, 1863, AP; Benjamin Moran, *The Journal of . . . , 1857–1865*, ed. Sarah Wallace and Frances Gillespie, 2 vols. (Chicago, 1948–49), Apr. 18, 1863.

2. *Education*, p. 31.

3. CFA to HA, Nov. 25, Dec. 23, 1877, Apr. 27, 1870, AP.

4. CFA to HA, Mar. 13, 1878, AP. Earl Harbert discusses Charles Francis Adams's scholarly bent in "Charles Francis Adams (1807–1886): A Forgotten Family Man of Letters," *Journal of American Studies* 6 (1972): 249–65.

5. CFA to HA, Mar. 1, 1870, AP.

6. CA, *An Autobiography*, ed. Worthington Chauncey Ford (Boston, 1916), p. 25.

7. CA, "Memorabilia," Mar. 14, 1897, AP.

8. CFA to HA, May 5, 1869, AP.

9. CFA to HA, Jan. 18, Jan 29, Feb. 13, 1878, AP; Perry Belmont, *An American Democrat* (New York, 1940), p. 140; CA, *Autobiography*, pp. 10, 13.

10. CA, *Autobiography*, p. 5; CA, "Memorabilia," Mar. 14, 1897.

11. CA, *Autobiography*, pp. 18–19.

12. *Education*, p. 36; HA to CA, Dec. 24, 1863, AP.

13. *Education*, p. 23; Martin Duberman, *Charles Francis Adams* (Boston, 1960), p. 339.

14. CFA to CA, Dec. 12, 1861, *Cycle*; CFA to HA, Apr. 5, 1870, AP.

15. *History*, 1:340–41.

16. CA, *Autobiography*, p. 44; *Education*, p. 35.

17. HA to CMG, May 10, 1907, Ford; *Education*, pp. 37, 15; HA to Robert Cunliffe, Mar. 22, 1885, AP. J. C. Levenson comments on the silver mugs in *The Mind and Art of Henry Adams*, p. 309.

18. HA to CA, Mar. 2, 1865, AP.

19. Cecil Spring-Rice to Margaret Spring-Rice, Dec. 15, [1887], *The Letters and Friendships of Sir Cecil Spring-Rice*, ed. Stephen Gwynn, 2 vols. (London, 1929).

20. Abigail Brooks Adams to J. G. Palfrey, Nov. 5, 1863, transcript, Harold Cater Papers, MHS.

21. HA to Mrs. Francis Lippitt, June 16, 1889, Cater; John Q. Adams to CFA, Jan. 5, 1872, AP; CA, *Autobiography*, p. 107 (quoting CA's diary).

22. HA to CA, July 19, 1862, Oct. 2, Dec. 11, 1863, AP.

23. HA to CA, July 2, 1861, to CFA, Jan. 21, 1872, AP.

24. HA to CA, Jan. 10, [1862], Sept. 4, 1867, AP.

25. CA, *Autobiography*, p. 166. See CA to HA, Sept. 18, 1864, to CFA, Nov. 2, 1864, *Cycle*.

26. Edward Kirkland, *Charles Francis Adams, Jr., 1835–1915* (Cambridge, Mass., 1965), chapters 2 and 4.

27. CA, *Autobiography*, p. 210.

28. HA to CA, Feb. 14, 1862, AP.

29. HA to CA, June 5, 1863, May 10, 1865, AP; HA to HCL, Thursday, Nov. [n.d.], 1915, Cater.

30. HA to CA, Oct. 15, 1861, CA to HA, Nov. 5, 1861, *Cycle*.

31. CA to CFA, Sept. 10, 1864, *Cycle*.

32. CA to HA, Aug. 13, 1864, *Cycle*.

33. HA to CA, Jan. 22, 1862, *Cycle*; HA to CA, May 8, 1867, AP; *History*, 4:442–43; CA to HA, Oct. 7, 1861, *Cycle*.

34. *History*, 1:160–61.

35. HA to CA, Oct. 5, 1861, Apr. 30, Nov. 16, 1867, AP.

36. CA to HA, June 4, 1880, HA to CA, Oct. 20, 1865, AP.

37. CA to E. L. Godkin, Oct. 30, 1880, E. L. Godkin Papers, Houghton Library, Harvard University; *The Nation*, Aug. 21, 1879.

38. HA to John Hay, Aug. 29, 1883, AP.

39. *History*, 5:49, 3:20, 6:36. Ernest Samuels examines Charles Adams's criticisms in *Henry Adams: The Middle Years* (Cambridge, Mass., 1958), pp. 391–95.

40. CA's marginal comments in the privately printed version of volumes 5 and 6 of the *History* (Cambridge, Mass., 1888) [5: first page of chapter xviii], MHS.

41. CA's and HA's marginal comments in the galleys of the *History*, 3:22, AP.

42. CA to HA, Friday, Jan. [n.d.], 1862, Jan. 23, 1863, *Cycle*; CA to Palfrey, Feb. 21, 1864, transcript, Cater Papers; HA to CA, May 8, 1867, AP.

43. As quoted in HA to CA, May 8, 1867, AP.

44. HA to CA, May 21, 1869, Ford.

45. HA to HCL, Thursday, Nov. [n.d.], 1915, Cater.

46. "Napoléon Ier et Saint-Domingue," *La Revue Historique* (April 1884), listed in Samuels, *Adams: Middle Years*, p. 424.

47. *History*, 1:394, 2:20–21.

48. CA, *Autobiography*, pp. 32–33.

49. *History*, 9:15, 46, 52. Earl Harbert analyzes Henry Adams's treatment of the episode in *The Force So Much Closer Home*, pp. 105–6, 112–14.

50. Bradford Perkins, *Castlereagh and Adams: England and the United States, 1812–1823* (Berkeley and Los Angeles, 1964), see esp. pp. 40–42n, 49–50n, 89–90, 116–17, 131, 152–53.

51. *History*, 5:419–20.

52. *History*, 4:240; HA, "Critique" (of Brooks Adams's MS biography of John Quincy Adams), pp. "289," "446," Adams Papers, Houghton Library, Harvard University. (In all references to this "Critique," the pagination is that of Brooks Adams's MS biography.) I am indebted to Earl Harbert for calling my attention to the "Critique."

53. HA to Elizabeth Cameron, Dec. 29, 1891, AP. Harbert discusses this letter in *The Force So Much Closer Home*, pp. 16–17.

54. "Critique," p. "429"; HA to Palfrey, July 1, 1874, Cater; John Quincy Adams, *Memoirs of . . .* , ed. Charles Francis Adams, 12 vols. (Philadelphia, 1874–77), Dec. 27, 1819.

55. *History*, 1:170–71, 187.

56. "Critique," p. "495."

57. HA to Brooks Adams, Feb. 18, 1909, Adams Papers, Harvard; "Critique," pp. "289," "429."

58. *History*, 1:98–99.

59. *Education*, pp. 316, 327.

60. HA to CA, Dec. 13, 1861, *Cycle*; HA to CA, Nov. 21, 1862, AP; "Critique," p. "495."

61. HA to CMG, Dec. 13, 1869, to HCL, Aug. 31, 1876, Ford.

62. HA, *John Randolph* (Boston, 1882), p. 20; *History*, 1:157, 180–81 ("intelligent" is used in the nineteenth-century sense of "well-informed"); *History*, 5:412.

CHAPTER 2 · *England*

1. *History*, 1:144, 146. See p. 120 below.

2. Lloyd Griscom, *Diplomatically Speaking*, p. 38, in Samuels, *Young Henry Adams*, p. 121; HA to CMG, Apr. 16, 1911, Ford.

3. HA to CA, Feb. 27, 1896, Ford.

4. HA to CA, Mar. 20, 1863, AP.

5. HA to CA, June 10, 1861, Ford; HA to J. G. Palfrey, Feb. 12, 1862, Cater; HA to CA, Jan. 10, Feb. 14, 1862, AP.

6. London *Times*, Jan. 10, 1862.

7. *Education*, p. 121; *History*, 7:5, 16.

8. *Education*, pp. 130–31.

9. HA to Abigail Adams, Mar. 6, 1860, Ford; HA to CA, Feb. 14, 1862, *Cycle*; HA to Frederick Seward, Apr. 4, 1862, in Charles Vandersee, "Henry Adams behind the Scenes," *Bulletin of the New York Public Library* (Apr. 1967).

10. HA to CA, Nov. 30, 1861, *Cycle*; HA to Seward, Jan. 30, Feb. 14, 1862, in Vandersee, "Behind the Scenes"; HA to CA, July 19, 1862, AP; HA to Seward, Mar. 20, 1863, in Vandersee, "Behind the Scenes."

11. Moran, *Journal*, May 4, 1863; Adams's report to Seward is in *New England Quarterly* 15 (1942): 725–28.

12. HA to CA, [Mar. (misdated Jan.)] 27, 1863, AP. That Adams exaggerated the potential sympathy of the English working classes for the North is strongly suggested by Mary Ellison's study of Lancashire, *Support for Secession* (Chicago, 1972).

13. HA to Abigail Adams, May 6, 1860, Ford.

14. HA to CA, May 22, 1862, AP.

15. HA to CA, May 1, 1863, AP.

16. John Q. Adams to CA, typescript, Feb. 15, 1864, AP; HA to CA, Mar. 20, 1863, Ford; HA to CA, June 3, 1864, AP.

17. HA to CA, May 10, 1865, AP.

18. *History*, 1:184.

19. HA to Robert Cunliffe, Nov. 12, 1882, to CMG, Aug. 21, 1878, to Cunliffe, Sept. 11, 1880, to CMG, Aug. 21, 1878, AP.

20. *History*, 4:59–60.

21. *Education*, p. 30.

22. HA to CA, Feb. 13, 1863, AP.

23. HA to CA, June 18, 1863, AP; *Education*, p. 144.

24. HA to CA, July 17, 1863, AP.

25. HA to CA, June 5, 1863, AP; HA to CA, Apr. 6, Apr. 22, 1859, Ford.

26. HA to CA, Oct. 23, 1863, CA to John Q. Adams, typescript, Feb. 15, 1864, AP; CA to Palfrey, Feb. 21, 1864, transcript, Cater Papers, MHS.

27. HA to CA, Mar. 20, June 25, 1863, Ford.

28. *Education*, p. 205; HA to CMG, Sept. 26, 1880, CMG to HA, May 8, July 18, 1890, AP; HA to CMG, June 29, 1909, Ford (2:519n).

29. MA to RH, Mar. 11, 1873, Thoron; and inferences from CMG "The Country Gentleman," *Nineteenth Century* 12 (1882):468.

30. CMG to HA, Oct. 24, 1892, AP.

31. *Education*, p. 207; Henry James, *The Portrait of a Lady* (New York, 1908), 1:143–44.

32. HA to CA, Sept. 30, Oct. 7, 1864, AP; HA to CMG, Mar. 28, 1870, Ford; *As You Like It* (New Cambridge ed.), III.ii.275; MA to RH, July 26, 1872, July 23, 1873, Thoron.

33. *History*, 1:181 (see p. 32 above); HA to CMG, Ford.

34. Henry James to his mother, Mar. 9, [1880], James Papers, Houghton Library, Harvard University.

35. Quoted in Leon Edel, *Henry James*, 5 vols. (London, 1953–72), 2:382 (the reader should note that pagination of this edition differs from that of the American edition).

36. James doubtless knew that the name of his friend's family had originally been "Milnes." "Gaskell" had been added in connection with an inheritance from a relation who bore that surname.

37. James to HA, July 15, [1877], Theodore Dwight Papers, MHS; and a letter (James to his mother, Jan. 18, 1879?) cited in Edel, *James*, 2:336; James, *Portrait of a Lady*, 1:9, 97, 102, 107, 155.

38. James, *Portrait of a Lady*, 1:181, 183, 97, 189.

39. HA to Elizabeth Cameron, Nov. 6, 12, 1891, AP.

40. HA to Cameron, Jan. 18, Jan. 11, 1892, AP.

41. F. O. Matthiessen and Kenneth B. Murdock, eds., *The Notebooks of Henry James* (New York, 1947), Feb. 5, 1892. The insertions within brackets are my inferences. See notes 42–44 below.

42. Frank Palgrave to HA, July 6, Sept. 27, 1871, Dwight Papers. "Otiose" is underlined in the original.

43. HA to CMG, Dec. 30, 1867, Ford; HA to Ralph Palmer, Nov. 21, 1868, AP.

44. HA to CMG, May 18, 1884, HA to Elizabeth Cameron, Jan. 18, 1892, AP. See also HA to Cameron, Jan. 23, 1892, and HA to CMG, Sept. 27, 1908, AP. Charles Vandersee kindly furnished the last of these references.

45. CMG to HA, Apr. 11, 1894, AP.

46. *North American Review*, Apr. 1874, p. 433.

47. HA to CA, May 29, 1863, AP. "Brilliant," in Adams's usage, did not connote "intelligent"; he meant "showy."

48. *North American Review*, July 1871, p. 211; *Hamlet* (New Cambridge ed.), V.ii.217–18; *History*, 1:79 (see p. 140 below); CMG, "The Position of the Whigs," *Nineteenth Century* 11(1881):903.

49. *History*, 4:27.

50. *North American Review*, Apr. 1872, p. 426.

51. CMG, "The Country Gentleman," p. 473.
52. CMG, "The Position of the Whigs," p. 912; James, *Portrait of a Lady*, 1:98.
53. CMG, "The Position of the Whigs," p. 902.
54. CMG, "The Country Gentleman," pp. 462, 466.
55. CMG, "The Position of the Whigs," p. 905.
56. *Education*, p. 211.
57. Cf. *History*, 1:183–84.
58. London *Courier*, July 27, 1813, in *History*, 7:359.
59. HA to CA, May 21, 1869, Ford; quoted p. 25 above.
60. HA to CMG, Nov. 25, 1877, AP; quoted p. 91 below.
61. See pp. 90–91 below.

CHAPTER 3 · *Clover*

1. HA to CMG, June 23, 1872, Ford.
2. Marian's first recorded meeting with Henry Adams apparently resulted from her dropping in to see Wendell Holmes, Jr., at the American legation in London on May 11, 1866. See Holmes's Diary, May 11, 1866, Holmes Papers, Harvard Law School.
3. Holmes, Diary, Dec. 25, 1866, Holmes Papers.
4. More than one observer wondered disapprovingly, during the long interval between 1866 and 1872, that Holmes did not declare his intentions to Miss Dixwell (Mark De Wolfe Howe, *Justice Oliver Wendell Holmes*, 2 vols. [Cambridge, Mass., 1957–63], 2:6). Marian Hooper was engaged to Henry Adams on February 27, 1872. Holmes became definitely engaged to Miss Dixwell a little before March 11, 1872.
5. Holmes, 1867 Diary, entries for 1872, Holmes Papers.
6. Eleanor Little, "The Early Reading of Justice Oliver Wendell Holmes," *Harvard Library Bulletin*, Spring 1954, p. 163. (In this article the Heineccius date is erroneously printed "June 14.")
7. Henry James to William James, Mar. 8, 1870, in Edel, *Henry James*, 1:326–27.
8. Henry James to William James, Apr. 9, 1873, June 15, [1879], to Henry James, Sr., Oct. 11, [1879], James Papers, Harvard.
9. Henry James to MA, Sept. 9, [1880], Dwight Papers, MHS. In the original manuscript "not" and "Do" are in script, with double underlining.
10. Henry James to MA, Nov. 6, 1881, Dwight Papers. Emphasis in the original.
11. Margaret Chanler, *Roman Spring* (Boston, 1934), pp. 301–3. See also Edel, *James*, 5:275.
12. Samuels, *Adams: Middle Years*, pp. 168–70.
13. Henry James, *Roderick Hudson* (New York, 1907), pp. 179–80. The novel was written in 1874–75.
14. HA to Abigail Adams, Nov. 8, 1859, Ford.
15. Edel, *James*, 2:179–80; cf. also 2:113–14, 358–59.
16. HA to HCL, Feb. 22, 1880, Ford.
17. Henry James to Elizabeth Boott, June 28, 1879, James Papers, Harvard; James, *Portrait of a Lady*, 1:74, 276.

18. Marian Hooper to Catharine Howard, Mar. 3, Mar. 8, 1869, Thoron, pp. 473–74.

19. The limited extent to which one or two of Osmond's traits may have derived from James's acquaintance with Henry Adams is suggested below, pp. 197–98, and chapter 8, n. 29.

20. Willie Lee Rose, *Rehearsal for Reconstruction* (New York: Vintage, 1964), pp. 50–51, 154, 178, 198, 221–22, 274.

21. HA to CMG, Mar. 26, 1872, Ford. (Russell Sturgis was the analogue of the banker Daniel Touchett in *The Portrait of a Lady*.)

22. George Cooke, ed., *The Poets of Transcendentalism* (Boston, 1903); the Higginson and Emerson quotations are on pp. 315–16.

23. CA, "Memorabilia," May 3, 1891, AP.

24. CA, "Memorabilia," quoted in Samuels, *Adams: Major Phase*, p. 604; idem, *Adams: Middle Years*, p. 327; idem, *Adams: Major Phase*, p. 249.

25. Marian Hooper to Eleanor [Shattuck], Sunday, Feb. 5, [1871], Shattuck Papers, MHS (emphasis in the original); HA to Brooks Adams, Mar. 3, 1872, AP.

26. Inference from Louise Hall Tharp, *The Peabody Sisters of Salem* (Boston, 1950), pp. 77, 348. Cf. Harold Schwartz, *Samuel Gridley Howe* (Cambridge, Mass., 1956), p. 104n, and John T. Morse, *Life and Letters of Oliver Wendell Holmes*, 2 vols. (Boston, 1896), 1:130, 142.

27. HA to CMG, May 10, 1885, AP.

28. *Education*, pp. 62–63. Henry attributes this view to the Transcendentalists.

29. CA, Diary, June 30, 1892, AP.

30. MA to RH, Apr. 20, 1873, Dec. 26, 1880, Thoron.

31. Marian Hooper to Catharine Howard, Mar. 3, 1869, Thoron, p. 473; HA to CMG, Apr. 27, 1872, Ford.

32. HA to CMG, June 23, 1872, Ford.

33. MA to RH, Oct. 20, Dec. 21, 1872, Thoron.

34. Henry Lee Higginson, address, in Bliss Perry, *Henry Lee Higginson* (Boston, 1921), pp. 372–73; Ellen Gurney to E. L. Godkin, June 9, [1886], Godkin Papers, Harvard.

35. Lucy Paton, *Elizabeth Cary Agassiz* (Boston, 1919), p. 402.

36. HA to CMG, Mar. 26, 1872, Ford; MA to RH, Dec. 28, 1879, Thoron.

37. MA to RH, Sept. 9, Sept. 15, 1872, Thoron.

38. MA to RH, Feb. 5, 1882, Thoron.

39. MA to RH, Nov. 2, Nov. 9, 1879, Thoron; *Education*, p. 16.

40. Marian Hooper to Eleanor Shattuck, Feb. 5, Mar. 5, 1871, Shattuck Papers.

41. Marion Hooper to Catharine Howard, Mar. 3, Mar. 8, Apr. 5, 1869, Thoron, pp. 473–75.

42. Marian Hooper to Eleanor Shattuck, Sunday, Feb. 5, [Jan. 10], 1871, Shattuck Papers.

43. MA to Godkin, Dec. 25, 1879, Godkin Papers.

44. MA to RH, June 1, 1873, Jan. 23, 1881, Feb. 17, 1881, May 14, 1873, Dec. 26, 1880, Thoron.

45. HA to Abigail Adams, Nov. 8, 1859, Ford; HA to CA, Apr. 9, 1865, Aug. 23, 1860 (translated from the French by Ben Sher; transcript courtesy of J. C. Levenson), Oct. 20, 1865, AP.

46. HA to Brooks Adams, Mar. 3, 1872, AP; Marian Hooper to Eleanor [Shattuck] Whiteside, Mar. 8, [1872], Shattuck Papers; HA to CMG, June 23, Mar. 26, Apr. 27, 1872, Ford.

47. HA to his niece, Mabel LaFarge, Sept. 26, 1908, Cater; CA to CFA, June 28, 1872, AP (in the original the word order stands "why is it necessary").

48. MA to RH, Sept. 8, Oct. 20, Nov. 5, 1872, Mar. 29, 1873, Thoron.

49. MA to RH, Oct. 20, 1872, Jan. 3, Jan. 1, Jan. 3, 1873, Thoron.

50. MA to RH, Nov. 5, Oct. 20, 1872, Feb. 16, Mar. 2, 1873, Thoron.

51. MA to RH, Mar. 11, 1873, Dec. 5, 1872, Thoron; HA to HCL, June 11, 1873, Ford.

52. MA to RH, Sept. 5, Nov. 5, 1872, Thoron.

53. MA to RH, Mar. 29, 1873, Thoron.

54. CA, "Memorabilia," May 3, 1891.

55. Clarence King to John Hay, July 4, [1886], transcript, Cater Papers, MHS; MA to RH, Feb. 27, 1881, Thoron.

56. HA to Godkin, Dec. 16, 1885, Cater; HA to Elizabeth Cameron, Nov. 21, 1891, AP; Elizabeth Cameron to Mrs. Hay, July 15, 1886, Dwight Papers; HA to Elizabeth Cameron, Dec. 19, 1891, to MA, Apr. 12, 1885, AP.

57. King to HA, Sept. 22, 1881, [Oct. 6, 1884], Mrs. Anne Proctor to MA, Aug. 15, 1882, Dwight Papers; CA, "Memorabilia," May 3, 1891; Mabel LaFarge, "A Niece's Memories," in HA, *Letters to a Niece* (Boston, 1920), p. 8.

58. HA to CMG, Nov. 25, 1877, AP.

59. MA to RH, Feb. 26, 1882, Thoron. Emphasis in the original.

60. MA to RH, Dec. 12, 1880, Thoron.

61. HA to MA, Apr. 9, 1885, AP.

62. MA to RH, Apr. 20, 1873, Thoron; J. Lawrence Laughlin, "Some Recollections of Henry Adams," *Scribner's Magazine* 69(1921):582; HA to John Hay, Oct. 31, 1883, AP.

63. MA to Godkin, Dec. 25, 1879, Godkin Papers; HA to Godkin, Nov. 22, 1880, Cater.

64. See CA to E. L. Godkin, Oct. 30, 1880, p. 22 above.

65. Wayne MacVeagh to HA, July 16, 1884, Dwight Papers; Chanler, *Roman Spring*, p. 303.

66. HA to CMG, Aug. 21, 1878, AP, and see *History*, 1:82–86.

67. MA to RH, Feb. 12, 1882, Thoron; John Hay to HA, Apr. 27, 1885, Dwight Papers; MA to RH, Nov. 18, 1883, Apr. 11, 1880, AP.

68. MA to RH, Feb. 13, 1881, Thoron; MA to Godkin, Dec. 25, 1879, Godkin Papers.

69. James Russell Lowell to Mrs. R. W. Gilder, Jan. 26, 1891, Lowell, *Letters*, ed. C. E. Norton, 2 vols. (New York, 1894); MA to RH, Jan. 18, Jan. 31, 1882, [Dec.] 21, [1880], Thoron.

70. HA to CMG, Sept. 9, 1883, to John Hay, n.d. [1882], to CMG, Oct. 6, 1878, to Robert Cunliffe, July 13, 1879, AP.

71. *History*, 1:95–96, 103–5.

72. HA to CMG, Nov. 28, 1878, AP; MA to RH, Apr. 24, 1881, Thoron; HA to MA, Apr. 10, [1885], Cater.

73. HA to MA, Apr. 12, Mar. 15, Mar. 18, Mar. 19, 1885, AP.

74. *History*, 1:193–94.
75. HA, *Life of Albert Gallatin* (Philadelphia, 1879), pp. 99–100.
76. HA to MA, Mar. 30, 1885, AP; MA to RH, Apr. 27, 1873, Thoron.
77. *Democracy*, ed. Ernest Samuels (Gloucester, Mass., 1961), pp. 99, 157, 106.
78. HA to HCL, May 13, 1880, Ford; *Education*, p. 207.
79. HA, *Mont-Saint-Michel and Chartres* (1913; rpt. Boston, 1933), p. 345.
80. Marian's description, during her wedding journey in Egypt, of her response to Henry's energetic sightseeing (MA to RH, Jan. 1, 1873, Thoron). See p. 69 above.
81. MA to RH, Nov. 17, 1872, Thoron.
82. HA to MA, Mar. 21, Apr. 10, Apr. 11, Apr. 12, 1885, AP.
83. HA to John Hay, Apr. 20, 1885, AP.
84. *History*, 6:2; E. Whitman Gurney to Godkin, Oct. 16, [1885] (misdated 1886), Godkin Papers.
85. CA, "Memorabilia," quoted in Samuels, *Adams: Major Phase*, p. 604; "Memorabilia," May 3, 1891, pp. 286–87, AP. See also CA, Diary, Oct. 14, 1885, AP.
86. CA, "Memorabilia," p. 282; HA to James Russell Lowell, Nov. 25, 1879, Cater; CA, "Memorabilia," pp. 281–82.
87. CA, "Memorabilia," May 3, 1891, in Samuels, *Adams: Major Phase*, p. 604.
88. Harold Cater, paraphrasing Rebecca Dodge Rae, Cater, p. li.
89. According to Rebecca Dodge Rae, ibid.
90. MA to RH, Mar. 16, 1873, Thoron.
91. Quoted in part in Ellen Gurney to Godkin, Dec. 30, 1885, Godkin Papers, in Samuels, *Adams: Middle Years*, p. 272.
92. HA to Brooks Adams, Feb. 18, 1909, Adams Papers, Harvard; *Education*, pp. 117, 493.
93. HA to Godkin, Dec. 16, 1885, Cater; Ellen Gurney to Godkin, Dec. 30, [1885], Godkin Papers; HA to Henry Holt, Mar. 8, [1886], Cater.
94. Ellen Gurney to Godkin, June 9, Oct. 28, 1886, Godkin Papers.
95. HA to HCL, Sept. 28, [1915], Cater; Ellen Gurney to Godkin, Jan. 10, [1887], Godkin Papers.

CHAPTER 4 · *Historian*

1. *Education*, p. 304.
2. J. Lawrence Laughlin, "Some Recollections of Henry Adams," p. 576; see p. 134 below. Henry Osborn Taylor, "The Education of Henry Adams," *Atlantic Monthly*, Oct. 1918, p. 490; idem, *Human Values and Verities*, p. 40, transcript, Cater Papers, MHS.
3. HA to Sir Henry Maine, Feb. 22, 1875, Cater; Ephraim Emerton, "History," in Samuel Eliot Morison, ed., *The Development of Harvard University* (Cambridge, Mass., 1930), pp. 154–57.
4. HA to CMG, June 20, 1871, Ford; HA to Robert Cunliffe, Mar. 13, 1871, AP; Laughlin, "Some Recollections of Henry Adams," pp. 578–80; Samuel Eliot Morison, *Three Centuries of Harvard* (Cambridge, Mass., 1936), p. 349.
5. HA to CMG, June 14, 1876, Ford.
6. *Education*, p. 16; HA to HCL, Oct. 6, 1879, to CMG, Apr. 14, 1877, Ford; HA

to Cunliffe, July 13, 1879, AP; Laughlin, "Some Recollections of Henry Adams," p. 578; J. Ellerton Lodge, interview with Harold D. Cater, June 27, 1942, Cater Papers.

7. *Education*, pp. 317, 327, 315–16, 323, 319, 329, 316.

8. HA, "Retrospect," *Harvard Magazine* 3(1857):66.

9. HA to George Bancroft, June 7, 1878, Cater; HA to CMG, June 18, 1878, Apr. 9, 1879, AP. The books to which Adams refers were his *Life of Gallatin* and his edition of Gallatin's writings. He spent the year 1879–80 in Europe doing research for the *History*.

10. HA to James Russell Lowell, Sept. 24, 1879, Cater; HA to HCL, May 13, 1880, Ford; HA to HCL, July 9, 1881, AP; HA to Francis Walker, June 6, 1881, Cater.

11. HA to HCL, Oct. 29, 1881, to CMG, Jan. 29, 1882, Apr. 30, 1882, Ford; HA to CMG, Dec. 3, 1882, AP.

12. MA to Elizabeth Cameron, July 26, 1883, AP.

13. *History*, 1:159, 183–84; HA to CMG, Nov. 25, 1877, Mar. 25, 1883, to John Hay, Apr. 8, 1883, AP; HA to Hay, Aug. 29, 1883, Ford.

14. HA to Theodore Dwight, July 10, 24, 1887, AP; Clarence King to HA, Sept. 25, [1889], transcript, King to Hay, Oct. 2, [1889], transcript, Cater Papers.

15. W. H. Prescott, *The Conquest of Mexico* (1843; rpt. Oxford, 1915), 2:261. In this chapter subsequent references are in the text.

16. Cf. David Levin, *History as Romantic Art* (1959; rpt. New York, 1963), chapter 7; on Prescott's imagery, pp. 181–83.

17. Emphasis added.

18. John Lothrop Motley, *The Rise of the Dutch Republic* (1856; rpt. London, 1896), 3:480–81, 490–95. In this chapter subsequent references are in the text.

19. Levin, *History as Romantic Art*, p. 196. This book has greatly influenced my judgments of Prescott, Motley, and Parkman.

20. Parkman's words to Barrett Wendell (Wendell, "Francis Parkman," in American Academy of Arts and Sciences, *Proceedings* 29 [1894]:439).

21. Francis Parkman, *Montcalm and Wolfe* (1884; rpt. Boston, 1922), 1:362–63, 528. In this chapter subsequent references are in the text.

22. See p. 104 below.

23. Francis Parkman, *The Old Regime in Canada* (1874; rpt. Boston, 1922), p. 465.

24. Ibid., pp. 377–78.

25. Levin, *History as Romantic Art*, p. 221. Levin restricts this judgment to Parkman's characterization of Pitt, Frederick, and Washington.

26. HA, "Reading in College," *Harvard Magazine* 3(1857):313–17; HA to CA, Jan. 17, 1861, Ford.

27. Cicero, *Of Duties*; Ludwig von Rönne, *The Prussian School System*; G. F. Puchta, *Lectures on the Institutes [of Justinian]*; HA to CA, Apr. 6, Apr. 9, 1859, Ford.

28. HA to CA, Feb. 20, July 10, June 5, July 23, 1863, AP.

29. HA to CMG, June 22, 1877, Ford; MA to RH, Aug. 7, 1872, Thoron; Edel, *James*, 2:333; F. T. Palgrave, *The Golden Treasury* (London, 1861), p. 8.

30. *Education*, pp. 214–15, 214.

31. HA to CMG, May 24, 1875, Cater; Palgrave to HA, Nov. 9, 1871, May 3, 1875, Nov. 9, 1871, Dwight Papers, MHS.

32. Palgrave to HA, May 3, 1875, Dwight Papers; HA to CMG, Mar. 26, 1867, Ford.

33. HA to CMG, Oct. 5, 1869, Ford.

34. HA to HCL, Monday, [June (?) 1875], Ford; Palgrave to HA, July 26, 1878, Dwight Papers; HA to HCL, May 13, 1880, Ford; MA to RH, May 9, 1880, AP; HA to Justin Winsor, June 26, 1882, photostat, Cater Papers; HA to [John] Field, Sept. 20, 1885, transcript, AP.

35. *History*, 5:119, 121–22.

36. *History*, 5:339–40.

37. *History*, 6:210–11.

38. HA to Brooks Adams, Feb. 18, 1909, Aug. 23, 1911, and the "Critique" accompanying the former letter, "p. 272," Adams Papers, Harvard; HA to E. D. Shaw, Dec. 20, 1904, Thoron, p. 458.

39. HA to HCL, July 31, 1876, Ford; CFA to HA, Jan. 13, 1869, AP.

40. Jacob Cooke, quoted in Vern Wagner, *The Suspension of Henry Adams* (Detroit, 1964), p. 41; HA to Brooks Adams, Feb. 18, 1909, Adams Papers, Harvard; HA to CMG, Aug. 25, 1867, Ford; HA, "Critique," "p. 36," "p. 10," "p. 40." See also Arthur Beringause, *Brooks Adams* (New York, 1955), pp. 317–20.

41. Samuels, *Young Henry Adams*, p. 32.

42. Richard Whately, *Elements of Rhetoric*, 1846 edition, ed. Douglas Ehninger (Carbondale, Ill., 1963), pp. 281, 306, 308.

43. HA to CA, Jan. 18, 1869, to CMG, May 22, 1871, Ford.

44. HA to HCL, Jan. 2, June 11, 1873, May 13, 1880, Ford.

45. HA to Brooks Adams, Feb. 18, 1909, Adams Papers, Harvard.

46. HA to HCL, June 25, [1874], Dec. 20, 1879, Ford.

47. *History*, 8:140.

48. HA to CA, Nov. 21, 1862, AP.

49. *History*, 5:256–57.

50. HA to HCL, June 2, 1872, to CA, May 21, 1869 (see p. 25 above), Ford; *Education*, p. 327.

51. *Education*, pp. 386, 221. See pp. 165–67 below.

52. *History*, 1:184 (see p. 39 above), 217.

CHAPTER 5 · *History as Art*

1. *History*, 1:30–31. In this chapter subsequent references are in the text.

2. Edward Gibbon, *Autobiography* (Oxford Univ. Press, 1962 ed.), p. 160. Cf. Levenson, *Mind and Art of Henry Adams*, p. 118.

3. HA to HCL, May 15, 1876, Ford.

4. See pp. 149–51 below. James Banner, *To the Hartford Convention* (New York, 1969).

5. Cf. William Ander Smith, "Henry Adams, Alexander Hamilton, and the American People as a 'Great Beast,'" *New England Quarterly* 48(1975):216–30.

6. See pp. 152–55 below.

7. See p. 32 above.

8. *History*, 1:181–83.

9. See, e.g., *History*, 1:74.

10. Thomas Jefferson to John Dickinson, Mar. 6, 1801, in *History*, 1:208.

11. Jefferson to Thomas Paine, Mar. 18, 1801, in *History*, 1:214.

12. Cf. Samuels, *Adams: Middle Years*, pp. 388–89.

13. Brooks Adams, "The Heritage of Henry Adams," in HA, *The Degradation of the Democratic Dogma* (1919; rpt. New York, 1949), p. 1.

14. See pp. 155–57 below.

15. Gibbon, *Autobiography*, p. 33.

16. *History*, 1:340–41; see p. 13 above.

17. J. G. Palfrey, *History of New England*, 5 vols. (Boston, 1858–90), 2:266.

18. HA, *The War of 1812*, ed. Major H. A. DeWeerd (Washington, D.C., 1944).

19. HA to Carl Schurz, May 16, 1871, Ford.

20. HA, *Mont-Saint-Michel and Chartres* (Boston, 1933), p. 50.

21. *Education*, pp. 28, 30.

22. HA to CA, Oct. 2, 1863, AP.

23. HA to CA, Apr. 9, 1865, AP; *Education*, p. 163.

24. *History*, 2:52–53, 9:207–17.

25. See, e.g., *History*, 5:157, 7:15.

26. Cf. Levenson, *Mind and Art of Henry Adams*, p. 153.

27. See James Baldwin, *The Fire Next Time* (Harmondsworth, 1964), p. 27; Malcolm X, *Autobiography* (Harmondsworth, 1968), pp. 339, 195.

28. See, e.g., *History*, 1:334, 2:52–54, 65, 4:298–99, 5:253–59.

29. See also *History*, 1:395–96.

30. See, e.g., *History*, 4:27, quoted p. 51 above.

31. *History*, 5:262.

32. Laughlin, "Some Recollections of Henry Adams," p. 576.

33. *History*, 8:120–55.

34. See, e.g., *History*, 1:79–80, 83.

35. See, e.g., *History*, 4:59–60, quoted p. 40 above. See also *History*, 1:278–79.

36. See p. 121 above.

37. See p. 106 above.

38. *History*, 6:372–75. See also *History*, 5:256–57, quoted p. 106–7 above.

39. See p. 50 above.

40. Emphasis added.

41. See also, e.g., his characterization of Harrison Gray Otis: *History*, 4:403, 8:292, 294.

42. *Education*, pp. 81, 109.

43. HA to Brooks Adams, "Critique" [Feb. 18, 1909], "201, line 19," Adams Papers, Harvard.

44. HA to CA, Nov. 16, 1867, quoted p. 22 above.

CHAPTER 6 · *History as Science*

1. Bradford Perkins, *The First Rapprochement* (Philadelphia, 1955); idem, *Prologue to War: England and the United States, 1805–1812* (Berkeley and Los Angeles, 1961); idem, *Castlereagh and Adams: England and the United States, 1812–1823*.

2. Perkins, *Prologue*, p. 434. See also pp. 14, 301, and *Castlereagh*, pp. 18, 61, 174.

3. Perkins, *Prologue*, p. 200. See also pp. 197, 304–5, 430.

4. Perkins, *Prologue*, pp. 100, 436–37; *Castlereagh*, p. vii. See also *Prologue,* pp. 50, 174, 367.

5. Perkins, *Prologue*, pp. 437, 156n. See also pp. 170, 172–73.

6. Ibid., pp. 94, 196.

7. Ibid., p. 259. See also pp. 252, 434.

8. Ibid., p. 290; *Castlereagh*, pp. 14, 54.

9. Perkins, *Prologue*, p. 392n.

10. Perkins, *Rapprochement*, p. 234; idem, *Prologue*, pp. 300n, 439.

11. For example, Adams attributes a British court's decision in the crucial *Essex* case to Sir William Scott; in fact, Sir William Grant pronounced judgment, and Adams is mistaken both as to the date of the ruling and the destination of the vessel.

12. *History*, 4:139.

13. James Banner, *To the Hartford Convention*, pp. 151–52. See also pp. 54, 155, 259.

14. Ibid., pp. 306–9, 343n.

15. Ibid., p. 343n.

16. Ibid., p. 349.

17. Those dealing with Adams's period are vols. 4–6: *James Madison: Secretary of State, James Madison: The President,* and *James Madison: Commander in Chief* (Indianapolis, 1953–61).

18. Brant, *Madison*, 4:509; Brant, "James Madison and His Times," *American Historical Review* 57(1951–52):866; Adams, *History*, 3:194. Cf. Samuels, *Adams: Middle Years*, pp. 398, 485–86.

19. Brant, *Madison*, 4:509, 5:63, 492.

20. Brant, *Madison,* 5:59, 63; Brant, "Madison," p. 867n; Adams, *History*, 5:37–38.

21. Brant, *Madison*, 5.135; Brant, "John W. Eppes, John Randolph, and Henry Adams," *Virginia Magazine of History and Biography* 63(1955):256; Adams, *History*, 5:200.

22. Brant, *Madison*, 6:307–8; Adams, *History*, 8:151. Brant's language is sometimes unconstrained as he assaults Adams's scholarship: thus he charges that the evidence "totally refutes" Adams's brilliant account of George Rose's mission to America in 1808. Brant shows that Adams summarizes inaccurately evidence that Adams himself quotes later in his same paragraph: Adams errs substantially in making the Americans seem far more yielding to the British than his own evidence proves them to have been. But Brant's subsequent polemic against Adams's account of the breakdown of negotiations carries little force; in avoiding prolixity, Adams simplifies but does not here distort the story. Much of the difference between Adams and his critic, respecting the Rose mission, lies not in facts but in interpretation. Adams presumes that, after such an outrage as Britain's peacetime attack upon an American frigate, the British were morally bound to make unconditional reparation; Jefferson should not have agreed to a quid pro quo. Brant on the other hand sees no loss of national self-respect in Jefferson's concession. Perhaps—as Adams believed—a weak nation like America in 1808 could hope for respectful treatment only by taking a tone high enough to pierce the British rulers' sense of contemptuous superiority (Brant, *Madison*, 4:412, 413; Adams, *History*, 4:191–92, 194).

23. HA, "Count Edward de Crillon," *American Historical Review* 1(1895):51–52.

24. Brant, *Madison*, 4:331; idem, "Madison," p. 867n.

25. HA to Samuel Tilden, Jan. 24, 1883, Cater.

26. *History*, 1:134; *Education*, pp. 44–45.

27. HA to J. G. Palfrey, Mar. 20, 1862, Cater.

28. HA, *Gallatin*, p. 267; Alexis de Tocqueville, *Democracy in America* (New York: Vintage, 1954), 1:280.

29. *History*, 1:89.

30. HA to Brooks Adams, Feb. 18, 1909, Adams Papers, Harvard.

31. *History*, 1:146.

32. *History*, 2:226.

33. *History*, 1:72–73; *Education*, p. 169; Louisa Thoron to Harold D. Cater, Jan. 18, 1939, Cater Papers, MHS; *History*, 1:142–43, 154.

34. HA to Brooks Adams, Feb. 17, 1909, Cater.

35. HA to George Bancroft, Apr. 25, 1879, Cater.

36. CA, *Massachusetts: Its Historians and Its History* (Boston, 1893), esp. pp. 41–42, 48–49. Cf. Kirkland, *Charles Francis Adams, Jr.*, p. 213.

37. HA to John Hay, Sept. 3, 1882, AP.

38. See also pp. 118–20 above.

39. Samuel Eliot Morison, "The Henry-Crillon Affair of 1812," MHS, *Proceedings* 69(1947–50):207–31.

40. Adams errs in taking John Henry's dispatches of 1808 as proof of an "alliance between the New England Federalists and the British Tories"—though he produces good evidence of improper Federalist communications to British representatives on other occasions. When he characterizes Henry as a "secret agent to obtain political information," he understates the Canadian governor's purposes (*History*, 4:248, 6:183; and see *History*, 4:232–37, 6:173–75). See also the error about Soubiron which Adams corrected in later printings of the *History*, 6:186: HA, "Count Edward de Crillon," pp. 51–69. There are mistakes—mostly proofreading errors—in the dates printed in four footnotes (*History*, 6:178–80, 184).

41. Brant does not acknowledge that President Madison was reckless in charging New England Federalists with near treason on the basis of insubstantial documentation. Madison's message to Congress was evidently a partisan effort to inflame anti-Federalist and anti-British sentiment, but Brant palliates the whole maneuver as an effort to achieve "national unity." The evidence does not totally refute Brant's version of the Henry-Crillon affair, still less does it suggest deliberate distortion. Yet information readily available to that author shows that Madison's role was far less creditable than he admits (Brant, *Madison*, 5:419).

42. HA to Oliver Wendell Holmes, Jr., Nov. 3, 1881, Holmes Papers, Harvard Law School.

43. *History*, 1:408–12, 2:1–3, 342–44, 348, 381, 3:61–64, 86, 140, 4:228–32.

44. Winthrop Jordan, *White over Black* (Chapel Hill, N.C., 1968), pp. 461–69.

45. Leonard Levy, *Jefferson and Civil Liberties: The Darker Side* (Cambridge, Mass., 1963).

46. For the Indians see *History*, 6:69–82, and p. 174 below; for the blacks in Haiti see *History*, 3:87–91, 140–43, and p. 145 above. Cf. David Brion Davis, *The Problem of Slavery in the Age of Revolution* (Ithaca, N.Y., 1975), pp. 171–84.

47. See, e.g., *History*, 3:1–2.

48. Marshall Smelser, *The Democratic Republic, 1801–1815* (New York, 1968), p. 351.

49. Ibid., p. 79.

50. *History*, 7:69, 9:242. The theme of democratic nationalism is stressed by William Jordy, *Adams: Scientific Historian*, pp. 81, 98, 118–19.

51. *History*, 6:69.

52. Samuels, *Adams: Middle Years*, pp. 358–59; *History*, 9:225.

53. See Jordy, *Adams: Scientific Historian*, pp. 113–19.

54. HA to CA, Oct. 2, Oct. 30, 1863, AP; HA to Oliver Wendell Holmes, Jan. 4, 1885, Cater; *History*, 7:69.

55. HA to CMG, Apr. 27, 1872, Ford; *History*, 7:70.

56. HA to CA, May 8, 1867, AP.

57. See *History*, 4:300–302, quoted p. 144 above. Ernest Samuels emphasizes Adams's determinism in *Adams: Middle Years*, esp. pp. 349–62, 372, 404–5.

58. See p. 20 above.

59. See Jordy, *Adams: Scientific Historian*, pp. 24–25.

60. When not quoting a primary source, Adams often devises a close paraphrase. His methods of paraphrasing are analyzed in Richard Vitzthum's *The American Compromise* (Norman, Okla., 1974), pp. 182–206.

61. *History*, 9:227.

62. *History*, 9:240.

63. Adams's fascination with human character and the criteria by which he judged it are discussed in Vitzthum, *American Compromise*, pp. 163–74.

CHAPTER 7 · *Macaulay and Gibbon*

1. HA to Charles Scribner, Dec. 19, 1888, in C. Waller Barrett, "The Making of a History," MHS, *Proceedings* 71(1957); HA to CMG, Jan. 21, 1883, Ford.

2. J. Cotter Morison, *Macaulay* (1882; rpt. London, 1896), pp. 38–39.

3. HA, "Reading in College," *Harvard Magazine*, pp. 313–17, quoted on p. 97 above.

4. *Education*, p. 221.

5. HA, Diary, Sept. 16, 1888 (filed at Feb. 12, 1888), AP, quoted on p. 220 below.

6. *Education*, pp. 91–92 (other references on pp. 367, 471, 477, 497); Gibbon, *Autobiography*, p. 160, quoted p. 112 above; HA to CA, May 19, 1860, AP, quoted in Kirkland, *Charles Francis Adams, Jr.*, p. 4.

7. *Education*, p. 386.

8. T. B. Macaulay, *History of England*, ed. C. H. Firth (London: 1914), p. 1196. In this chapter subsequent references are in the text.

9. Emphasis added.

10. Emphasis added.

11. Emphasis added.

12. My literal translation of the report on p. 1170n.

13. HA, *History*, 6:70–72.

14. See, e.g., his reference to the Earl of Oxford, p. 1168.

15. Edward Gibbon, *The Decline and Fall of the Roman Empire*, ed. J. B. Bury, 7 vols. (London, 1896–1900), 6:219n, 5:396n. In this chapter subsequent references are in the text.

16. Ibid., 7:159. Gibbon employs the phrase in describing Mahomet II.

17. Emphasis added.

18. Quoted in part in J. B. Black, *The Art of History* (New York, 1926), p. 177.

19. See, e.g., the passage on Athanasius: *Decline and Fall*, 2:363–64.

20. But for other objects of Gibbon's humor see John Clive, "Gibbon's Humor," *Daedalus*, 105, no. 3(1976):27–35.

21. Ibid., pp. 31–34, explores the relation of Gibbon's humor to his underlying philosophy.

22. See Gibbon, *Autobiography*, p. 180.

23. Emphasis added.

24. HA to Brooks Adams, Feb. 18, 1909, Adams Papers, Harvard, quoted p. 105 above.

CHAPTER 8 · Mont-Saint-Michel and Chartres *and* The Education of Henry Adams

1. Ernest Samuels, "Henry Adams and the Gossip Mills," in *Essays . . . presented to B. R. McElderry*, ed. Max Schulz (Athens, Ohio, 1967), pp. 59–75.

2. HA to John Hay, Apr. 8, 1883, AP; cf. *Education*, p. 334.

3. HA to Hay, Jan. 7, 1883, to Elizabeth Cameron, Dec. 7, 1884, AP.

4. HA to Hay, Nov. 22, 1885, AP.

5. Henry Adams's reference to C. K. Adams was transcribed "C. F. Adams" in Cater. This error led Ernest Samuels to conclude that Henry's brother Charles attended the convention (HA to Theodore Dwight, Sept. 13, 1885, Cater; Samuels, *Adams: Middle Years*, p. 269). See the original letter of HA to Dwight, AP.

6. HA to Dwight, Sept. 13, 1885, Cater; HA to Hay, Sept. 19, 1885, Ford.

7. HA to Elizabeth Cameron, Christmas, 1885, AP.

8. Elizabeth Cameron to Mrs. Hay, July 15, 1886, filed with Hay to HA, July 18, 1886, Dwight Papers, MHS.

9. Elizabeth Cameron to HA, Aug. 16, [1886], Dwight Papers; HA to Elizabeth Cameron, Nov. 5, 1891, AP.

10. J. Lawrence Laughlin, "Some Recollections of Henry Adams," pp. 576, 582.

11. HA, in Harvard Classbook, quoted in George Elsey, "The First Education of Henry Adams," *New England Quarterly*, Dec. 1941, pp. 683–84; HA to CA, Oct. 21, 1864, AP; HA to CMG, Apr. 23, 1865, Mar. 30, 1869, Ford; HA to CA, Feb. 13, 1863, AP.

12. HA to Abigail Adams, Nov. 8, 1859, Ford; HA to CA, Jan. 23, May 14, 1863, AP; HA to Charles Eliot Norton, Feb. 28, 1867, Cater.

13. HA to CMG, Nov. 23, 1869, Ford; HA to CA, July 23, Sept. 3, 1863, Mar. 2, 1865, AP.

14. Abigail Homans, *Education by Uncles* (Boston, 1966), p. 20; HA to [John] Field, Sept. 20, 1885, transcript, AP.

15. Winslow Warren, in William Kellen, "Winslow Warren," MHS, *Proceedings* 64:53; HA to CA, May 15–17, 1859, Ford; HA to CA, July 23, 1863, AP; HA to CMG, Friday, [n.d., 1873], Ford, 1:246; HA to CMG, Oct. 24, 1879, Ford.

16. HA to Jacob Cox, Oct. 31, Nov. 17, 1870, Cater.

17. HA to CMG, Aug. 25, 1867, Ford.

18. Ibid.; HA to CA, May 3, 1869, AP; HA to CA, Apr. 30, 1867, to HCL, Apr. [n.d.], 1876, Ford.

19. Mark A. De Wolfe Howe, *Portrait of an Independent: Moorfield Storey*, p. 129, transcript, in Cater Papers, MHS.

20. CFA, Diary, June 21, 1877, AP; CA to HA, Aug. 2, 1863, *Cycle*; Brooks Adams to Barrett Wendell, Apr. 3, 1918, transcript, Cater Papers; Abigail Adams to HA, July 19, [1870], CFA to HA, Aug. 4, 1870, AP.

21. Hay to HA, Dec. 9, 1885, AP; Clarence King to Hay, May 16, [1894], transcript, Cater Papers. On King see Samuels, *Adams: Major Phase*, p. 367.

22. Louisa Hooper Thoron to Harold D. Cater, Nov. 10, [1942?], Mabel Hooper to HA, Sept. 8, 1898, transcript, Cater Papers; Laughlin, "Some Recollections of Henry Adams," p. 576, quoted pp. 86, 134 above.

23. *History*, 4:402, quoted p. 126 above; *Education*, p. 16, quoted p. 88 above.

24. HA to CA, May 14, 1863, AP; HA to CMG, May 17, 1869, to HCL, June 11, 1873, Ford; HA to Oliver Wendell Holmes, Jr., Jan. 4, 1883, Holmes Papers, Harvard Law School; HA to Robert Cunliffe, Mar. 22, 1885, AP.

25. HA to Hay, June 25, 1882, AP.

26. *History*, 1:144, 4:454. See p. 120 above.

27. *History*, 4:464–66.

28. HA to HCL, Aug. 31, 1879, Ford; *Education*, p. 257; James, *Portrait of a Lady*, 1:382. James wrote the novel in 1880–81. See pp. 46–47, 55–58 above.

29. James, *Portrait of a Lady*, 2:197; HA to CMG, Sept. 9, 1883, to CA, May 7, 1869, James to HA, June 15, 1892, AP. The suggestion that James derived Osmond's lust for consideration—and perhaps one or two of his other traits—partly from study of Adams's personality, requires not to be misunderstood. Osmond's viciousness and hatred bore no resemblance to Adams's character, as James well knew. Osmond lacked every one of Adams's redeeming qualities: Adams's gentleness and loyalty to his wife, to several members of his family, and to his closest friends; his sharp intelligence; his deep laughter at the absurdities of the world; his "intellectual sensuousness"—a phrase Adams applied to Jefferson—; his imaginative power; his perfectionism as a literary craftsman; the "silences of purpose and conscientiousness of effort" with which he worked to fulfill his artistic aspirations. These qualities were ascendant during the happy years of his marriage to Clover, though perhaps James did not perceive them all. The impetus from Adams's marriage lasted until 1890, when he brought the *History* to completion. Thereafter some of his positive characteristics atrophied, while bitterness and age brought to the fore his more Osmond-like traits. Yet after Clover died James came to appreciate Adams much more than when she, the focus of their covert rivalry, was still alive (*History*, 1:144, quoted p. 120 above; see George Hochfield, *Henry Adams: An Introduction and Interpretation* [New York, 1962], p. 3; Clarence King to HA, Sept. 25, [1889], transcript, Cater Papers, quoted p. 91 above).

30. HA to HCL, Oct. 6, 1879, Ford, quoted p. 88 above; HA to Hay, Oct. 8, 1882, AP.

31. HA to Henry Holt, Jan. 6, 1885, Cater; HA to Hay, Jan. 8, [1884, misdated 1883], AP.

32. HA to CA, Jan. 10, 1862, *Cycle*. See pp. 35–36 above.

33. HA to Hay, Oct. 10, 1885, AP.

34. HA to Wayne MacVeagh, Sept. 25, 1881, Cater; *History*, 4:469; HA to HCL, Jan. 6, 1878, Ford.

35. *History*, 1:397–98.

36. HA to Henry Osborn Taylor, Apr. 5, 1911, Cater.

37. Computed from data in Samuels, *Adams: Middle Years*, pp. 338–39. Cf. Samuels, *Adams: Major Phase*, pp. 365–67.

38. HA, *Mont-Saint-Michel and Chartres* (Boston, 1933), p. xvi; Samuel Eliot Morison, "A Letter," *New England Quarterly*, Mar. 1954, p. 97.

39. CA, "Memorabilia," June 1, 1893, AP.

40. HA to CMG, Feb. 3, 1884, to Elizabeth Cameron, Feb. 13, 1891, Ford.

41. *Mont-Saint-Michel and Chartres* (Boston, 1933), p. 92. In this chapter subsequent references are in the text.

42. Ibid., p. 263.

43. Adams's private anti-Semitism, which was of long standing, coexisted for years with a medley of less illiberal attitudes. He and Marian made a point of visiting the ghetto of Frankfurt an der Oder in 1872. He believed Jewishness contributed to making the character of his respected mentor Palgrave "quite different from the ordinary" and therefore especially interesting. He thought Jews were a "down-trodden" group. He detected a parallel between his own position, as an outsider to the main lines of America's late nineteenth-century development, and that of Jews (HA to CMG, Sept. 9, 1883, Feb. 10, 1881, AP).

But his anti-Semitism was evident as early as 1875 when, privately, he expressed his "terror" lest the *North American Review* "should die on my hands or go to some Jew." In 1879 he and Marian made an adventurous trip from Spain into North Africa—Marian believed she was the first European woman to have entered the town of Tétouan in years—and they stayed there with a Jew. The experience displeased Adams, and he jested contemptuously to Robert Cunliffe that "I have now seen enough of Jews and Moors to entertain more liberal views in regard to the Inquisition, and to feel that, though the ignorant may murmur, the Spaniards saw and pursued a noble aim" (HA to HCL, May 26, 1875, Ford; HA to Cunliffe, Nov. 21[?], 1879, AP).

During the happier years of his life Adams kept these prejudices out of the public eye; and in the *History*—as J. C. Levenson has noted—Adams "was quick to catch Jefferson for a scornful reference to Jews." But as bitterness and old age afflicted him, and as the decencies and inhibitions of public expression were shaken both in America and Europe by waves of anti-Semitism, Adams permitted himself to be swept into the current. His comparison of himself with a Jew in the opening passage of *The Education of Henry Adams*—where he claims to have been branded at his birth in Boston, like some Israel Cohen "born in Jerusalem under the shadow of the Temple and circumcised in the Synagogue by his uncle the high priest"—might at first seem a mere literary conceit. But Adams's resentment, his retroactive sense of handicap in the nineteenth-century stakes, found coarser expression later in the *Education*. He alleged that when he had returned to America in 1868, after nearly ten years abroad, he found his old world dead: "Not a Polish Jew fresh from Warsaw or Cracow—not a furtive Yacoob or Ysaac still reeking of the Ghetto, snarling a weird Yiddish to the officers of the customs—but had a keener instinct, an intenser energy, and a freer hand than he—American of Americans, with Heaven knew how many Puritans and Patriots behind him" (Levenson, *Mind and Art of Henry Adams*, p. 224, referring to *History*, 1:312; *Education*, pp. 1, 238. Cf. Samuels, *Adams: Major Phase,* pp. 356–58. Levenson analyzes Adams's anti-Semitism, especially in the 1890s, pp. 224–26).

44. George Santayana, *The Life of Reason: Reason in Religion* (New York, 1905), p. 91. See also pp. 4, 13.

45. See also *Mont-Saint-Michel,* pp. 128, 143, 245, and Robert Mane, *Henry Adams on the Road to Chartres* (Cambridge, Mass., 1971), pp. 197–203.

46. HA to HCL, Sept. 28, [1915], Cater.

47. HA to HCL, Mar. 1, 1915, Cater; see also Samuels, *Adams: Major Phase*, pp. 559–60.

48. *Education*, pp. 20–21. In this chapter subsequent references are in the text.

49. Ibid., pp. 204–7.

50. John Stuart Mill, *Autobiography* (New York, 1924), pp. 108–9.

51. Robert Sayre, *The Examined Self: Benjamin Franklin, Henry Adams, Henry James* (Princeton, 1964), p. 201.

52. Oliver Wendell Holmes, Jr. to Frederick Pollock, June 27, 1919, *Pollock-Holmes Letters,* ed. Mark De Wolfe Howe (Cambridge, 1942).

53. See Levenson, *Mind and Art of Henry Adams,* p. 320n; Sayre, *The Examined Self,* pp. 114–15, 115n.

54. Said of the Chicago Exposition of 1893, in *Education,* p. 340.

55. *Education,* p. 382; see HA to Brooks Adams, Feb. 18, 1909, quoted p. 103 above.

56. HA to CA, Oct. 2, Dec. 11, 1863, AP, quoted p. 16 above.

57. Levenson, *Mind and Art of Henry Adams,* p. 348; Sayre, *The Examined Self,* p. 201.

58. See his comments, in a different context, quoted p. 217 below.

59. Paraphrased, and in part quoted, from *Education,* pp. 498, 501.

60. Interpretations different from this one are set forth, supported by a wealth of valuable detail, in Levenson, *Mind and Art of Henry Adams,* pp. 289–350; Samuels, *Adams: Major Phase,* pp. 346–95; and Sayre, *The Examined Self,* esp. pp. 90–136, 196–202.

61. *History,* 2:65; HA to John Hay, Jan. 23, [1884, misdated 1883], AP. Adams did not place the word *autobiography* on the title page of the *Education* (it was put there by the publisher of the posthumous work), and his purpose was not simply self-portraiture. But the book's form and content are autobiographical, and perhaps it is not willful to evaluate it, in part, by criteria appropriate to this genre.

62. Henri Troyat, *Tolstoy* (1967; rpt. Harmondsworth, 1970), pp. 548–49.

63. HA to CA, May 21, 1869, Ford, quoted p. 25 above.

64. HA to CMG, June 18, 1878, AP; HA to CMG, Apr. 30, 1882, Ford, quoted pp. 89–90 above.

CHAPTER 9 · *The Sense of Failure*

1. HA to CA, Oct. 22, 1867, transcript, AP. Charles Vandersee kindly drew this recently discovered letter to my attention.

2. HA to Albert Bushnell Hart, Dec. 3, 1886, John Hay Papers, Brown University.

3. HA, Diary, Sept. 16, May 20, June 3, 1888 (filed at Feb. 12, 1888), AP. See also Samuels, *Adams: Middle Years*, 2:331.

Bibliographical Note

All of my references to the Adams Papers are to the family collection at the Massachusetts Historical Society, unless otherwise specified in the notes. Other important collections at the Society are those of Theodore Dwight, Adams's secretary; Harold D. Cater, Adams's editor and biographer; and the Shattuck family. At Harvard the Houghton Library holds additional Henry Adams papers as well as the papers of E. L. Godkin and Henry James. Other Henry Adams letters are at the University of Virginia and in the John Hay Papers at Brown University. The Oliver Wendell Holmes, Jr., Papers are at the Harvard Law School.

A new edition of Henry Adams's letters, soon to be published by the Harvard University Press under the editorship of Ernest Samuels, Charles Vandersee, J. C. Levenson, and Viola Winner, will supersede earlier collections.

Ernest Samuels's accurate and detailed three-volume biography is an invaluable study: *The Young Henry Adams, Henry Adams: The Middle Years*, and *Henry Adams: The Major Phase* (Cambridge, Mass., 1948–64). J. C. Levenson's *The Mind and Art of Henry Adams* (Boston, 1957) presents the most influential general interpretation of Adams's work and contains in addition a host of shrewd observations on specific points. William H. Jordy's *Henry Adams: Scientific Historian* (New Haven, 1952) treats authoritatively the scientific side of Adams's historical work and is of wider scope than its title suggests. David Levin's *History as Romantic Art* (Stanford, Calif., 1959) offers a fine critical examination of Adams's New England predecessors, especially Prescott, Motley, and Parkman.

Guides to the many other useful studies of Adams are found in Samuels's and Jordy's books and in three bibliographical aids: Earl Harbert, "Henry Adams," in Robert Rees and Earl Harbert, eds., *Fifteen American Authors before 1900: Bibliographic Essays* (Madison, Wis., 1971); Charles Vandersee, "Henry Adams," *American Literary Realism, 1870–1910*, 2:89–120, 8:13–34.

Index

Numbers in italics refer to major discussions.

Adams, Abigail Brooks (Henry's
  mother), *12–17*, 33, 70, 192, 194
Adams, Brooks (Henry's brother), 26,
  30, 88, 194
Adams, Charles Francis (Henry's
  father), *8–14*
  attitudes, 60, 127
  and *Education*, 14, 217
  influence on Henry, 33, 103, 194,
    219, 221
Adams, Charles Francis, Jr. (Henry's
  brother), *17–26*, 33, 219
  attitude toward father, 11, 13
  as historian, 9–10, 18, 154
  and Marian Adams, 68, 72, 81–82
  relationship with Henry, 60, 73–74,
    189, 194, 200, 217
Adams, Henry
  career, 7, 187
    academic, 9, 25, 71, *86–87*
    literary, 25, 31, 39, *88–91*, *101–7*,
      219
    political, 87–88, 106, 198
  education
    by father, 8–10, 97, 99–100
    by brother Charles, 19–25
    at Harvard, 97, 103–4

in Germany, 98
in England, 38, 41–42, 52–53,
  98–100
feelings
  about Adams family, 31–32,
    59–60
  about England, 34–37, 53,
    128–31, 149, 207–8
  about New England, 10–11,
    113–15, 130, 200, 206–8,
    210–12
  about the South, 152–54; *see also*
    Adams, Henry, ideas: na-
    tionalism and secession
  about the United States, 30–31,
    90–91, 107, 129–31, 145,
    154, 160, 200–201; *see also*
    Adams, Henry, ideas: de-
    mocracy and republicanism
ideas
  anti-Semitism, 203, 242–43
  democracy and republicanism,
    21, 32–33, *36–40*, 53, 90,
    111–12, 118–19, 153, 158
  determinism and free will, 16,
    131, 144, 158–59
  irrationalism, 210, 212–15

Adams, Henry (*cont.*)
  ideas (*cont.*)
    nationalism and secession, 113,
      150–51, 154, 157–58
    slavery and race, 26–27, 35–37,
      131–32, 145
    women and sex, 14–17, 66–68,
      192, 203–4, 211–12
  income, 8, 14
  literary style, 20–21, 50–51, 103–7,
    111–45; *see also* Adams, Henry,
    writings: *Education, History,*
    Mont-Saint-Michel
  personality, 120, *190–201*
    capacity to inspire affection,
      194–95
    craving for public acclaim,
      195–201
    critical spirit, 10–11, 38, 120,
      143, 157, 159–61, 192–94
    deficiency in sympathy, 183,
      220–21
    melancholy, 16–17, 24–25, 91,
      191–92, 213–14
    objectivity, 12–13, 27, 86–87,
      157, 173–74
    reserve, 84, 89, 191–93, 198–99
    self-esteem, 10, 53, 193, 216–17
    sense of failure, 4, 31, 83, 85,
      199–200, 219–21
    sense of humor, 13, 76–77,
      86–87, 133–34, 192
    social ambitions, 40–41
    tenderness, 83, 195
    unconventional manner, 68, 87
    ungraciousness, 75, 192–93
  physical appearance, 24, 42, 75,
    190–91, 193
  and scientific history, 24, 101, *105,*
    107, *159–60,* 182–83, 220
  self-portrait, 210–11, 215–17, 221;
    see also Adams, Henry, writ-
    ings: *Education*
  writings
    Democracy, 66, 73, 74, 76, *79,* 85,
      152, 196
    Education of Henry Adams, The,
      206–18
      assessments of, 1–2
      privately printed, 51, 199
      as self-portrait, 83–84, 86,
        88–89
      tone, 16, 41, 64, 166, 221
    Esther, 71, *79–80,* 85, 188, 201,-
      206, 221
    History of the United
      States,111–61, 182–84
      assessments of, 1, 3
      Charles Adams's influence,
        23–24
      John Quincy Adams's influ-
        ence, 27–30
      Marian Adams's influence, 73,
        76–77
      writing of, 84–85, *88–91*
      literary style of, 101–3, 106–7
      Adams's revulsion against, 85,
        200–201, 219–21
      see also Canning, George; Jef-
        ferson, Thomas; Madison,
        James; Napoleon Bona-
        parte; Pickering, Timothy
    John Randolph, 198
    Life of Albert Gallatin, 20, 22–23,
      73, 78, 88
    Mont-Saint-Michel and Chartres,
      43, 51, 188, 199, *201–6,* 221
    New England Federalism, 10, 113,
      199
Adams, John (Henry's great-grandfather), 9, 32, 118–19, 154
Adams, John Quincy (Henry's grandfather), 9–11, 14, *26–33,* 126, 207
Adams, John Quincy, II (Henry's
  brother), 13, 27, 33, 200
Adams, Louisa (Henry's sister), 13,
  194, 212, 217–18
Adams, Louisa Johnson (Henry's
  grandmother), 12
Adams, Marian Hooper, 3, *54–85,*
  219
  and Elizabeth Cameron, 187–90

and *Education*, 89, 212
and *Esther*, 79–80, 201
and *Mont-Saint-Michel*, 205–6
personality, 192–93, 195
relationship with Henry, 22, 49,
    212, 220
Adams, Mary (Henry's sister), 14–16
Agassiz, Louis, 65, 78

Bancroft, George, 53, 63, 73, 219
Banner, James, 113, 149–51, 157
Becker, Carl, 1–2
Boott, Elizabeth, 68
Brant, Irving, 148, 151–52, 155, 157,
    237, 238
Bright, John, 36, 208
Brooks, Phillips, 79
Browning, Robert, 75, 196

Cameron, Donald, 188–89
Cameron, Elizabeth Sherman, 28, 60,
    71, *187–90*
Cameron, Martha, 189
Canning, George, 39–40, 127
Channing, Edward, 87, 147
Comte, Auguste, 98, 158
Cunliffe, Sir Robert, 42, 45–46

Dana, Richard Henry, 8, 14, 21, 208
Darwin, Charles, 158
Doyle, Sir Francis, 42, 48, 98
DuBois, W. E. B., 34

Eliot, George, 101
    Middlemarch, 70, 80, 85

Gardner, Isabella, 47
Gaskell, Charles Milnes, *42–53*, 99,
    100, 207
Gaskell, Lady Catherine, 44, 47
Gibbon, Edward, *176–84*
    Adams's attitude toward, 107, 113,
        165–67, 220
    Autobiography, 112, 121
    style of, 137, 140
Godkin, Edwin L., 22, 66, 74, 75

Gurney, Ellen Hooper (Marian's sis-
    ter), 58–59, *62*, 71, 84–85
Gurney, Ephraim Whitman, 54, 62,
    84

Hay, John, 31, 189, 194–95
Hervey, Augusta, 48–49
Hervey, Lady Mary, 44, 48
Hervey, Wilhelmina, 48–49
Hewitt, Abram, 31, 73
Holmes, Oliver Wendell, Jr., 1–2,
    54–55, 211
Hooper, Edward, 54, 58–59, 200
Hooper, Ellen (Marian's sister), *see*
    Gurney, Ellen Hooper
Hooper, Ellen Sturgis (Marian's
    mother), 58
Hooper, Marian, *see* Adams, Marian
    Hooper
Hooper, Robert William, *57–62*, 79
Houghton, Lord, *see* Milnes, Richard
    Monckton
Howard, Catharine, 64–65

James, Henry, *55–58*
    Bostonians, The, 63
    literary career, 34, 92, 146, 165
    Portrait of a Lady, The, 11, 31,
        45–47, 52, *57–58*, *197–98*, 241;
        see also Boott, Elizabeth;
        Lowe, Elena
    relationship with Adams, 48, 74,
        76, 128
    relationship with Marian, 68, 70
    Roderick Hudson, 56–57
Jefferson, Thomas, *115–20*, *152–57*
    Adams's affinity for, 34, 120,
        196–97, 199
    mentioned in *History*, 29–30,
        39–40, 107, 129, 148
Jordy, William, 2

King, Clarence, 72, 91, 194–95,
    208–9
Kuhn, Charles, 203

Kuhn, Louisa Adams, *see* Adams, Louisa

LaFarge, John, 60, 79
Laughlin, J. Lawrence, 87, 88, 190
Levenson, J. C., 2, 214
Levin, David, 4, 95, 97
Lodge, Henry Cabot, 84, 105, 196–97, 206
Lowe, Elena, 55, 57, 66
Lowell, James Russell, 50, 82

Macaulay, Thomas Babington, *167–76*
   Henry Adams's attitude toward, 104, 107, *165–66*, 199
   influence on Charles Adams, 9–10, 23
   method, 136
   style of, 137, 141, 178, 182–84
MacVeagh, Wayne, 31, 74
Madison, James, 132, 143, 148, 151–55
Mill, John Stuart, 38, 40, 42, 208–9
Milnes, Richard Monckton, Lord Houghton, 41, 45, 46, 52
Morison, Samuel Eliot, 155
Morton, Levi, 75
Motley, John Lothrop, 65, 92, *93–95*, 97, 107

Napoleon Bonaparte, 39–40, 106–7, 120–23, 131–32, 199, 215
Nordhoff, Charles, 74

Palfrey, John Gorham, 8, 14, 123

Palgrave, Francis Turner, 42, *98–100*, 203
Palmer, Ralph, 42
Parkman, Francis, 53, 92, *95–97*, 107
Perkins, Bradford, 27–28, 148–49, 157
Pickering, Timothy, 21, 113, 126–27, 156
Prescott, William Hickling, *91–93*, 97, 107

Renan, Ernest, 74
Richardson, Henry Hobson, 53, 74, 80, 194

Samuels, Ernest, 2–3, 188
Santayana, George, 34, 58, 181, 205
Sayre, Robert, 214
Schurz, Carl, 73
Shattuck, Dr. Frederick, 64, 67
Smelser, Marshall, 156–57
Spencer, Herbert, 75, 158
Story, William Wetmore, 128
Sturgis, Russell, 58, 59, 231
Sturgis, Mrs. Russell, 11
Sumner, Alice, 70
Sumner, Charles, 8, 14, 21, 40, 127

Times (London), 20–21, 35–36, 198
Tocqueville, Alexis de, 38, 153, 158

War of 1812, 143–44, 148–49, 182
Wenlock Abbey, 43–47
Whately, Richard
   Elements of Rhetoric, 103–5
Winter, Yvor, 1–2